style, naturally

style, naturally

by **SUMMER RAYNE OAKES**

the savvy shopping guide to sustainable fashion and beauty

CHRONICLE BOOKS
SAN FRANCISCO

Photography credits: see page 344, which constitutes a continuation of the copyright page.

Library of Congress Cataloging-in-Publication Data:

Oakes, Summer Rayne.
   Style, naturally : the savvy shopping guide to sustainable fashion and beauty
/ Summer Rayne Oakes.
     p. cm.
   Includes index.
   ISBN: 978-0-8118-6524-1
   1. Fashion. 2. Beauty, Personal. 3. Clothing and dress—Environmental aspects.
   4. Cosmetics—Environmental aspects. 5. Sustainable living. I. Title.

GT511.O34 2008
391—dc22   2008010490

Manufactured in China

Design by JAY PETER SALVAS
Front cover Photographer: Seth Karecha, Hair/Makeup: Katie Jarvis, Jacket: Levis ECO,
Jewelry: Ombre Claire
Author photo Photographer: Jon Moe, Hair/Makeup: Chris Newburg, Dress: Anna Cohen
This book was typeset in Chaparral MM 9/13, Myriad Pro 7.5/9,
and AmarilloUSAF

10 9 8 7 6 5 4 3 2 1

CHRONICLE BOOKS LLC
680 SECOND STREET
SAN FRANCISCO, CALIFORNIA 94107

WWW.CHRONICLEBOOKS.COM

This book is dedicated to everyone who cares about our planet and wants to look good while doing better.

A special thanks to Alex for being there for me every step of the way. Your mentorship and friendship deserve much greater recognition than what I can say on this page.

this spread: Summer Rayne plants trees on a reforestation/sustainable development area in the Sofala Province at the Mezimbite Forest Centre. She wears Levis Eco, American Apparel, and TOMS shoes.

Contents

background photo: Many of Carolina K Designs are hand-knit and embroidered
by Peruvian artisans **www.carolinak.com**

A NOTE TO THE READER

I grew up in northeastern Pennsylvania an outdoor-loving, natural-history junkie. I left no plant, animal, mushroom, or insect mystery unsolved. In college, people knew me as the rainforest girl with the bug net in her backpack who studied sewage sludge. I didn't pay attention to the latest trends—whether round toes were in this season and out the next. So just how did I come to write a book on style, you may ask?

The truth is, my insatiable passion for the environment and my driving motivation to bring about real, positive change drove me to write this book. I felt that if I wanted to have a broad impact as an individual, I would need to break out of the lab and reach out to people in new ways. (Bug nets in backpacks only get a person so far.) As I researched toxic organic contaminants in sewage sludge (which, by the way, has everything to do with our clothes and beauty products), I came to the conclusion that fashion might be a good vehicle for talking environment. So I slung my hiking boots over my travel pack, hung up my bug net (if only for a while), took to the runways, and put pen to paper with a mission—and one mission only: to elevate the profiles of environmental and social issues through style.

This book is much more than a run-of-the-mill style guide. My aim is to show the wide-ranging effects on the environment of what we wear and what we put on our bodies. For me, fashion and beauty have always placed second, behind my health and the health of our world. It's not my love for fashion that made me passionate about the environment. Rather, it's my passion for the environment that made me love fashion for its potential to create change.

Many of us struggle to align our beliefs and values with our everyday choices, and today we have more options than ever. Using organic products on our bodies, wearing more eco-conscious garments, and getting involved in the whole process may seem trivial at first, but in the end, every effort truly does make a difference. I've seen how the simple purchase of the right product can yield positive results. I've seen how a group of committed women who care about what's in their makeup can get regulatory laws passed. I've seen how one designer can change the lives of hundreds of families once stricken by poverty. These are just some of the stories I look forward to sharing with you. Hopefully, you will be inspired to become a part of it all.

When I was able to figure out how to combine style with sustainability, I began down a path to a more fulfilling lifestyle. Who I was—my style, so to speak—was no longer conflicting with the way I wanted to live my life. I could finally look good, feel good, and do good—simultaneously: a win-win-win situation!

I hope this book will not only help you to see style in a new light but also arm you with the knowledge to make a difference. May you lead by example, and do so in style.

Much love,
Summer Rayne Oakes

INTRODUCTION

I've wanted to write a book about sustainable style and beauty for a while, but it didn't seem like the world was ready for it. As recently as a few years ago, the fashion and beauty industry regarded sustainable style about as warmly as it would a flannel-loving, fanny-pack wearer in the front row at Fashion Week. Sustainability and style just didn't seem to go together. Consumers had a hard time grasping the concept because not much in the way of quality product existed. The words *green* or *eco* brought to mind oversized, oatmeal-colored tees, patchouli, and Jesus sandals. Very few good brands existed (and I use the term brand very loosely). There was a dearth of research and development of high-quality organic, eco-friendly materials, lower-impact dyes, and eco-conscious packaging. Unless you made a garment out of Grandma's old quilt or whipped up an avocado masque in your kitchen, there just wasn't much sustainable style or ecologically sound product to be found.

Dressing chicly and beautifying sustainably is getting easier by the day. The Burlap Sack Theory, which my friend, Green-design-guru Josh Dorfman, defines as the tightly held belief that environmentally aware products must be unattractive and frumpy, is a thing of the past. More and more designers recognize the consumer's wish for products that are both stylish and eco-friendly.

The Eco-Fashion section of this book will shed light on the history and future of eco-conscious design; explain what the terms eco-fashion and sustainable style mean; offer up Designer Profiles of people who have been exemplars of their way of design and thinking; and give you some helpful style tips along the way.

This book will also give you details on the core concepts and philosophies that define eco-fashion, offering the inside scoop so that you may become an eco-style taste-maker and trendsetter in your own right. You'll also see hundreds of gorgeous pieces from top designers across the globe, and even get a peek at some real-life stylish women.

The Eco-Beauty section of this book will reveal the big picture of the cosmetics industry. It will take you through your daily regimen to show how your health is directly affected by your beauty products. It will give you the know-how to choose ingredients that will nourish your body; introduce you to new eco-conscious personal-care alternatives for your skin, hair, and nails; teach you tips of the trade; and share stories and profiles from inspiring forerunners in the eco-conscious beauty arena. You'll also get details on the core concepts that define eco-beauty to make certain that you are equipped with all the necessary information to be healthy and fabulously radiant.

I hope you enjoy the hundreds of photos and stories I've included in this book. Consider this a colorful, and in no way comprehensive, window into the world of eco-style. While you'll find tons of resources in this book, I've no doubt that by the time it is printed, there will be countless more resources and eco-brands in addition to those you'll find here.

Sustainable style will keep evolving. So consider this book a primer on eco-conscious philosophies and products. This is an opportunity to redefine what style means to you. Dive into new frontiers that fly in the face of what you considered to be "fashion" and "beauty." Explore ways in which you can do good, look good, and feel good. Once you open your mind to eco-consciousness, the opportunities for positive, fashion-forward change are limitless. Go ahead: Explore. Learn. Embrace. Redefine. Inspire. Be.

That's Style, Naturally.

Hand-graded and -draped silk chiffon crêpe dress **www.leila-hafzi.com**

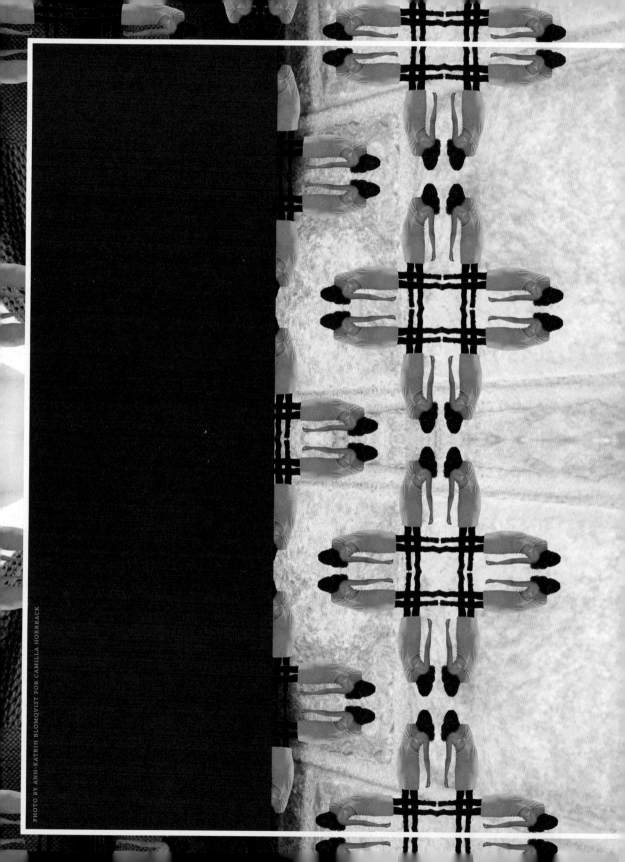

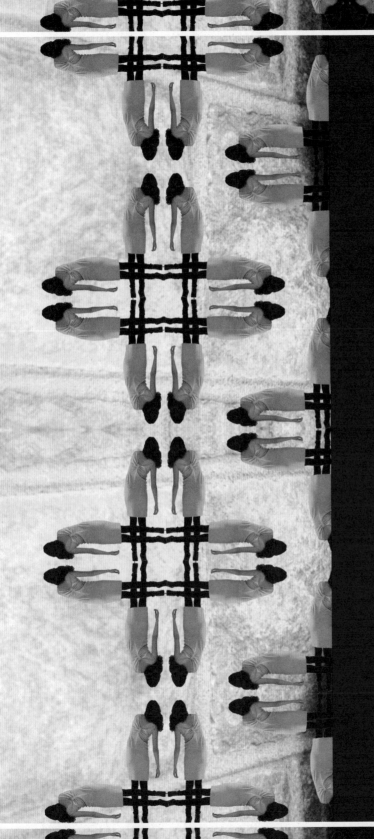

eco-fashion

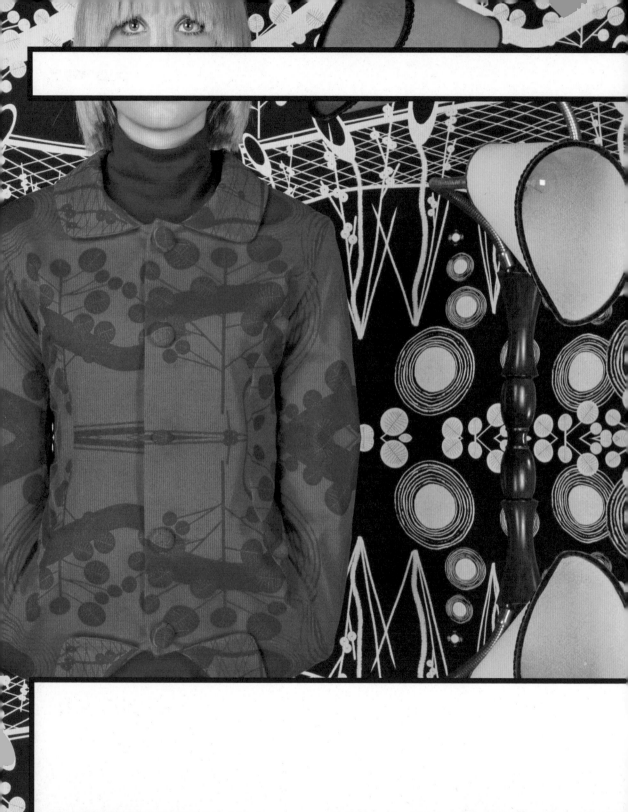

PHOTO BY FRAN FLYNN FOR BIRD TEXTILES

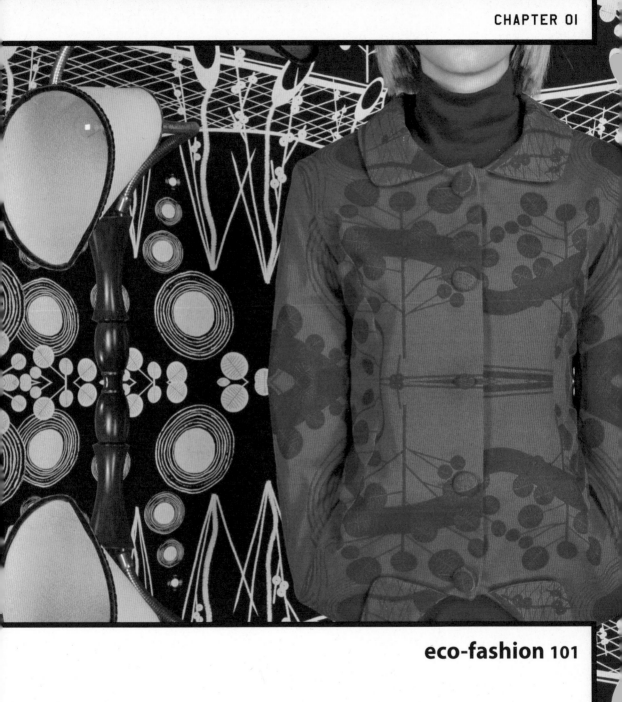

eco-fashion 101

"EVERY MORNING I AWAKE TORN BETWEEN A DESIRE TO SAVE THE WORLD AND AN INCLINATION TO SAVOR IT.
THIS MAKES IT HARD TO PLAN THE DAY."
—E. B. WHITE, AMERICAN WRITER, 1899–1985

Getting to the Root of Eco-Fashion:
A Brief History

The year is 1989, and acclaimed British designer Katharine Hamnett, known for her oversized tees with large block-letter political slogans, emerges from the haze of her success. Upon reading that the fashion industry is responsible for great environmental destruction, she begins lobbying for change and later terminates all her existing licensing arrangements in favor of cleaner production practices. That same year, Deborah Lindquist, whose father almost lost a limb from a pesticide spill while working on their farm, heads from New York to Los Angeles to create a clothing line entirely out of vintage fabric.

The following year, Lynda Grose, a San Francisco native, cofounds and successfully launches the Esprit Ecollection, the first completely ecologically sound clothing line distributed internationally by a major corporation. Then in 1991, across the Pacific, UK-born Safia Minney, daughter of an Indian Mauritian father and a Swiss mother, introduces the concept of ecologically sound, fair-trade fashion to Tokyo, Japan, with a collection of handwoven, naturally dyed clothes made by Bangladeshi women's groups. Two years later, UK-based Sarah Ratty starts the Conscious Earthwear label, which later gives way to her current label, Ciel. That same year, Yvon Chouinard, owner and founder of Patagonia, sees firsthand the destruction generated by conventional (read: pesticide-intensive) cotton farms and the effects on the people and land of California's Central Valley. In 1994, he decides to switch the entire Patagonia conventional cotton line to organic cotton. Then in 1996, Marci Zaroff, founder of Under the Canopy, uses the term "eco-fashion" to describe her line of organic cotton tees.

The following year, Leila Hafzi presents her first fair-trade, ethical collection on the runways in Stavanger, Norway, giving a couture twist to environmentally conscious fashion.

As you can see, ethical and eco-conscious fashion was sprouting up all over the place, but it wasn't being transmitted from designer to designer as it is now. Instead, a collective consciousness was spontaneously erupting in all corners of the world. Each designer had his or her own awakening, brought about by awareness of an issue that had far greater reach than their clientele's closets. What set this phenomenon apart from the popular fashion trends at the time was its unassuming, grassroots nature. The ideas did not come from the big clothing conglomerates or the high-end designers that crowded the glossy pages of *Vogue* and *Elle* each month. The ideas came from a crop of daring, innovative, tireless activists looking to make a difference. What they didn't know was that their collective actions created a quiet revolution that would challenge fashion's status quo.

Fast-forward to present day. The sustainable fashion movement has hit the mainstream. Ideas are exchanged swiftly and across oceans via print and the Internet. New players hit the scene every day. A few years ago, I could name all the eco-designers off the top of my head; now it's too difficult to keep track of them all. Some come on board because it's trendy, others because they are passionate about making a difference through design or, at the very least, are trying to figure out how to leave a lighter footprint on the planet.

The movement continues to evolve and grow, both in diversity and complexity. It's not just about organic cotton fields and fiber any longer. It's about incorporating more environmentally and socially responsible principles and practices throughout the manufacturing process and life cycle of a product—from materials to construction to design to how we care for our clothes and what we do with them when we don't want them any longer. It is not necessarily about producing and consuming more eco-friendly products, but about producing better and consuming better. This is a broad way of looking at eco-fashion or sustainable style, but because the concept of sustainability in apparel is so complex and multifaceted, a broad view works best.

The ever-evolving innovations of this movement breed new ways of addressing myriad issues, including organics standards (free of pesticides, chemical fertilizers, and genetically modified ingredients); fair and ethical labor practices (no sweatshops, free to form unions, fair pay, overtime pay, benefits); recycling initiatives (of excess fabric, materials, and old or used garments); community development (reinvesting in or assisting communities); philanthropic giving; and local sourcing and energy efficiency to reduce carbon emissions.

Image from Katharine Hamnett archive (1984): Hamnett meets with former prime minister, Margaret Thatcher, wearing her own design, a reference to polls showing public opposition in the UK against the basing of Pershing missiles in the country.

(2007): A revival of some of the looks that made Katharine Hamnett so popular in the 1980s. In a 2008 interview for *Vs*. magazine, Hamnett says that she uses statements " . . . to give people a voice. Saying you 'know' is one thing, doing something about it is another."

Milestones: In 2006, Marks and Spencer became the first major UK retailer to sell fair-trade cotton clothing. In 2007, they issued a report called Plan A, which was a comprehensive plan to address climate change, resource use, waste, fair trade, and health. Since that time, they have made significant headway—both internalizing and externalizing the idea of sustainability— including reducing CO_2 emissions from their stores and offices by 55,000 tons; opening three pilot "eco-stores"; supporting fair-trade farmers; and helping to shift the percentage of clothing washes done at 30 degrees Celcius from 23 percent to 31 percent.

With all of these issues at stake, it's difficult to discern one single best practice. One person's priority may be another person's problem. You could argue that fair trade is important because it helps people in marginalized areas gain access to the marketplace and make a living, but it's not really sustainable because the associated long-distance shipping bumps up carbon emissions. You could take the stance that sourcing and manufacturing everything in China is efficient and cuts down on energy, but labor practices there are questionable. You could argue that vegan products are best because they do not harm animals, but these products may not be eco-friendly because they use petroleum-based materials in place of leathers. Don't worry; I don't plan on arguing which approach is holiest. I will tell the story, show you the product, and let you decide what sustainable style means to you and how best to support the movement.

A New Spin on Fashion

It's funny to see how some people in the industry get all shaken up about eco-fashion, either because it's new (and therefore exciting) or because it's foreign (and therefore threatening). Whether I'm speaking at a conference, giving a workshop at a university, or making small talk at an event, the following conversation never fails to take place.

A Marks and Spencer tag **www.marksandspencer.com**

Person: "So, do you think this Green fashion stuff is a trend or here to stay?"

Me: "What? You mean a trend like brightly colored spandex, jelly shoes, and dirty trucker hats? In one season and (thankfully) out the next?"

Person: "Yeah."

Me: "Have companies ever specifically assembled divisions to address how brightly colored spandex affects the rest of the company?"

Person: "What?! No."

Me: "Precisely. Companies are, however, assembling entire divisions to address sustainability, not only in their products, but across their company's practices. Newer design lines have incorporated sustainability into the core of their business from the get-go. I would argue that the most successful companies use sustainability as a source of innovation, and it's these principles that help guide them through better practices and design. I highly doubt that companies are going to disassemble those divisions and those design philosophies two seasons from now because it's 'out of style.'"

Of course, it might be easy to see this eco-fashion stuff as a trend, because that's the way the fashion industry works, right? Fashion is an unforgiving world, where you are measured by how many seasons you have under your vintage leather belt. It's like clockwork. Tick, tock, tick, tock: counting down the days until you can turn the page to see the next big thing. But when you recognize that sustainability goes far beyond the element of fashion, it makes perfect sense: It's not design for the sake of design any longer. It is true design, a way of thinking and a way of doing business that sets out to solve a problem, remedy an issue, or make a difference. That's part of the reason why this eco-stuff is so cool. It's much bigger than fashion. It goes far beyond trends. It's got legs.

Sustainability is not going to be "in" one season and "out" the next. What will change is how it is packaged and perceived.

Green Is the New Invisible

I don't know who first used the phrase, "Green Is the New Black," to describe the eco-fashion movement, but the first time it was used, it was brilliant. The second and third time, it was cute. After the fiftieth time it showed up, it just became (yaaaaawwwwnnnn), well, excuse me for saying this, but sooooooo two seasons ago. Yes, of course I am happy that eco-stuff is showing up everywhere. The point is that as our knowledge of the issues grows, our expectations shift. Our perception of sustainability will shift, as should the language. Smart companies and designers will adjust to the changes. One day, we'll wake up and Green will not be the new black, it will be the new invisible. Meaning, no longer will sustainable be the exception or something that's considered au courant; instead, it will be a matter of course—something that all designers incorporate into their design ethos.

Is Sustainable Style an Oxymoron?

This is another question that I am often asked. The short answer is: Yes. Sustainable style is an oxymoron, that is, if it's held up to today's fashion norms of "cheap chic" and "fast fashion," which embody three words: More, faster, quicker. What does that mean? Well, a number of companies have snubbed the two-season runway rule and instead pump out merchandise faster than ever. Many brands have mastered the art of disposable "fast fashion." They haul shipments of the newest styles off to the retailer several times a week. If "old" styles don't sell, then they slash their prices drastically and push them out of the store as quickly as possible. Sound like any place you shop? Don't worry, I'm not going to jump all over you and tell you where to shop. I merely would like to bring to your attention, that in the long run, shopping this way just doesn't make sense.

Buying well means not having to buy all the time. A good shopper is an edited shopper. Meaning she buys higher quality products that last longer. She buys things with a lot of meaning, like a handwoven sari purchased during a trip to Dubai, a pair of organic cotton jeans made in an old town in Georgia, or a T-shirt that helps build awareness for breast cancer or HIV/AIDS. Or she buys a versatile garment she'll get a lot of use out of—something that she can mix and match.

Take it from the fashion authority, Tim Gunn: "The key is to shop wisely, which means—brace yourself—to shop less."

That said, please know that I'm not asking you to throw away your entire wardrobe (though if you want to, Chapter Three: Tips of the Trade outlines the best ways to dispose of your unwanted garments). I'm not even asking you to buy Green all the time. That is neither possible nor practical. What I am asking you to do is expect more from your clothes, not less!

TREND FORECAST

Julie Gilhart, *Barneys New York, senior vice president and fashion director*

"Fashion and the business of fashion are all about trends. Green acts like a trend. It acts like a cargo pant or skinny-leg jean or chandelier earring. It has the same energy. As a fashion director, I look for energy. And with Green, you can't get enough of it—you want a piece of it. It is the only trend I have ever seen that is a movement. In fashion, movements are never really talked about. But this is real. And it has the energy of a trend, but will change and garner even more energy. It is going to get more sophisticated and edgier. People are going to figure out how to internalize it and externalize it. It is not going to go away. If a store like Barneys is feeling that on all different levels, then you can be sure that it is here for good."

Tiffany Chanelle Brown: Dancing Queen

Dance instructor; entertainer

No one moves quite like Tiffany on the dance floor. With a head bob, hip sway, and move your body this way, I knew I was destined to get me some dance lessons. An entertainer by nature, Tiffany has studied many genres of dance and has danced for artists like Lil' Mo and Ryan Leslie.

Where are you from?

I was born and raised in Baltimore, Maryland.

What are you wearing?

Look #1:

In my first look, I'm wearing a beautiful Bahar Shahpar silk dress with an organic cotton lining. It's a fun, flirty print and I love the way it moves when I dance. I paired the dress with a vegan, pale pink, patent-leather shoe.

Look #2 (page 23):

The second look is my favorite. I am wearing a gorgeous purple American Apparel halter dress. I paired that look with a pair of opaque black tights and fabulous black patent-leather Mary Janes. To tie the look together, I accentuated my waist with a sexy leopard-print belt with just a hint of black patent leather.

Who are your favorite designers?

Betsey Johnson: I love her dresses because they are so sexy and vibrant.

What are your favorite places to shop?

I tend to shop at American Apparel a lot because they have great dance clothes. It's a plus that everything is made here in the United States, too. Otherwise, I like heading down to SoHo in New York, which has a number of cute boutiques.

What fashion era or icon do you love?

I love the styles of Old Hollywood. Dorothy Dandridge comes to mind. I admire her; she was feminine and classy. I also love all the urban influences coming out of New York City. I try to blend those two worlds together and create my own style of urban glam.

What fashion rules do you follow?

The only fashion rule I follow is: Do not follow rules. Be yourself and express yourself through your clothing. Wear what complements your body shape and makes you feel comfortable.

The Goods on the Goods

When you flip through the Clothing and Accessories section, I hope you'll not only fall in love with the designs, but also with the designers, their philosophies, and the process behind the designs. When I have this background information, I find that suddenly my clothes have meaning and I'll wear a piece with pride—and I'll want to tell people all about it. I also find that I have a new interest in hanging onto and caring for that piece for years to come.

Somehow, most of us have managed to forget about everyone involved in the process right up until the salesgirl rings us up. (And, let's face it, not many of us will even remember her.) The design and manufacturing processes have become invisible. I mean, the back of our tag—"Made in Indonesia," "Made in China," or the rarer "Made in the USA"—only tells us so much about what we're about to buy. Did you know that over 26.5 million people across the world manufacture our textiles and clothes? 26.5 million people! My brain can barely process the enormity of that number. And that's not even counting the millions of other faceless people who work the farms that supply our fiber, import and export garments, design our clothes, advertise them, style the pieces on models and celebrities, write about the clothes, lobby for their fibers, and retail the garments. Bah! Give me design full of life! Give me design with vitality! Give me design with a purpose!

I decided I wanted more from my clothes. I had been buying eco-conscious designs for many years already, but three years ago, I made up my mind to make a valiant effort to expect more from my clothes. I came to this conclusion in the back of a long line at H&M (with which, I'm sure, you're all familiar).

That morning I had dressed quickly, got on the subway, and headed over to Broadway to the nearest H&M. I had an event later that night, and I needed a pair of black trousers. From the time I woke up to the time I got to the store, I barely even thought about my purchase. I opened the shiny glass doors and made my way through the store, pushing past all the hands feverishly flipping through the racks. That's all I remember: No faces, just hands flipping this way and that, like fish out of water, through a sea of endless clothes. The worst part about it: my hand was one of those fish.

I grabbed trousers in my size, cut in on the line to the changing room (hey, I was in a rush), and checked under the bright fluorescent lights to make sure the pants made my butt look at least moderately good. They passed the test; I tore them off, slid back into my pants, and walked outside to the checkout line. Whoops, didn't even look at the price. Oh, $14.99. Okay.

From the time I walked through the door to the time I got in line, a whole five minutes had elapsed, and most of those five minutes were spent looking at myself in the mirror. Then I stood and waited as six or seven people bought armloads of clothes. Some people had the exact same clothes as the person behind them. One girl even had two of the same skirt in different sizes. "Can I return this if it doesn't fit?" she asked shrilly.

I looked at the tag in the pants, almost as a way of fooling myself into believing I had considered where the garment came from. That's when it set in: I wanted something more from this experience. I actually felt regretful for the entire 20 minutes I was in line. I went ahead, much to my growing disgust, and bought the pants. You know what? I never ended up wearing them.

I wore a dress (that I absolutely love) that night. I packed up the pants a few weeks later and dropped them off at the Salvation Army, price tag still attached.

I'm not suggesting you not shop at H&M (by the way, they're beginning to use organic cotton) or any other store for that matter. That's not the point. What I'm asking is that you think before you buy. Be fully aware of your actions. Ask yourself where the item came from, whether you really need or want it, and whether you're going to get much use out of it. This simple step will save you time, money, and closet space.

I now do my best to be actively aware while I'm shopping. Even when I can't buy eco-conscious products (e.g., when they're not available, are too expensive, are not the right fit, or I'm looking for a different style), I still ask myself the same important questions and try to exhaust all possibilities before buying something—whether that means trawling the vintage shops or swapping some styles with friends.

Case in point: This past holiday season, I went to Nordstrom in search of a warm overcoat. After a little deliberation, I decided that I wanted a black, floor-length trench coat. It was a calculated purchase on my part. I've started attending events and dinners that require a more formal wardrobe, and I didn't have the proper jacket for the winter months. Sure, I may have looked glamorous at that red-carpet fundraiser for Riverkeeper, but truth be told, I froze my butt off trying to hail a cab before and after the event. Not fun!

But I didn't want to get a special-events-only jacket either. I wanted something I could wear on many occasions. The black trench would be a perfect fit. It's a timeless piece that epitomizes sophistication. It would transition from one winter to the next effortlessly, without skipping a style beat. And it's versatile: It looks just as appropriate with an evening dress as it does with a pair of jeans, black boots, and a sweater.

Nordstrom had no shortage of black trench coats. I asked the lady in the women's apparel department if they carried any eco-conscious designers, or at least any jackets in organic wool or organic cotton canvas. She was very receptive to the idea but said they didn't carry any such styles or brands. I looked around some more just to see if anything struck my fancy, but I came up empty. I headed home and did a quick search on some eco-fashion retail Web sites to see if any designers were offering black trench coats. Camilla Norrback, Linda Loudermilk, and Noir all had black jackets but not exactly what I was looking for. I then went to the Barneys Web site and checked out "Barneys Green," a special section devoted to eco-conscious design (which, according to Julie Gilhart, is part of a larger initiative). I found a piece by Loomstate—a beautiful black anorak in organic cotton canvas. It wasn't floor-length, but it was on sale. I made a point to visit Barneys after the holidays to try on the jacket and look around for other brands. I didn't end up finding anything that I fancied, so I'm holding off for another season.

The point is, even though I didn't end up buying anything, at least I was fully aware throughout the decision-making process. And I asked the important questions. This is a big step from blindly making another purchase. And that's important. You know why? Because I expect more from my clothes. And you can quote me on that.

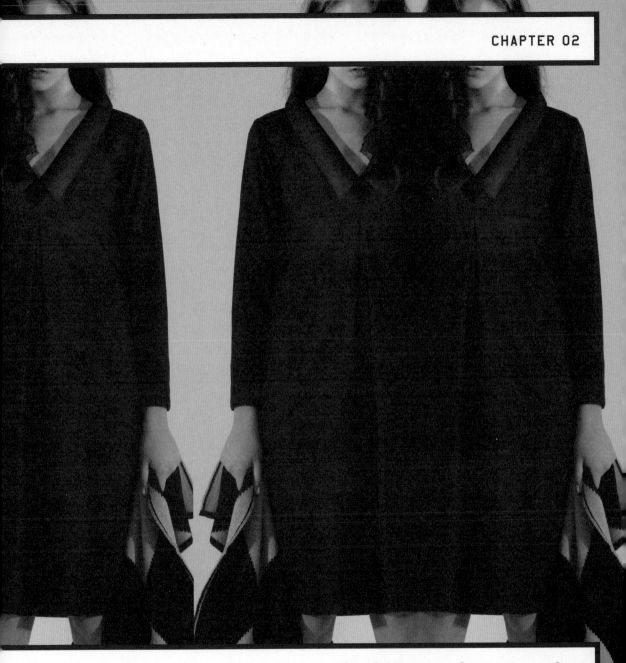

clothing *and* accessories

"PEOPLE WHO GIVE A SHIT ARE SEXY."
—SCOTT HAHN AND ROGAN GREGORY, COFOUNDERS OF LOOMSTATE

The Goods on the Goods

While *fashion* is something that can be bought, sold, traded, tucked, and tailored, *style* is something that's particular to each of us. Style is the way we put our look together. You could think of it as a language: The necklace, the shoes, the handbag—these are simply words that, on their own, may not have significance. You have to put them together to create a story.

Style doesn't start with big-name, fancy brands, as some advertisers would have you believe. Style starts with you. It starts with who you are, what you choose to wear and how you wear it, how you carry yourself, how you go about the day, what you do with your time, and how you feel in your clothes and your skin. That is style.

How we dress and adorn ourselves says a lot about our culture, our lifestyles, and our society. It can also connect us on a personal level to other people. How many times has someone come up to you and said, "Nice shoes," "Cute jacket," or "Oh, my gosh, where did you get that purse?!?" Those are instances when fashion, or more likely, style, started a conversation that otherwise we may not have had.

Something as simple as, "Oh, my gosh, where did you get that purse?!?" may not seem monumental, but it is precisely why fashion is such an excellent medium for sending strong messages. "Oh, this purse? Funny you should mention it. I saw it a few days ago and absolutely fell in love with it. It's made from discarded candy wrappers and was crafted using an ancient Mayan basket-weaving technique. It was produced by a family-run business that works with hundreds of artisans in Mexico. If you look closely, you'll see that each one of the wrappers is folded and weaved by hand. It's stunning, isn't it?"

Nahui Ollin candy-wrapper bags **www.nahuiollin.com**

This sort of conversation not only says something both about the wearer and the company's design philosophy, but also gives insight to another culture and puts the spotlight on people in a different part of the world. Discarded candy wrappers? Well, that makes a statement about waste. Working with local craftspeople? That says something about the label's cultural sensitivity. The fashion piece—in this case, the bag—had a personal story to tell that the wearer communicated through her style.

The most common misconception about sustainable fashion is that it comes in one color and looks one way: neutral, boxy, baggy, shapeless. On the contrary! The best sustainable fashion is invisible. Great design is just that—great design! It's vibrant, classy, and meticulously tailored. In this section, I'll show you a dazzling array of fashions and accessories that are all these things, not to mention sustainable. Read on; I think you'll find that the eco-designer profiles, details about their processes, and information about their environmental ethos will give you an enriching look behind the products.

An organic cotton blouse by Camilla Norrback **www.camillanorrback.com**

DENIM: BABY'S GOT THE BLUES!

Ahhh, blue jeans! Denim is one of the most iconic pieces of apparel of all time. Though developed in the 19th century as working-class wear, the denim market has greatly evolved over the last 150 years and has influenced almost every genre: cowboys, rebels, hipsters, hippies, freedom fighters, and fashionistas. Denim is one of those versatile materials that anyone can wear, which is why blue jeans are the most widely produced piece of apparel in the world: over 1.5 billion pairs sold worldwide!

A lightweight, organic cotton chambray, crossback dungaree skirt with a detachable bib and lots of pockets **www.howies.co.uk**

Fitted, organic cotton, stretch blazer by Fair Indigo **www.fairindigo.com**

Lauren denim skirt by Howies **www.howies.co.uk**

Lightweight organic denim jeans by Howies **www.howies.co.uk**

Custom-fit handwoven organic denim shorts with natural indigo dyes **www.goindigojeans.com**

Machja light-wash organic denim jeans **www.machja.com**

Machja skinny-fit dark-wash organic denim jeans **www.machja.com**

Loose-fit jeans made out of organic cotton, perfect for the summer months **www.howies.co.uk**

Eco-Stylephile: LEVI STRAUSS AND CO.

Levi's Design Challenge: Source cleaner, pesticide-free cotton.

Cotton, the most widely used fiber crop for our clothes, may seem natural, but it is one of the most heavily sprayed crops in the world. It accounts for only 3 percent of worldwide crops, but it uses approximately 25 percent of the world's insecticides and more than 10 percent of world's pesticides (herbicides, insecticides, and defoliants). Many of the pesticides used on cotton are likely to cause cancer. Tens of thousands of deaths occur each year in cotton-producing countries due to poisoning or improper use of pesticides.

Organic cotton in the field **www.marksandspencer.com**

Levi's Design Solution: Use only organic cotton (free of pesticides) or cleaner cotton alternatives (minimal pesticide use combined with natural pest control).

Organic cotton is grown without the use of chemicals and is now farmed in over 22 countries. In November of 2006, San Francisco–based Levi Strauss developed a line called Levi's Eco that uses organic cotton. They launched the products in the U.S., European, and Japanese marketplaces. Though they weren't the first company to develop, sell, and market an organic denim line, they were one of the biggest. Because they were in a position to influence smaller manufacturers and distributors to make the change, too, they recognized it as an important step for their company. In addition to the organic cotton they use in this line of denim, Levi's also uses recycled buttons, rivets, and zippers, and in some styles, natural organic indigo to eliminate the use of chemical dyes. The company's commitment is a reflection of a larger trend in this arena: Estimated global retail sales of organic cotton products increased from $1.1 billion in 2006 to $2.0 billion in 2007, and this number is predicted to grow to $6.8 billion by 2010.

www.levis.com

What Can You Do?

▬ Support organic farmers by purchasing organic products.

▬ Write to your favorite designers and companies and insist that they use organic or cleaner cotton in their product lines.

▬ Ask stores whether they carry organic cotton clothes. The more people ask, the more the store will become aware of the demand.

▬ Get involved in the organic cotton movement. Check out what these organizations are doing: Co-Op America, Organic Exchange, Sustainable Cotton Project, Pesticide Action Network, Organic Consumers Association, Better Cotton Initiative, Organic Trade Association, International Federation of Organic Agriculture Movements, and the Ethical Fashion Forum. For detailed information, visit the Resources section.

▬ Attend trade and fashion shows that support and sell organic products. Here are some popular ones: Ethical Fashion Show, Estethica, Green Festival, and All Things Organic. To get more information, check out the Resources section.

COTTON MOUTH

Even though cotton is not regulated as a food crop, its by-products easily find their way onto our dinner tables and into our beauty and cleaning products. Pietra Rivoli, author of *The Travels of a T-shirt in the Global Economy*, maps the connection between what we wear and what we eat:

The oil from the [cotton]seed, about 16 percent of the seed's weight . . . comes back in Snickers bars, Ragu spaghetti sauce, Peter Pan peanut butter, Girl Scout Cookies, Certs breath mints, and almost any kind of crispy snack food. The biggest buyer of cottonseed oil in the world is Frito-Lay.

Cottonseed oil is also the primary input in the production of olestra, a frying fat that leaves no trace of fat calories, and is also an important source of vitamin E for pharmaceutical producers. And finally, the oil is also processed into "soap stock" that turns up in soaps and detergents of all kinds. Colgate-Palmolive is also a major customer.

The meal of cottonseed constitutes almost half of the seed's weight. It contains high-quality protein and is used to feed cows, horses, hogs, chickens, turkeys, sheep, mules, and fish—many animals that are used to supply food for the public.

So next time you're trying to decide whether or not to buy those organic cotton jeans, think of your next bite of chicken tagine.

My Style, Naturally: I got my first pair of organic cotton jeans in 2005, four years after I started getting into sustainable fashion. It was a pair of Mantras from Loomstate. The jeans were a dark-washed organic denim with a wide flare at the ankle and contrasted yellow stitching—a classic pant I could wear several times a week. The perfectly placed signature, "Nature Calls," stitched inside the button fly, and the polka-dot pocket liners, however, were the details I fell in love with. I quickly learned that Loomstate cofounders, Scott Hahn and Rogan Gregory, were pioneers in eco-denim. "So many people were coming out with denim lines," they remembered. "We figured, if companies were going to knock us off, we'd do it the right way: with organic cotton and sound ecological principles. We really wanted to raise the bar."

www.loomstate.org

Design Label: Loomstate

When Scott Hahn and Rogan Gregory launched Loomstate, the first premium, organic denim line, in late 2003, they were faced with an authentic challenge: how to be a sustainable company. "When we started the brand, 100-percent-certified organic cotton didn't exist in commercially competitive denim," says Scott.

Scott and Rogan flew to Turkey and worked with textile engineer Mehmet Ali Babaoglu, who embraced their idea for a fully certified organic cotton line. The resulting effort yielded a beautiful, 13-ounce ringspun fabric, upon which they founded the company. Loomstate's first collection was made from Mehmet's denim and two weights of jersey that had been made from 100-percent-certified organic cotton from Africa.

Once the logistics on a viable organic cotton line were figured out, Scott and Rogan realized fairly quickly that Loomstate could help induce a massive change in the consciousness of the consumer and to supply partners. In order to do that, however, they needed every step of their process to be profitable, environmentally responsible, and socially accountable to the local and global communities. "Good design does more than catch an eye or fit snuggly on your bottom. It solves problems and utilizes people and resources in thoughtful, constructive ways," asserts Scott.

From their first brand, ROGAN, the two learned that good ideas would be copied by other brands, oftentimes by much larger players in the industry. "ROGAN had qualities that quickly became sought after and copied—from the design aesthetic to the understated attitude to our drive toward authenticity and function," says Scott. "This was a sign to us that if we were to compete in a shallow industry void of ethics, we would have to raise the bar and reinvent what it meant to provide a quality product to the market. The world certainly did not need another denim brand," he concludes.

Scott's own personal connection and commitment to the environment and to the communities from which they source runs deep. "I gained much as a boy growing up in a national park," he explains. "My grandfather Howard T. Rose built a marina for the National Park Service on Fire Island in 1964. He and my family proceeded to manage and operate the marina and concession for close to fifty years. The unique ecological and sociological dynamic was one that provided knowledge to the importance of conservation, civil service, and progressive social culture. I would not be who I am today without that experience, and Loomstate may have been just another clothing brand."

www.loomstate.org

Scott Hahn of Loomstate

SHOES: IF THE SHOE FITS, WEAR IT!

Shoes may well be the most important accessory in a woman's wardrobe. Someone once told me: Never skimp on your shoes or your bed because you're either in one or the other. Okay, okay, so it's not Confucian, but it sure as hell makes a lot of sense. After all, we all want happy feet and happy sleep.

- Form and Fauna microfiber vegan shoes with embellished brass grommet and rounded wooden heel **www.formandfauna.com**
- The Ibo by Terra Plana has a natural latex (rubber) sole, recycled foam foot beds, and vegetable-tanned leather. **www.terraplana.com**
- The Maputo sandal by Terra Plana is sourced as close to where it is manufactured as possible to reduce carbon emissions. It has a latex rice-husk sole and is vegetable-tanned. **www.terraplana.com**
- This cute, flat, open-toe sling-back sandal is made with an organic cotton upper and patent linen borders. **www.izzylane.com**
- Not crazy about leather? No worries. Mink has a great leather-alternative for the summer months. **www.minkshoes.com**
- Black linen flat shoe with patent-leather toe cap, handmade in Britain **www.izzylane.com**

■ A half d'Orsay open-toe platform, with laser-cut faux leather over canvas, by Charmoné is a striking accessory, especially with a cream-colored dress. **www.charmone.com**

▬ A handmade, solid cherry wedge, with recycled rubber sole and faux-suede liner **www.mohop.com**

■ The Yellow Peacock by Form and Fauna is comprised of a biodegradable synthetic upper and a heel designed from scrap alder wood. **www.formandfauna.com**

▬ This Form and Fauna shoe has a vintage feel and will look great with anything from trousers to sundresses. The upper part is made from biodegradable synthetic material, and the heel is made from second-generation scrap alder. **www.formandfauna.com**

▬ Faux patent-leather stiletto heel by Mink **www.minkshoes.com**

▬ Make a splash in these Hetty Rose heels, made from vintage kimono fabric. **www.hettyrose.co.uk**

■ Stir some envy in Charmoné's velvet d'Orsay Cinnamon heels with satin ruffles. They may quite possibly be some of the sexiest shoes on the planet. **www.charmone.com**

■ Sling-back heel created from a 1960s Scandinavian-design cotton **www.kitty-cooper.co.uk**

■ These comfortable flats are made from a 1950s barkcloth. **www.kitty-cooper.co.uk**

■ These may have been your grandmother's curtains, but they surely aren't your grandmother's shoes. **www.kitty-cooper.co.uk**

■ Even Cinderella would have been envious of these heels made from a 1930s dove-blue satin and 1950s fuchsia silk heel. **www.kitty-cooper.co.uk**

■ This seriously cute organic denim platform, with contrasting red stitching and a second-generation scrap-alder wedge, is a lovely complement to some short shorts. **www.formandfauna.com**

Niki Robinson's fun platform shoes are made of recycled materials. She says that she "goes to [flea] markets in search of unexpected treasure, which may evolve into the design of a shoe." **www.tecasan.com**

A Niki Robinson flat as bright as the Brazilian flag and made out of recycled materials **www.tecasan.com**

Cork wedge heel with crisscross straps **www.minkshoes.com**

A sweet vegan pump made with vintage fabric by Beyond Skin **www.beyondskin.co.uk**

A sparkly vegan pump by Mink **www.minkshoes.com**

Turn up the color with Hetty Rose heels, made from vintage kimono fabric. **www.hettyrose.co.uk**

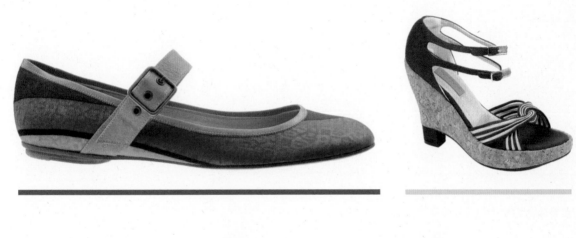

- Veja's Volley shoes were inspired by a Brazilian model of the 1970s. The canvas is made of organic cotton, and the sole is made from natural latex. **www.veja.fr**
- Terra Plana's Worn Again Bicycle shoes are made out of recycled denim, tires, and seat belts. **www.terraplana.com**
- A peephole vintage kimono classic heel by Hetty Rose **www.hettyrose.co.uk**
- These Moyi Ekolo boots seem to just fold over and hug the foot. They are made from vegetable-tanned leather by artisans in Namibia. **www.moyiekolo.fr**

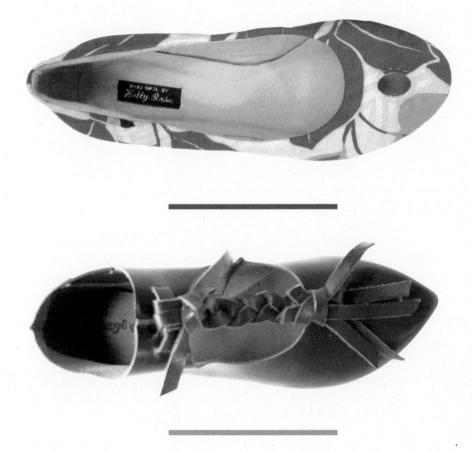

OTHER NOTABLE DESIGNERS: Kenneth Cole "Gentle Souls," Natalie Portman for Té Casan, MooShoes, Novacas, Simple Shoes

Eco-Stylephile: NIKE CONSIDERED

Nike's Design Challenge: Minimize ecological impact through the entire life cycle of the shoe.

It is not uncommon to have anywhere from 30 to 80 different components in one pair of shoes. Raw materials as varied as leather, rubber, and cotton come together to form the inner soles, outer soles, and shoelaces. Because shoes use so many widely varied materials from so many different places, designers are posed an especially big challenge when considering how to minimize environmental impact. They need to keep in mind all phases, from material sourcing to shipping to manufacturing.

Nike's Design Solution: Weave sustainable innovation into every phase of shoe production.

Nike Considered was started in 2005 with the goal of making the most sustainable shoe possible, without sacrificing design innovation. That year, the Nike Considered Boot won the Industrial Designers Society of America (IDSA) award for design ingenuity. A hemp lace woven into the leather upper made this handcrafted shoe a one-of-a-kind design that molds to the foot. The leather came from a manufacturing center that recycles its wastewater and uses vegetable-based dyes to tan the shoes. Better yet, Nike sourced the majority of the materials within 200 miles of its factory to reduce transportation costs and energy expenditures. The designers of the shoe reduced manufacturing waste by 61 percent, energy consumption by 35 percent, and the use of solvents by 89 percent.

Additionally, the shoe fit more effectively within Nike's Reuse-A-Shoe program, which recycles shoes after they have run their course. Due to positive consumer feedback and interest, the Nike Considered program is now a company-wide commitment that drives sustainable innovation across all of Nike's products and practices.
www.nike.com

What Can You Do?

- Encourage your favorite shoe companies to get off on the right foot and strengthen their social, environmental, and energy-efficiency standards.

- Join or start a campaign like the Clean Clothes Campaign (www.cleanclothes.org).

- Turn your sneakers into an athletic track: Nike has a shoe-recycling program that grinds up your old trainers and turns them into tracks and basketball courts (www.nikereuseashoe.com).

- Worn out your sole or broken a heel? Maintain your shoes and take them to a cobbler instead of throwing them away.

Did You Know? Nike has recycled about 20 million shoes to make 250 sport surfaces.

CRADLE TO CRADLE

The book, *Cradle to Cradle: Remaking the Way We Make Things*, by William McDonough and Michael Braungart, heralded a new and smarter design philosophy for the world.

In rethinking shoe design, Michael recalls his trip to a chromium-extraction factory. Chromium is the heavy metal used in shoe-leather tanning processes. He noticed that only older men, wearing gas masks, were working there. When he asked why this was, the supervisor explained that it took, on average, about twenty years for workers to develop cancer from chromium exposure. The company, therefore, made the decision to allow only workers older than fifty to do this job. Hmmmm.

Michael suggested that the design of the shoe could be more "intelligent" so as not to create any environmental or health impacts. Why not create a sole made or coated with biodegradable materials that could be detached after use? Why not create the rest of the shoe in plastics and polymers that were not harmful, and which could be recycled into new shoes?

Nike has taken McDonough and Braungart up on the idea, as have a number of textile materials companies, like the American Fibers and Yarns Company, Designtex, Milliken, Mission Rubber Company, Rohner Textil, Spectrum Yarns, and Victor Innovatex.
www.mbdc.com

Nike has committed to designing all footwear to meet the Nike Considered design-standard baseline (or higher) by 2011. Shoes like the trainers featured here use environmentally preferred materials, minimize waste, and focus on sustainable manufacturing processes.

The Nike Trash Talk is the first performance basketball shoe made from manufacturing waste. Nike footwear designer Kasey Jarvis says that she was "able to create a shoe that stands up to the stringent on-court performance requirements but is also more environmentally friendly." The upper part of the shoe is pieced together from leather and synthetic leather waste; the midsole uses ground foam scraps from factory production; the outsole uses natural rubber, which can be recycled into Nike Grind tracks afterward; and the shoelaces and sock liners are made from environmentally preferred materials, like organic fibers. The entire shoe is packaged in a fully recycled cardboard box. **www.nikeresponsibility.com**

Design Label: TOMS Shoes

My Style, Naturally: In the summer of 2007, I stepped onto the subway wearing my Flower Power TOMS. A girl next to me looked over and said, "Nice TOMS." I thanked her and we both went on our way. It was clear that the two of us knew the story of TOMS. It was like sharing an intimate secret with a stranger who suddenly feels like a friend. Three months later, I went on the TOMS shoe drop in South Africa. We partnered with Food 4 Africa and helped hand-deliver 50,000 shoes to school-aged children, from Johannesburg to informal settlements outside of Port Elizabeth, Empangeni, and Ingwavuma. At a school in Ingwavuma, the school's headmistress said, "These kids have never felt shoes on their feet. I thank you for coming here."

Several years ago, Blake Mycoskie was running around the world with his sister on the show *The Amazing Race*. "[That show] really inspired me to get out and see the world more," he says. In 2006, when Blake's fourth company was coming to life—the first-ever driver's education course strictly using hybrid vehicles—he was in his glory. "I thought I would celebrate my success by going to play polo in Argentina," he laughs. So Blake took the trip, but it was a trip that would take him on an entirely different journey.

Two hundred barefoot children: that's what it took to change Blake's perspective. "I saw all these kids in the village with no shoes, running around with cuts and dirt on their feet." TOMS, or Shoes for Tomorrow, began as a project with his polo instructor, Alejo Nitti. "We figured if I could just sell 250 pairs of shoes in the states, it would be enough to buy a plane ticket back to Argentina and give this one village shoes."

Blake did more than sell 250 pairs of shoes, however. An article in the *Los Angeles Times* helped sell 2,000 pairs in one day. "Even after that," Blake recollects, "I thought 'OK, this is exciting,' but it wasn't until October 2006 when I went to give away the shoes that I knew I wanted to do this full-time."

Blake's first moments in Argentina, playing with the kids and putting shoes on their feet, were very emotional. "It was like a dream coming true, and that's when I realized that this was much more significant than giving someone a pair of shoes."

A spring print by TOMS shoes

Blake Mycoskie, founder of TOMS

Knowing that TOMS was his future, Blake flew back to Los Angeles and sold his shares of the driver's ed company to his two partners. The deal was closed in January 2007, and Blake started concentrating solely on TOMS. "The shoes are just a vehicle to spend time with the kids, to enjoy life, and make everyone feel more comfortable. That's really what TOMS is all about," he says smiling. And TOMS still stays true to its original mission of one-for-one. For every shoe that is sold, one is given away to a child who doesn't have shoes.

After countless shoe drops in Argentina and one in South Africa, Blake is now giving all of his attention to the launch of a new TOMS boot. "I was speaking in a church in Northern California, and this woman came up to me and told me about people in Ethiopia who were suffering from a disease called podoconiosis, commonly called 'podo' or 'Mossy Foot.' It was terrible. I never saw anything like it before, and it is a completely preventable disease."

Podo is a debilitating disease that occurs in individuals who are regularly exposed to red-clay soils that come from volcanic rock, like the soils found in Ethiopia. The foot becomes inflamed and requires plastic surgery after prolonged irritation. In Ethiopia alone, approximately 11 million people, or 18 percent of the population, are at risk for it. "Now we are giving these special boots that are changing lives in a significant way and, in some ways, are saving lives because people who have the disease can't work, can't support themselves, and get ostracized from the rest of the community. We can teach kids to wash and wear their shoes, and they'll never get the disease. And for those who have it really bad, orthopedic surgery can be done. My dad happens to be an orthopedic surgeon. To think, what are the chances!?!" he exclaims. "[My dad is] very excited. All his life he was looking for a way to use his skills to do something besides make money. Ethiopia is going to be Argentina all over again for me, but it's a new frontier."

www.tomsshoes.com

Blake and a boy in Argentina after a shoe drop

The original TOMS shoe was designed after the *alpargata*, a flat-soled canvas shoe, commonly worn by farmers in rural Argentina.

The wrap boot is a departure from the *alpargata* and the first move by TOMS to compete in the higher-design marketplace. Unconventional in its look, the idea behind it is also, well, unconventional. "There are all these beautiful women in Argentina who are married to the polo players, but they get neglected during the polo season. So you see all these lovely ladies hanging out together in the bar. The idea for the wrap boot came from that. Design a boot that looks like the bandage wrap on the polo-pony's leg, so they can get more attention from their polo-playing husbands. And I tell you," assures Blake, "the boot really looks sexy."

Design Lines: Terra Plana, Worn Again, VivoBarefoot

He may come from a long line of shoe designers (try seven generations of shoe gurus), but Galahad Clark has carved out his own space in the shoe business with Terra Plana.

In 1825, the Quaker brothers James and Cyrus Clark created the first Clarks shoe—a sheepskin slipper. Housed in Somerset, England, the company has grown into a global brand, known not only for their high-quality shoes, but also their community-based ethos.

"I never intended to work in the shoe business," Galahad says. "I fought it for a while. I spent some time at university in Chapel Hill and got really into the music of the Wu-Tang Clan. As funny as it sounds, it was one of the things that really inspired me [to get back into shoes]. They were wearing shoes that my father had designed. They even shot a video in a shoe factory and came out with an album cover of these shoes that [my father] designed and doctored in a thousand different ways with bright and amazing colors. They were heroes of mine. I called them up pretending to have my father's endorsement. That was my chance to go meet them and make shoes with them. It was an extraordinary time."

Terra Plana was an existing company that his father was involved in, originally founded by sculptor Charles Bergman. In 2001, Galahad took over. "The original Terra Plana shoes were quite organic and made in a very artisanal way with organic materials and natural latex soles. I loved the concept of Terra Plana. I loved what it stood for. It really resonated with me, and I fell in love with the shoes." Galahad decided to carry on the Terra Plana philosophy but to infuse it with a deeper flavor of design and further explore the realm of sustainability.

"I went through a period of studying and learning about sustainability, which is a massively interesting, ultra-complex, multifaceted minefield really," he says. "Suddenly we were thinking about sustainable design from all kinds of angles: life-cycle analysis, materials efficiency, and energy efficiency.

My Style, Naturally: It took me a while to realize how much attention a great pair of shoes will get you. My first pair of eco-conscious heels was made by Terra Plana. The shoes were a black vegetable-tanned-leather ankle boot that laced in the front and had a recycled cork heel. The real draw, however, was the brightly patterned recycled quilt that had been used to make the entire front half of the shoe, resulting in each shoe having a slightly different pattern. I was often stopped and asked where I got them—maybe because people are not accustomed to seeing quilted boots. Whatever the reason, it wasn't hard to spread the good word about Terra Plana.

Galahad Clark of Terra Plana

"You are trying to minimize waste: waste energy, waste material, or just waste product at the root of it all. Ideally, you want the consumer attitudes to change and you want them to buy things that last, that they become attached to, and that they can repair."

Terra Plana now tries to incorporate all of these principles into their design ethos. "Your average shoe has 30 different components," says Galahad. Terra Plana now looks into repairability, lightness, anatomical design, and materials and durability to minimize toxins and waste. On the materials side, Terra Plana uses chrome-free leathers, pure latex soling, recycled rubber soles, and recycled foam foot beds. They've also introduced E-leather, which is a unique blend of leather and textile fibers re-woven and finished to look and feel like quality leather.

www.terraplana.com

"The first Terra Plana soles were made with *Lactae hevea*—the purest, self-sustaining natural rubber in the world, sitting for three weeks in the turning mold like cheese," laughs Galahad. "Since then, we have made soles out of all sorts of materials, respecting sustainability. My favorites are the ultrathin TPU soles on Vivo Barefoot—the puncture-resistance and thinness give you all the benefits of walking barefoot and all the protection of normal shoes. What could be more sustainable than shoes that are healthy for you and outlast the rest? Plus, your feet scuff less when barefoot due to a natural gait correction and extra grace in walking and running."

"We set out to make the minimum shoe possible, meaning minimum waste but maximum efficiency," Galahad says. "The strap is optional. Some kids in the Philippines perfected hang tens on longboards in the first strapless Dopies. Beat that!"

"These boots are made with vegetable-tanned leather and recycled quilts," Galahad points out. "They are made with a genuine stitch down canasta construction and girls love them. Every pair is unique, handmade, and particularly 'real' and repairable."

"This is a genuine turn shoe with chrome-free leather and hand-stitched details," says Galahad of the Mumbai. "It's a beautiful shoe and a distinctive style that is Terra Plana–femininity defined."

The Ursa has a lightweight, high-performance heel and a flexible sole.

"We partnered with Anti-Apathy on this shoe, which was called Worn Again. The first version was made of recycled parachutes, leather from car scraps, reclaimed rubber soles, tweed jackets, and prison blankets. They were 'rubbish' and people seemed to like that. We were the first brand to make shoes out of bicycle tires as well."

This is a comfortable walking shoe, made out of recycled quilts and other reclaimed materials.

SOUL OF AFRICA

Following a visit to a South African orphanage in 2003, Galahad's father, Lance Clark, decided he wanted to help with the plight of AIDS orphans. So he designed a moccasin, named the Khulani after the orphanage that inspired his initiative. "I cried when I first visited the orphanage," he says. "The little kids clung to my legs. They had no blankets, no books, there was only enough for basic food. I wanted to see if I could help them to help themselves and not just depend on foreign charity." Thus was born the Soul of Africa initiative. Clarks prepares shoe kits that are then hand-stitched by unemployed women from KwaZulu-Natal, South Africa.

For every pair sold (at an approximate $45 cost), nearly $10 goes toward the care and support of South African children orphaned due to AIDS. Additionally, each pair sold helps to provide employment for local villagers, many of whom are helping to care for family members also affected by the AIDS virus.

"It's a wonderfully successful project," says Galahad. "That project last year raised over a million dollars."

www.soulofafrica.org.za

BAGS: IT'S IN THE BAG!

According to Shop, Etc., three out of four women have a favorite handbag. And if we could choose only one designer item, 22 percent of us would choose a handbag over shoes. Considering that the average woman owns six bags (yes, we know you're not the average woman!), *Style, Naturally* has plenty of sustainable style solutions to satiate your love affair with the accessory that keeps us together.

Paper and plastic are soooo last season. Shop with a graphic-print reusable bag, like this bamboo-print bag by Envirosax. **www.envirosax.com**

Here's another stellar graphic print by Envirosax. **www.envirosax.com**

Anya Hindmarch's "I'm Not a Plastic Bag" caused a fury across continents in 2007. **www.anyahindmarch.com**

RetroActif takes discarded PVC art banners and turns them into classic, fun, and fashionable handbags. **www.retroactif.net**

These carryalls are made out of food bags by skilled artisans in Cambodia. **www.collpart.com**

b. happybags are a stylish alternative to paper and plastic. **www.bhappybags.com**

shopping bags

These handcrafted purses are made from silk and buffalo horn, created by artisans from the Nam Dinh province in Vietnam. Part of the profits from the bags go toward caring for disabled orphans in the community. **www.worldofgoodinc.com**

This uniquely designed bag is created by women in North Calcutta who were once sold or forced into prostitution because of extreme poverty. These bags give the women a chance for a better future. **www.freesetbags.com**

These great summer totes from Mad Imports are made by artisans in Madagascar out of a finely woven crochet and have a decorative coconut button. **www.buildanest.com**

This beautiful little bag is made in a community near Delhi, India, out of old saris. Each one is unique. **www.worldofgoodinc.com**

A basic, classy bag, handmade by Issan weavers of Northern Thailand **www.worldofgoodinc.com**

fair-trade bags

- Simple contemporary shape made out of felted wool **www.feltstudio.com**
- This felted Josh Jakus UM bag is perfect for traveling. It unzips to lay flat. **www.joshjakus.com**
- This lovely, rounded, felted-wool bag gives a contemporary look to everyday outfits. **www.piawallen.se**
- A lovely bamboo slat bag made in Bali **www.fiveaccessories.com**
- The Lily organic cotton bag, with PVC-free synthetic-leather trim and recycled PET lining, by Helen E. Riegle **www.her-design.com**

eco-friendly materials

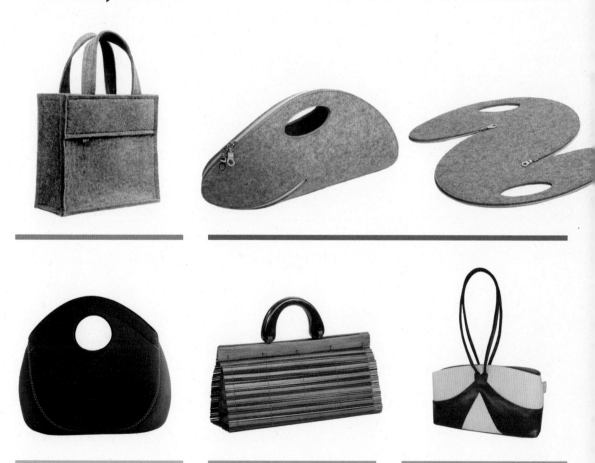

Need a chic way to charge your cell phone? Try a Solarjo. **www.solarjo.com**

A handsome satchel for that special guy in your life. Perfect for charging iPods and cell phones. The leather is vegetable-dyed (free of chrome and heavy metals), and the hemp/cotton fabric is hand-shibori-dyed with natural pigments. **www.noonsolar.com**

This is the perfect backpack to take on a picnic, day hiking, or camping. **www.rewarestore.com**

A beautiful tote with vegetable-dyed leather and naturally dyed hemp/cotton mix **www.noonsolar.com**

These high-powered showstoppers can charge many of your gizmos and gadgets. **www.voltaicsystems.com**

solar bags

My Style, Naturally: If I had to pick the piece from my collection that attracts the most attention, it would probably be Shayne McQuade's Voltaic solar bag, which is smartly designed with solar panels on the back. I have three of them, which may seem excessive, but I have put them all to good use. I use the small Daypack for short hikes or day trips. I use the Generator laptop bag for work, and the large Backpack for extended trips. The latter came in very handy in Africa. Whether I was in a hotel or in the bush, I was able to charge my camera, BlackBerry, and phone via my bag, with no problem whatsoever. One hour in direct sun will power over 3 hours of iPod playtime or over 1.5 hours of talk time on a typical cell phone. The number one question I am asked: "Does it charge your laptop?" The response: Voltaic's Generator bag uses a single solar panel to produce up to 14.7 watts of power. That means one full day of sunlight can fully charge a typical laptop. ***www.voltaicsystems.com***

The Hobo bag is made from PVC art banners. **www.retroactif.net**

Seattle-based Alchemy Goods turns recycled billboards and seat belts into carry totes. This particular bag is made out of 95 percent recycled materials, denoted by the little Ag 95 label in the right-hand corner. **www.alchemygoods.com**

French-based Bilum works with local artists to create these fancy billboard bags. **www.bilum.fr**

Australian-based 2xO (two times around) turns billboards into functional street-wear designs. **www.2xo.com.au**

No two billboard bags are ever the same. **www.2xo.com.au**

recycled: billboard and poster bags

▰▰ Toothpaste containers, juice boxes, and dish-detergent containers are turned into functional laptop bags. **www.xsprojectgroup.com**

▰▰ The perfect carryall for your gym clothes, made by artisans in Cambodia out of fish-feed bags **www.collpart.com**

▰▰ It's hard to top this basket-bag, crafted by artisans from Harare, Zimbabwe. Each bottle cap is straightened, cleaned, punched, and threaded by hand. **www.worldofgoodinc.com**

▰▰ A woven candy-wrapper bag created by artisans in Mexico **www.nahuiollin.com**

▰▰ A chain-linked candy-wrapper bag **www.ecoist.com**

▰▰ A recycled juice-pack bag, made by a women's cooperative in the Philippines **www.doybags.com**

recycled: consumer packaging

A recycled chain-link candy-wrapper purse **www.ecoist.com**

A recycled rice bag, made by artisans in Cambodia **www.collpart.com**

A chic wrapper bag with recycled leather straps **www.nahuiollin.com**

With trash, you find there is no "away." Here, tomato sauce packaging has been turned into a lunch container. **www.doybags.com**

Shopping for groceries in the city? Use this cart to get your stuff from the store to your front door. **www.collpart.com**

A hot little spring-loaded clutch, made from fabric sourced for the 1975 AMC Gremlin **www.kimwhitehandbags.com**

The checkered pattern of this bag comes from the seat fabric of a 1984 Ford. **www.kimwhitehandbags.com**

This is the ultimate little purse for girls who love cars. The fabric is reupholstered from a 1975 Buick Skylark and a Buick Apollo. **www.kimwhitehandbags.com**

This is a fancy little number. **http://shop.littlearth.com**

Harveys makes the best bags, out of woven seat belts. **www.seatbeltbags.com**

A classic cyclone purse, made from a recycled license plate **http://shop.littlearth.com**

recycled: car-part and tire bags

▰▰▰▰ A beautifully designed chocolate-colored seat-belt purse **www.seatbeltbags.com**

▰▰▰▰ A luxe little license-plate purse, with a little bling **http://shop.littlearth.com**

▰▰▰▰ The Uptown Bag by Passchal is made from truck-tire inner tubes and lined with leather. **www.passchal.com**

▰▰▰▰ A slim little recycled-tire purse for a night out **www.gimmegoods.com**

Did You Know? In 2003, the U.S. generated approximately 290 million scrap tires.

Did You Know? Tires should never be burned. Tire fumes can be hazardous and release harmful pollutants into the air and water.

Did You Know? Historically, scrap tires took up space in landfills, were stockpiled, or dumped illegally. Now markets exist for 80.4 percent of these scrap tires.

This little recycled-tire bag by English Retreads is perfect for those on the go. **www.englishretreads.com**

A very contemporary carrying case **www.gimmegoods.com**

This is a sweet "it" bag that is paparazzi-ready. The handles are made from repurposed bicycle tubes, and the rest is made from recycled tires. Check out the different colors it comes in at **www.englishretreads.com**

The Tri Bag, made out of truck inner tubes and lined with leather, is fiercely chic. **www.passchal.com**

Designer Katja Aga Sachse Thom achieves this bag's sophisticated, rounded design by using automobile inner tubes and stitching the seams together with traditional saddlemaker's techniques. **www.kastd.com**

Designer Valerie Doehler rescues old rubber tires and reincarnates them as handbags. **www.lucuma.com**

■■■■ Très chic "bowling" bag by Vegan Queen. The bag is made out of PVC-free polymer, vegetable rubber, organic cotton French terry, and recycled medallions. **www.veganqueen.com**

A vintage-belt bag **www.tinglondon.com**

A handbag made out of vintage slides **www.redcamper.com**

A fairly-traded and -designed handbag by Alessandra Bravo and Peruvian artisans. *Arpillera* folk art began in the 1970s, when social upheaval in Peru pushed the Andean communities to the cities. Women began learning sewing skills at home. Fabric is hand-stitched onto natural silk to give each bag a delicate look. **www.lucuma.com**

This carryall bag is perfect for hauling groceries or beach gear. It's made out of recycled ship sails. **www.reiter8.com**

miscellaneous bags

A bag made out of recycled fire hose and old billboards **www.2xo.com.au**

An out-of-this-world shoulder bag made from a landing parachute from the *Soyuz* International Space Station mission of April 2004. Don't believe it? It comes with an authenticated, signed certificate from A. Kaleri, Russian cosmonaut and flight engineer of the *Soyuz* TMA-3. **www.everquestdesign.com**

Finished reading your favorite book? Have it rebound into a purse by Caitlin over at **www.rebound-designs.com**

This bag is on fire. Feuerwear designer, Martin Klusener turns recycled fire hoses into durable bags. **www.feuerwear.de**

Fire hoses and seat belt straps make this little purse perfect for the streetwise style maven. **www.feuerwear.de**

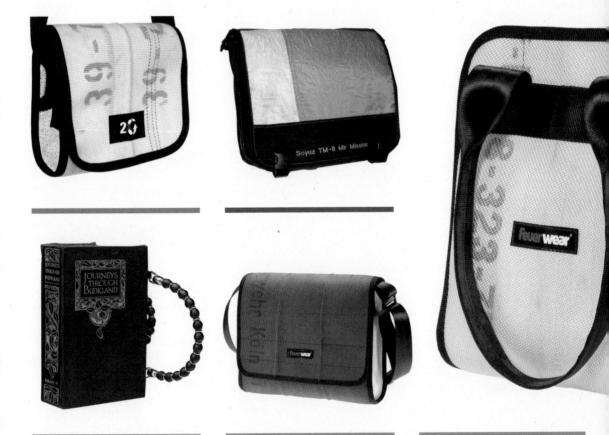

A reclaimed vintage handbag, with an original hand-painted motif by Vivien Cheng **www.viviencheng.com**

A perfect little clutch made from vintage fabric and old belt-buckle detailing **www.againnyc.com**

A terrific, metallic, vintage-fabric yoga-mat carrying case with solid brass hardware **www.sarahdonegan.com**

A metallic back pouch, recreated out of vintage fabric **www.sarahdonegan.com**

Piece Lily makes sweet little purses like this one out of found vintage fabrics. **www.piecelily.com**

recycled: vintage bags

Black vegetable-tanned leather, vintage purple lambskin, and an organic cotton twill liner make this bag truly special. **www.teichdesign.com**

The metal clasp from a vintage belt buckle finishes off this look. **www.love-eco.co.uk**

The chic, asymmetrical, butterfly-wing flap on this Vivien Cheng handbag is an eye-catcher. **www.viviencheng.com**

A drawstring bag made from vintage fabric **www.sarahdonegan.com**

A magenta, vintage lambskin clutch with organic cotton lining **www.teichdesign.com**

A vegetable-tanned leather clutch with vintage kimono fabric bow **www.hettyrose.co.uk**

The Bambi is a beautifully feminine bag. **www.sarahdonegan.com**

A vintage fabric bag by Enamore **www.enamore.co.uk**

An exclusive Amy Kathryn print with faux-leather shoulder strap **www.amykathryn.com**

Eco-Stylephile: XSPROJECT

XSProject's Design Challenge: Clean up waste and help fight poverty.

Artist and environmentalist Ann Wizer has lived in Asia for over 23 years. On moving to Jakarta in 2000, she witnessed the more than 350,000 *pemulung* (trash pickers), who collect and sell consumer waste for a living. Each trash picker's family survives on 35 to 45 American dollars per month. With an estimated 80,000 tons of non-biodegradable, nonrecyclable, flexible-plastic packaging manufactured in Indonesia every year, Ann decided to try an out-of-studio "intervention," tying together waste cleanup with increasing income opportunities for the disadvantaged.

XSProject's Design Solution: Take trash from the dump to high design.

Ann's "intervention" has evolved into XSProject, a non-profit social enterprise that buys flexible-plastic packaging waste collected by Jakarta's trash pickers, providing them with much-needed extra income. Working with other small-scale nongovernmental organizations (NGOs) and small cottage industries, XSProject transforms this waste into accessories that make a strong social and environmental statement.

In addition to creating income opportunities and reducing waste, XSProject works closely with schools, communities, companies, and NGOs to promote environmental awareness and recycling programs, and to help improve the lives of the trash pickers.

XSProject uses discarded waste packaging from detergents, shampoo, toothpaste, and cooking oil, collected from more than 30 companies. Since 2002,

XSProject has designed over 40 products, reused 14 tons of trash, and sold over 23,000 items throughout the world. These products help address environmental care, public education, and poverty issues. Projects like this help us reconsider our consumer choices, what we throw away, and how we define corporate responsibility.

What Ann Has to Say:

"Leaving my studio was imperative. One needs to be deeply involved, not alone in a studio separated from life on the street. I wanted my art to be relevant, to respond to social issues, not merely comment on them from the privileged position of the white-walled gallery. . . . Poverty is often despairingly patronized, or at best, romanticized, when packaged, photographed, and sanitized for the international culture audience. It doesn't smell anymore. . . . "

www.xsprojectgroup.com

What Can You Do?

- Always recycle. Who knew those shampoo bottles could end up in another nation's backyard?

- Don't use plastic bags for your purchases. Bring a reusable canvas or cloth bag to reduce waste.

- Plastic comes from oil. Look for alternatives that handle like plastic, such as compostable corn (Ingeo).

- Write your local government officials to help put a ban on plastic bags and other plastic packaging. It was shown that the plan to outlaw plastic bags in San Francisco, an ordinance that was approved by the city's Board of Supervisors in 2007, would reduce oil consumption by nearly 800,000 gallons a year. Banning plastic is possible. Some countries are already doing it, including Rwanda, Bhutan, Bangladesh, South Africa, and cities like Mumbai, Paris, and San Francisco.

- Ask companies to take action. Insist they have recycling programs or switch to packaging that is biodegradable or that can be reused, reduced, or recycled.

- If you don't already have one, start a recycling program in your community, in the workplace, or at local universities and schools. Check out if programs like Recyclebank are in your community. **www.recyclebank.com**

- Get a local school to sponsor an XSOutreach Program, an educational, environmental awareness activity that gets students involved in waste collection, recycling, and designing products. Revenues go to participating NGOs and into scholarship funds for local trash pickers' children. XSProject also has products that can be sold for school fundraisers, making students more aware of how to solve environmental problems through education and design. **www.xsprojectgroup.com/uc/xsoutreach.shtml**

- Support designers like Ann Wizer. Your purchase can make a world of difference to someone in another part of the world.

Did You Know? According to the *Wall Street Journal*, the United States goes through 100 billion plastic shopping bags annually. If we cut out all those plastic bags, we would save 1.5 billion liters of oil and eliminate 9.24 billion pounds of carbon dioxide annually.

XSProject's vibrant, durable bags are made out of nonrecyclable flexi-packaging.

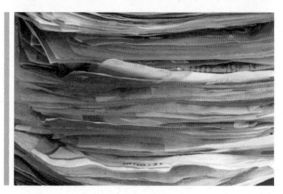

Local citizens collect and wash non-flexible packaging waste from the streets of Jakarta, Indonesia, for XSProject.

After collection, employees of XSProject prepare packages for washing and sanitation.

XSProject design utensils

Sewing the XSProject bags

Packages are dried and organized.

Ann Wizer does a lot of arts and crafts projects, like these flowers, in the local schools to raise awareness about trash and poverty.

JEWELRY: BAUBLES, BLING, AND SHINY THINGS!

We ladies can be magpies when it comes to jewelry. See something sparkly or colorful, and it's hard to pass by. Check out some of these pieces made from recycled glass, recycled metal, sustainably harvested wood, bowling balls, and other crazy materials.

A hand-carved ring **www.fiveaccessories.com**

Hand-crafted silver earrings by Denise Disharoon **www.fiveaccessories.com**

A bracelet made from old hardware and transistors **www.wiredresistance.com**

Soft rubber bracelet hand-linked with stainless steel **www.wiredresistance.com**

A Geraldine Rincon Costa Orange tagua nut necklace **www.geraldinerincon.com**

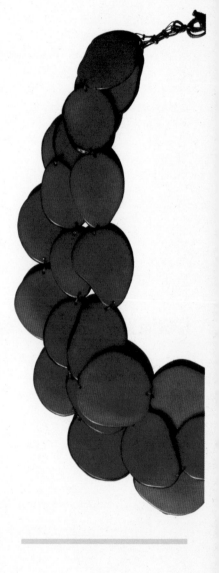

CHRISTINE J. BRANDT

A piece by Christine J. Brandt could easily qualify as one of the Seven Natural Wonders of the World. Each piece is its own architectural landscape. The shapes are reminiscent of ancient rock formations, magnificent glaciers, and burning red sand dunes.

Christine's jewelry is unique and handcrafted from ethically mined stones and sustainably harvested woods. Over the summer of 2007, she had the privilege of designing the "O" bracelet, exclusively for *Oprah* magazine, with women artisans of Rwanda. Christine explains, "The bracelet that I designed is called Sunset Sky and is a multi-strand design of Hessonite garnet and wood beads from Africa. Each bracelet is hand-beaded by the women of Rwanda."

www.christinejbrandt.com

The Sunset Sky bracelet is available at www.macys.com.

KIRSTEN MUENSTER

Kirsten is like a modern-day Michelangelo. She carves mini-masterpieces with a keen attention to detail and a deep appreciation for the color, pattern, shape, and history of each piece.

Kirsten finds her stones in the United States through trusted stone dealers, or she'll cut her own. She also occasionally recycles stones from vintage pieces; the silver she uses is always recycled. Sometimes Kirsten experiments with unexpected materials, such as "Fordite" and copper-fire brick, by-products of automotive paint plants and copper smelting, respectively. She has also worked with a material called "Bowlerine," made from recycled bowling balls.

"I've come to acknowledge the fact that the choices I make in my own work have an impact," says Kirsten. "I may be drawn in by the color, pattern, shape, and story behind my materials, but the choices I make regarding my jewelry can be best understood in terms of my attempt to achieve more eco-conscious selections."

www.kirstenmuenster.com

BE CARBON NEUTRAL™

Massimo LoBuglio, a climate psychologist by trade and the mastermind behind the BE CARBON NEUTRAL concept, is one of the few people in this world who can get me revved up over seemingly insignificant things, like how the color blue affects people's moods or a new billboard for Apple computers. With all his crazy energy and enthusiasm, you know that BE CARBON NEUTRAL has got to be brilliant.

The BE CARBON NEUTRAL campaign started off with a spinning-windmill pin design, hand-carved in NYC by Anthony Aletto, a fourth-generation Neapolitan fine-jewelry designer. The pin quickly became the "it" piece among environmental leaders: The campaign uses recycled metals and eco-friendly packaging and printing materials. And to top it off, production, manufacturing, and shipping are all carbon neutral.

The idea behind BE CARBON NEUTRAL is to get consumers engaged every step of the way. "It's about taking a Green journey," says Massimo. "We can inspire people all we want, but in order to create change, we must spring them into action."

With each BE CARBON NEUTRAL purchase, the campaign makes you carbon neutral for one month by supporting projects like reforestation, which helps soak up carbon before it clogs the atmosphere, or through investing in wind farms. The campaign's initial pieces are unique and handcrafted, ranging from the exquisite spinning-windmill cuff links to boho-chic pendants with insignia like "Love," "Peace," and "Be Eco-Friendly." The bridal program even offers luminous conflict-free diamonds and bespoke designs, as well as tools to carbon neutralize the wedding event.

www.eliminatecarbon.com

PALMA COLLECTION

The Palma Collection is completely on par with my sense of style: artisanal, vibrantly exotic, and steeped with a raw edge.

If you take a trip down the Pacific Coast of South America, you'll likely come upon the *Phytelephas macrocarpa*—a short, bushy palm tree that normally grows under the canopy of the dense, tropical rainforest. For centuries, locals have used the tree for a variety of things—from shade to carving figurines. When the fruit ripens, it drops to the ground and the locals collect it.

The secret to the Palma Collection lies in the nuts stored in this ripe fruit. Tagua nuts (or vegetable ivory as many people like to call it because of its durability and resemblance to animal ivory) are dried for about two months, until they are extremely hard. The outer shell is separated, and the dark skin is shaved off to reveal a beautiful, creamy ivory color.

The artisans polish the tagua to get a clean, shiny look and then dye them an array of vivid colors to use for making necklaces, hair accessories, bracelets, rings, and other incredible pieces.

http://store.palmacollection.com

SMART GLASS JEWELRY

It's like finding colored glass wash up on the beach, only better! Each Smart Glass Jewelry piece is handmade by Kathleen Plate. Many of her pieces are made from recycled glass, like Coca-Cola bottles and glass bottles from beauty products.

www.smartglassjewelry.com

Eco-Stylephile: A.D. SCHWARZ

a.d. schwarz's Design Challenge: Limit deforestation and help stop poverty.

Deforestation is wreaking havoc, at an alarming rate, on land and communities in tropical regions. One such region is the Miombo woodland in Southern Africa, the largest contiguous patch of deciduous tropical forest in the world. The destruction directly threatens the environment and the people living there. In November 2007, I drove down the coast of Mozambique and saw whole forests being burned for agriculture and charcoal. Piles of trees lay on the sides of the roads, burning throughout the night and making the area look like a war zone. These actions have serious consequences, such as higher soil temperatures, flash floods, late rains, and poorer soils.

a.d. schwarz's Design Solution: Create the highest value product out of sustainably harvested wood.

Allan Schwarz is a real-life Indiana Jones of architecture and design, minus the Hollywood hype. In 1994, the South African–born designer left his position as teaching fellow of a class, entitled Design with Nature, at the Massachusetts Institute of Technology (MIT) and set out on a mission to create a model for sustainable development. He leased a plot of land in Mezimbite, Mozambique, and started a nursery and workshop to produce sustainably harvested bracelets, furniture, essential oils, and other products. Soon after, he developed the Mezimbite Forest Centre to take detailed tree inventories and to create management plans to balance timber harvesting with replanting. Allan has trained

CHRISTO HARVEY

many people in the area, providing them with the skills to produce higher quality designs. His business and program aim to preserve indigenous forests and give locals skills, confidence, and economic incentives to manage the forests instead of cutting them down.

The simple elegance of his work is expressed in the a.d. schwarz heirloom label, which includes bracelets and kitchenware. The pieces possess an enviable beauty and are handcrafted from more than 40 different indigenous hardwoods. All products in the a.d. schwarz line carry the *Carimbo verde*, or "Green stamp," issued by the Franchise Development Programme (FDS), a local Mozambique NGO. All finishes are natural, made from indigenous vegetable oils and beeswax, and produced right on site by the region's co-op participants. Allan shows that, by design, populations can both preserve a region and make a living for themselves.

What Allan Has to Say:

"Poverty is at the root of forest destruction. My dream is to break the economic necessity of such destruction by economically empowering the forest's inhabitants, while building a culture of giving back what is taken or used from the forest and the landscape."

www.adschwarz.com

What Can You Do?

- If you are buying designs made out of wood, ask the retailer or designer if the wood is Forest Stewardship Council (FSC) certified or if it has some other trusted "Green stamp."

- Write to your favorite designers and companies and insist that they use sustainably harvested wood in their products.

- Get involved in sustainable forestry initiatives. See what organizations like Forest Ethics, Forest Stewardship Council, Greenpeace, Rainforest Action Network, and Rainforest Alliance are doing and see how you can get involved.

Preparing to plant some of the seedlings for the forest replanting program at the Mezimbite Forest Centre in Sofala Province, Mozambique

Bracelets made out of sustainably harvested African blackwood

A seedling at the Mezimbite Forest Centre

Design Label: Monique Péan

After a tragedy in the family, Monique Péan, a former financier at Goldman Sachs, found solace in making jewelry with a mission. "My little sister Vanessa passed away unexpectedly in a car accident. She was 16 at the time, and it totally changed my life. I couldn't sleep at night; designing jewelry kept me busy. It provided an escape for me that eventually became my passion."

Even after her sister's untimely passing, Monique learned from her. "She was in the process of setting up a foundation to provide scholarships to underprivileged students in Haiti. Inspired by her efforts, I sought to create a fine-jewelry line that would combine my love for design with my sister's philanthropic vision."

That vision led Monique to the far reaches of the Arctic Circle, where she met local villagers of Shishmaref, a traditional Inupiat Eskimo village. The village, which is only three miles long and a quarter-mile wide, is eroding up to ten feet per year due to intense flooding caused by global warming. The population of 600 now faces evacuation from their homeland and the loss of their cultural heritage.

Though the villagers were skeptical of Monique, she quickly connected with them as an artist. The area shares a rich history in indigenous art and is world-renowned for carvings in whale bones and walrus ivory. "Albert, one of the villagers, welcomed me into his home," Monique says. "He began unwrapping tiny treasures that were hidden in his one-room home. He showed me woolly mammoth tusks that were over 25,000 years old. It was as if I was in the backroom of the Smithsonian!"

Monique says that the fossilized ivory has been in the earth for tens of thousands of years but is coming to the surface now because of the intense erosion. "The island is in such a perilous state, and the entire village needs to be relocated."

Monique was keen on getting the Alaskan natives' story told. She now sources materials that are in their natural state from indigenous artists and works closely with the artisans of Alaska to create her pieces. "I combine art with awareness," she says. "If I can employ an indigenous artist or raise awareness of an environmental issue, then I am achieving what I set out to do."

> *My Style, Naturally:* Monique Péan is a woman with a big heart. I met her at my fund-raiser for Power Shift '07, the first-ever youth climate-change summit and lobby day. She gave a piece to the organization for auction. I didn't realize how much climate change plays a significant role in the development of her line until she told me her story.

Designer Monique Péan

A Little Goes a Long Way: One of Monique's latest collections is with Charity: Water, an organization that gives 100 percent of its donations toward providing clean water and sanitation facilities to people around the world. For this line, Monique chose to use recycled gold, since mining for gold releases mercury into the water system. Each piece from the Charity: Water collection will provide clean drinking water to at least 10 people for 20 years. "There's something a little bit infectious about combining art and community development," remarks Monique. "It makes me wonder why I ever pursued anything else professionally."

www.moniquepean.com

Eco-Stylephile: BRILLIANT EARTH

Brilliant Earth's Design Challenge: Source diamonds and gemstones that have been mined responsibly.

According to a report by the Gem and Jewelry Export Promotion Council and KPMG International, a Swiss-based financial and auditing firm, worldwide jewelry sales will grow 4.6 percent per year to reach $185 billion in 2010 and $230 billion in 2015. The global retail market for diamond jewelry has recently been estimated at $70 billion, according to the Diamond Information Center. A number of diamonds from conflict zones, particularly within Africa, have made their way into the market. The wars for these diamonds have cost an estimated 3.7 million lives.

In 2002, an association of diamond-producing and -trading countries developed the Kimberley Process Certification Scheme (KPCS), which has helped establish standards to stop trade in conflict diamonds. The process has reportedly reduced the number of conflict diamonds to an estimated one percent of the world's rough diamond supply, but it is a voluntary system that is self-regulated and only deals with designated conflict areas, not issues of environmental sustainability or social justice. As a result, many designers feel that it is not effective enough. Amnesty International conducted a survey of 246 jewelry stores across 50 cities and 18 states to find out more about the diamond market. They discovered that only 27 percent of shops were able to assure that they had a policy on conflict diamonds. When asked whether consumers inquired about conflict diamonds, 83 percent of respondents answered rarely or never. One hundred and ten shops refused outright to take the survey.

Brilliant Earth's Design Solutions: Create shining examples of conflict-free, environmentally responsible diamond jewelry.

Disturbed after not being able to find a reliable source for her wedding ring, Beth Gerstein and her business partner, Eric Grossberg, formed the conflict-free diamond company, Brilliant Earth. Through research, they found an area in the Canadian Arctic where they could trace the journey of each diamond to ensure that it had minimal impact on the environment and could be guaranteed conflict-free.

Brilliant Earth complies with environmental and labor laws of the Canadian government and indigenous tribal groups. The company designs and creates its jewelry domestically with audited business practices. Even the jewelry's gold and platinum come from recycled and renewed metals to help eliminate harsh mining. The company also helped cofound the Diamonds for Africa Fund,

The Digger's Pendant features the imprint of the palm of a diamond digger, fashioned from black oxidized silver and showcasing a conflict-free diamond.

a fund that gives back to local communities that have been directly harmed by the diamond trade. The company dedicates 5 percent of its profits to the fund, in addition to participating in a national effort to support communities affected by the trade.

www.brilliantearth.com

What Can You Do?

- Make sure that your diamond or precious-stone supplier can legitimately certify your gem from extraction to point of sale.

- Get involved in promoting responsible mining practices. Check out **www.nodirtygold.org**.

- Write your representatives to ask that they take a role in monitoring the diamond industry. If you are in the United States, you can find out who your representatives are at **www.house.gov/writerep**.

- Get involved in the conflict-free diamond movement. Donate to or check out what the following organizations are doing: Amnesty International, Conflict-Free Diamond Council, and Diamonds for Africa Fund.

Did You Know? The production of one gold ring generates 20 tons of mine waste.

An ethically and environmentally sourced Brilliant Earth diamond pendant

An ethically sourced Brilliant Earth platinum sapphire and diamond ring

A cascade of beautiful platinum around a Brilliant Earth diamond, sourced ethically and environmentally

Summer Rayne Oakes with a Brilliant Earth Digger's Pendant

BRAS AND PANTIES: OH, THE UNMENTIONABLES!

So what if you're the only person who gets to see what you're wearing underneath? Take it from the French women, who love their lingerie: The key to feeling feminine and sexy is what lies underneath. Slip into some of these sensuous numbers—made out of organic cottons, hemp-silks, and other luxurious materials.

Hemp-silk pink panties with ties **www.enamore.co.uk**

Organic cotton undies **www.howies.co.uk**

Graphic black-and-white-print silk panties **www.eco-boudoir.com**

Tie your partner up when you're feeling naughty, using these silk ties. **www.eco-boudoir.com**

A beautiful eye mask made from vintage fabric **www.enamore.co.uk**

Ruffled organic silk undies **www.greenknickers.org**

▬▬ Blue hemp-silk panties with tie sides **www.enamore.co.uk**

▬▬ A pink hemp-silk eye mask **www.enamore.co.uk**

▬▬ A delicate, black hemp-silk bra with scalloped lacing **www.enamore.co.uk**

▬▬ Ruffled black silk panties with heart-shaped earth **www.greenknickers.org**

▬▬ A bamboo-fiber bra with silk lining **www.eco-boudoir.com**

▬▬ Soft merino thong by Vera & William **www.verawilliam.no**

- A 100 percent natural-silk gown **www.eco-boudoir.com**
- A hemp/Tencel dress with organic cotton lace and satin bow does double-duty as a day dress and a sexy chemise. **www.enamore.co.uk**
- Printed silk tie camisole **www.eco-boudoir.com**
- Sophisticated hemp-silk lounge pants **www.eco-boudoir.com**
- A white hemp-silk eye mask **www.enamore.co.uk**
- Printed silk panties **www.eco-boudoir.com**

OTHER NOTABLE DESIGNERS: Eberjey, Nichole de Carle, BuenoStyle, Elise Aucouturier, Peau Ethique

ATHLETIC GEAR: DON'T SWEAT IT!

It doesn't matter if you hike, bike, run, climb, surf, or jump. There is environmentally friendly gear for all of your athletic pursuits. Get a good stretch or sweat going in some of these pieces, which utilize the latest high-performance fibers—like organic cotton jersey, bamboo, and recycled PET (plastic bottles).

The Alana organic cotton hoodie is perfect for warm-ups and lounging around. **www.prana.com**

You gotta have a pair of organic cotton cords. **www.howies.co.uk**

The soft, comfy Alana pant **www.prana.com**

These flip-top mittens are great for running in colder climates. **www.howies.co.uk**

An organic cotton jacket for cooler weather **www.howies.co.uk**

A form-flattering, organic cotton yoga top, with excellent coverage **www.prana.com**

Look pretty in pink while out on a walk/run. **www.howies.co.uk**

An organic cotton jersey fitted turtleneck **www.prana.com**

Organic cotton "Divine" pants **www.prana.com**

A great little run tank, brought to you by Howies **www.howies.co.uk**

A fitted organic cotton tracksuit **www.howies.co.uk**

A PVC-free yoga mat, made from carbon- and hydrogen-bonded compounds known as thermal plastic elastomer (TPE). Totally slip-resistant **www.prana.com**

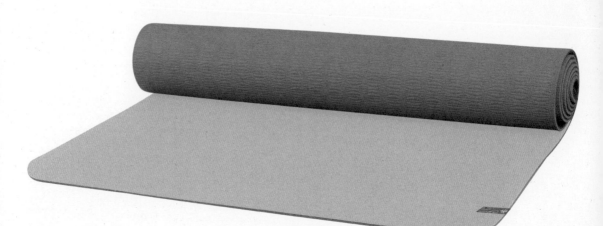

OTHER NOTABLE DESIGNERS: Nike, Adidas, Quiksilver

EVERYDAY WEAR: FUN, FLIRTY, AND COMFORTABLE

Sometimes we girls just want to throw on the no-fuss dress and look great. Check out these designers for great clothes you can wear day and night.

An organic cotton tie-waist dress **www.stellamccartney.com**

A silk dress made in the USA by Doie Designs **www.doiedesigns.com**

Bamboo-fiber V-neck dress **www.doiedesigns.com**

This bamboo deep V-neck dress with silk sleeves effortlessly transitions from day to night. Dress it up with accessories. **www.doiedesigns.com**

This bat-sleeve jacket is perfect for colder days. **www.stellamccartney.com**

Lara Miller answers a busy woman's need for function and versatility. Her buttery bamboo knits may be worn myriad ways. Most pieces can be wrapped, untied, and flipped to create entirely new garments. I always have a blast trying her stuff on. **www.laramiller.net**

A shirt by Skin and Threads **www.skinandthreads.com**

Contrasting black-and-white organic cotton garments **www.laramiller.net**

Organic cotton dress and jacket **www.skinandthreads.com**

A feminine, ruffled blouse made from silk and organic cotton by Camilla Norrback **www.camillanorrback.com**

Katharine Hamnett's organic cotton tees, hoodies, and vest dresses are eye-catching pieces that always seem to get a few looks. I love pairing her shirts with great jeans and topping it all off with high heels. **www.katharinehamnett.com**

OTHER NOTABLE DESIGNERS: Beau Soleil, Loyale, John Patrick Organic, Undesigned, The Battalion, ecoSKIN, Stewart and Brown, Toggery, SameUnderneath, Chloe Angus

SPECIAL PIECES: TO BE CHERISHED FOREVER

We've all walked through a store and glimpsed a garment that seemed to be made just for us. Perhaps it's something that is truly one of a kind, lovingly sewn together from vintage fabrics and found lace; or maybe it's a piece that has been hand-embroidered or -embellished by artisans from another country. Whatever it may be, you know it will be part of your wardrobe—and memories—forever; feeling good just never seems to go out of style.

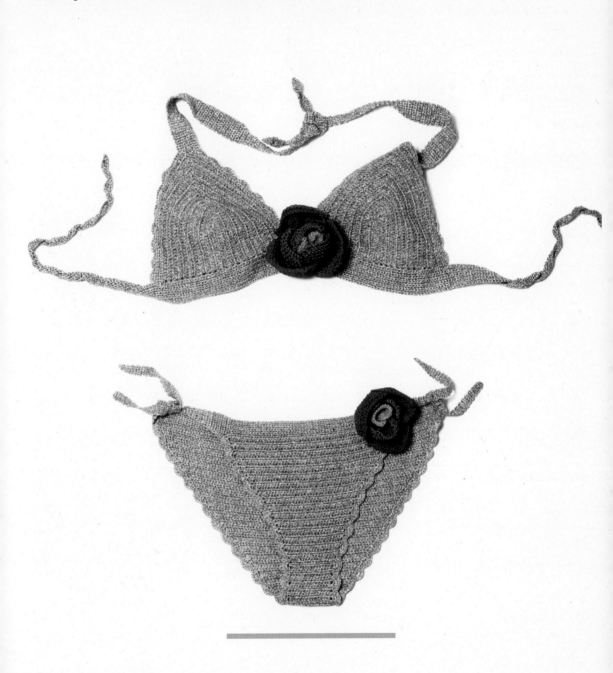

■■■■■■ A Super Lucky Cat recycled scarf blouse **www.greenwithglamour.com**

■■■■■■ A recycled cashmere sweater, with floral embellishments **www.deborahlindquist.com**

■■■■■■ A beautiful, vintage floral-print dress **www.enamore.co.uk**

■■■■■■ Marigold-swirled vintage fabric, tailored into a lovely summer dress **www.enamore.co.uk**

■■■■■■ A signature-tailored jacket with double cuffs made from vintage kimono fabrics by AOI **www.devidoll.com**

OTHER NOTABLE DESIGNERS: Myco Anna, On and On, Ekovaruhuset, Bird Textile, Caravana, Carolina K, Velvet Leaf

Design Label: Alabama Chanin

Natalie "Alabama" Chanin says she got her design background from the women in her family. "I think what I realized is that their hands were always moving, always making something to enrich our lives," she begins. "They were always tatting lace or making quilts or shelling peas or making preserves. They were really well-versed in the domestic arts, and that has had a strong influence on my design."

The Alabama Chanin label (formerly known as Project Alabama) pays homage to the traditional handcraft and quilting history of the rural South. Recycled cotton shirts are re-dyed, stitched, beaded, and transformed into exquisite couture pieces. "The garments we make are extremely time-consuming," says Natalie. "We have some garments that take sixteen women up to three weeks to make. We don't want to make our products all exclusive, so we've figured out how to do more accessible designs and kits, too."

The label got its start with a T-shirt. Natalie, who was born and raised in Alabama, and later worked in fashion design in New York and Europe, was on sabbatical in New York and about to go to a party. "I had nothing to wear," she reminisces, "so I took this T-shirt apart and sewed it back together again."

People were so curious and enthusiastic about the shirt that she started making versions for her friends and family. "The best part of it," she says, "was that I really enjoyed stitching it."

Natalie took the idea of one-of-a-kind, hand-stitched shirts to different manufacturing facilities in New York. They thought she was crazy. The process was too time-consuming and very difficult to do.

"The more I looked at it, the more I realized it looked like a quilting stitch," Natalie recollects. That brought Natalie back to the memories of quilting circles in her hometown. She called up the ladies in Florence, Alabama, and sure enough, she found people who wanted to sew. They made 200 hand-stitched shirts and took them to New York's February 2001 Fashion Week. She sold every single one, but on top of that, people began placing wholesale orders.

Natalie set up a production office in Alabama, and after 22 years of being away, she knew she was home. "I think I speak for all of us that we love this company. It is quite incredible to sit on County Road 200 and be able to do a work that you love."

Alabama Chanin has now extended their line to include jewelry, home textiles, and furniture—items all made by hand in Alabama. "These kinds of handcrafts are a dying art," she says. "I would like to hope that what we are doing—preserving this handcraft—is being able to preserve a piece of history—a part of the rural South and rural America."

www.alabamachanin.com

Natalie Chanin of the Alabama Chanin label

Alabama Chanin's signature look is a handcrafted quilting stitch. Sometimes six women may have touched the garment before it is even finished.

Handcrafted floral corsagés

Close-up of hand-stitching

One of Alabama Chanin's signature reclaimed jewelry pieces.

Design Label: People Tree

My Style, Naturally: It was December 2005, and I was in Hong Kong for the World Trade Organization Ministerial Conference, a meeting between nations that determines what trade will look like over the next decade. A mob, more than ten thousand strong and representing 160 nations, protested outside the meeting halls, chanting, "Down, down with the WTO." Inside one of the buildings, I was backstage preparing for a fair-trade fashion show with designs by People Tree. That's where I met Safia for the first time. Instead of joining the mob to chant "Down, down," we focused on bringing attention to the positive results that fair trade can bring to people and communities.

You could say that Safia Minney single-handedly brought fair-trade fashion to Japan. Heck, you could even say that Safia Minney helped put the words *fair trade* and *fashion* in the same sentence!

Safia realized early on that fair trade helps transform lives. "My father . . . came from a corrugated iron–roofed house that is synonymous with the poor or economically disadvantaged in Third World countries," she said in an interview for *Lucire* magazine. "[Where you're born is] just the luck of the draw."

People Tree now works with 50 different cooperatives across 15 countries, with headquarters in both London and Japan, which she will admit is no small feat. "We started very simply in the Japanese market over twelve years ago. It was a modest line of caftan tops made by women in Swallows, a small isolated village in Northern Bangladesh. We managed the operation out of my garage for three years. It's incredibly expensive to set up infrastructure and employ the traditional skills of people."

Swallows holds a special place in Safia's heart and is an area with which she still works to this day. "The women were left with no husbands or older sons after the Indo-Pakistani War of 1971," she says. "They were faced with the challenge of rebuilding the economy from the ground up."

The women's resilience is a true testament to the unbreakable human spirit. They began weaving, a skill normally left to men. "In a couple years, they became extremely good," she muses. "People Tree got involved to help them with quality and design direction."

Safia in harvested organic cotton

"Along the way, we gradually introduced pattern-cutting skills, improvement of handwoven fabrics, embroidery, beadwork, and even organic cotton initiatives." The women of Swallows also recently started a day-care center for children. "They are incredibly pro-women and pro-environment," Safia says. "In terms of women's issues, they have literacy programs, run micro-credit loans, and educate about child trafficking, which is common in the area. They do it all themselves," she beams.

Within the past year, Safia learned that the funding for the school in the area would disappear in five years. She acted quickly. "We put a premium on the products made in Bangladesh and give that money to the school. You can't just sit there and see a child's future go out the door. There are over 300 children here, and they are incredibly bright. Some go on to teach, some go into nursing, some work in the nonprofit sector for the region, and still others work in the handicrafts unit."

People Tree continues to work with the women of Swallows and is expanding organic cotton programs in the area so that farmers and their families are not exposed to pesticides.

From the Rag Trade to the Runways

One of Safia's greatest joys is taking People Tree catalogs and magazine editorials of their product back to the artisans in the villages. "They are just so extremely proud that their work is made in the environment that it is made in and looking so glamorous," she says. "Oftentimes, the men and women of the area can't imagine that they can give anything back to such a wealthy country as the UK or Japan. You know, they will see Toyota cars and trucks on the road and turn to me and say, 'We are giving something back to the country that makes those cars. It's a miracle.'"

www.peopletree.co.uk

Model Ann Markley wears People Tree

A handwoven 100 percent cotton shirt, with a decadent ruffle, created in collaboration with designer Richard Nicoll and Bangladeshi weavers **www.peopletree.co.uk**

A fair-trade, 100 percent organic cotton jersey bubble-sleeve dress, created in collaboration with New York–based designer Thakoon and Assisi Garments in Southern India **www.peopletree.co.uk**

A fair-trade, 100 percent organic cotton jersey dress, made in India **www.peopletree.co.uk**

A handwoven silk organic cotton shirt, made by artisans in Folk, Bangladesh **www.peopletree.co.uk**

A fair-trade handwoven silk blouse made in India **www.peopletree.co.uk**

A handwoven sweater **www.peopletree.co.uk**

A fair-trade, 100 percent handwoven, cotton blouse, with coconut-shell buttons **www.peopletree.co.uk**

Benita Singh:

Fair-trade consultant; account executive at BBMG; cofounder of Mercado Global; cofounder of League of Artisans

A good friend from college put Benita in touch with me. I had been working on eco-fashion stuff while she was in the midst of setting up Mercado Global, a nonprofit organization that helps develop and market fair-trade products to the U.S. market. The summer before her senior year in college, she took a formative trip to Guatemala. "I saw things that were more beautiful and so much more demonstrative of art and culture than anywhere in the States, but the women there could not market the products," she says.

Where are you from?

I grew up on Long Island, but my parents are from India. I spent a lot of time in India growing up, and I go back at least once a year.

What are you wearing?

This is an organic cotton Calvin Klein dress I got in Bombay. The shoes I got at Shoe Mania in Union Square. The red pendant I bought from a woman on the beach in Goa, India. The bag was made by a cooperative in Pondicherry on the southern tip of India. I got it at ABC Carpet and Home.

What are your favorite places to shop?

NEW YORK

Takashimaya (www.ny-takashimaya.com) is a great place to shop. It isn't about the label, it's about quality materials and just the uniqueness and value of the designers they have there. The store brings in undiscovered names and really believes in new designers.

ABC Carpet and Home (www.abchome.com) because you are surrounded in every single sense with a sustainable lifestyle.

LONDON

Portobello Market because you get these amazing one-off vintage pieces that no one else will have. The vendors have incredible stories about each piece. The ambience is wonderful because you are shopping with people who appreciate the same things you do.

INDIA

Hauz Khas (www.hauzkhas.com), a market in Delhi, is a strip of designers who value the handmade craft. It is not "designer" clothes in the sense that it is a brand, but you look at it, and you find so much value in it. You can look at a piece and see how much time went into making it.

Who are your favorite designers?

I like classic designers, like Donna Karan and Michael Kors.

Which fashion era or icon do you love?

Any era that embraced color and fine tailoring—maybe a bit of the Victorian era.

Take me through your closet.

My closet is a reflection of my travels. I use my wardrobe to remember where I have been. I have fine-tailored British hunting jackets, hand-beaded kurtas from India, and Guatemalan peasant shirts.

Which fashion rules do you follow?

• Better to be overdressed than underdressed.
• Reuse and donate. I usually give directly to people who I know need it.
• Accessorize. Focus more on your accessories than your outfit. You can wear the same thing two days in a row and totally change the look just by accessories alone. There is so much potential to change the world through accessories too because so many artisans around the world are capable of making them.

What are your favorite fashion pieces?

A *kalamkari* silk scarf from League of Artisans (www.lotusbyloa.com): it is hand-painted in pomegranate and vegetable dyes. My bag from the Lenore Collection (www.lenorecollection.com): she takes newspaper ads and makes them into bags; the weaving is all done by a women's cooperative in Thailand.

What motto do you live by?

I do yoga, so I have a lot of mantras that I follow. Don't be overconfident, but be fearless. Share. Live in the moment.

Ethika Boutique: In October 2005, an earthquake rocked Pakistan, leaving many casualties and destroying nearly 6,000 schools, most of which have not been rebuilt. The government and aid agencies will be tackling the work of reconstruction in the coming years, but grassroots work in the form of innovative business models can create immediate change. Ethika works with skilled Pakistani women, largely in rural areas, to create high-end, limited-run design pieces that create a livelihood for the women and children in the area.

www.ethikaboutique.com

A contemporary tunic inspired by Morocco

A handwoven silk jacket is perfect for wearing over an elegant dress. The puff-sleeved shoulders, cinched waist, and slight bustle below the waist give women the loveliest curves.

A chic jacket with hand-embroidered floral detailing

A black georgette shirt with raw-silk ruffles, necktie, cuffs and beautiful embroidery on the sleeves

OTHER NOTABLE DESIGNERS: Arne and Carlos, BLLACK, Ciel, FIN, Les Racines du Ciel, Rodnik, Sakina M'sa, Stella McCartney, Swati Argade, Maggie Norris, Deborah Milner

Design Label: Bahar Shahpar

Bahar Shahpar got her start in the fashion industry by being a jill-of-all-trades. "Makeup, art direction, styling, custom accessory designs," she says with a smile in her eyes. In 2004, she launched design lines, I Love Raw Meat and Agricult, which eventually developed into her self-titled label, Bahar Shahpar, in the spring/summer of 2007. "As I was doing the research to get a line started, I learned how destructive the textiles industry could be. . . . It was a no-brainer to try to follow a philosophy of sustainable design."

Originally from Iran, Bahar's parents immigrated to the United States when she was a young girl. "I essentially grew up in an immigrant family," she says. "There are doctrines inherent in that—working hard and living the American Dream. As much as my parents embraced the American lifestyle and encouraged us to explore—there was a definite old-world sensibility. I didn't grow up thinking about environmental issues. . . . Recycling is about all it took."

What Bahar did grow up with, however, was an innate curiosity about society, constantly questioning why things are the way they are. "I tend to be academic. [She has a degree in psychology.] But this is really a lifestyle issue, and sustainability is about a lifestyle change. It's so easy to get caught up in the headiness of it, the philosophy, and the emotion of it—it all feels good. That is why people have latched onto it as a popular consumer trend. It feels good."

She will admit that the "feeling good" part takes some work. "There are a lot of tough choices, sacrifices, and compromises," she asserts. "That part of it was a real reality check for me. It's easy to talk about it, but to do it is a different thing."

Different Generations, Same Philosophy

"My mom and I talk a lot about what I do," Bahar says. "Even though we don't share the same experiences, we can relate to one another. She once said to me: 'Bahar, when I grew up, we carried canvas bags to the store. It doesn't make sense to use plastic bags.' They had that practicality—and they had that appreciation for resources—that I don't think we have here," remarks Shahpar. "I'm glad I grew up with that as my basis. I have an appreciation not only for the way things were but an appreciation for practicality."

Bahar Shahpar in one of her signature designs

Now Bahar tries to address many aspects of sustainability, not just as a designer, but also as a showroom manager. In the spring of 2007, she co-launched The Four Hundred, a sales showroom and brand-development agency focusing on high-end sustainable design lines. "I saw a huge void in the marketplace for representation. I really understand the unique challenges that these designers have while they are trying to adhere to a philosophy of sustainability," she says.

"The showroom gives us a place to have a really edited point of view on what is happening in sustainable design. We focus on high-end, innovative design, high-quality construction and craftsmanship—and of course, people who really share a passion and aspiration toward sustainability in their manufacturing and production. In order for these brands to succeed, they have to integrate into the mainstream market and be able to hang alongside all the other contemporary brands."

So far, Bahar has received high praise from buyers—from eco-boutiques to Saks. "It's not just the product we are selling," she assures me. "It is a lifestyle and philosophy behind the product."

What's in Bahar's Closet? She calls it a "flea market by the highway." "It's a mix of things that I have had for the last twenty years or so. It is a mix of rolls of fabric, things I can't bear to get rid of (always in a pile), boxes of vintage collections—like sunglasses and scarves—and bags of containers. My tote and container collection is crazy! And I am definitely a bag lady. I'm one of those people who always wants to be prepared. You never know if you'll get too hot, if you'll need a change of wardrobe, or if your lips will get chapped."

www.baharshahpar.com
www.showroomfourhundred.com

A silk blouse and organic cotton screen-print pencil skirt by Bahar Shahpar

Design Label: Leila Hafzi Designs

I first met Norwegian-born Leila Hafzi at the Ethical Fashion Show in Paris, October 2007. Her taste in design is impeccable, and I was drawn to her intricate dresses knitted out of nettle. One in particular caught my eye: a floor-length dress hand-dyed in a natural chartreuse color, reminiscent in color to the Dior dress Nicole Kidman wore at the Academy Awards in 1997. It was dramatic. It was sophisticated. I couldn't believe it was made from nettle, a plant that is often associated with pricking bare legs in the summer. But here it was being used as haute couture design material.

Back in the 1990s, Leila had to create a small collection in order to get into design school. She made up her mind to go to Kathmandu, since her friends told her that was where she would find the finest fabrics and tailors. "My first experience in Nepal shook me," she reflects. "I met all these talented craftsmen and women and I experienced Tibetan art and Buddhist philosophy, the poor people and young street children, disabled men crawling through the dusty streets. . . . It captured my feelings and sorrow because you realize you can't save them all."

Nepal didn't become just a place for Leila to source fabric, it became her mission. She was convinced that she could make a difference, however small. "I wanted to prove that Nepal could produce and export top-class designer garments that appeal to Western sensibilities. Through this, I knew I could make a few small changes and inspire others to do the same."

While in Nepal, Leila met Shobha Pandey, a young Nepali woman who had recently started a small-scale knitting project using hemp and nettle thread. "I liked the untreated rough material. Most of all, I love being able to give knitting work to the women." Sure enough, within a short period of time, Leila and Shobha's project grew to include around 200 women. "Once Shobha told me, 'Leila, I have a good house now and don't need to work as much as I am, but without this business, the women have no work to go to and cannot send their children to school.'" Leila also started working with a tailor who used recycled silk saris, which she often uses in her line. With her assistance, he was able to triple the size of his small workshop and opened up a tailor business in Delhi two years later.

When Leila came back to Norway in 1997, she presented a show to 400 guests. Her company was the first to present such unique, eco-conscious fabrics with a cultural- and community-development focus. Her designs continue to be a fusion of cultures, highly symbolic to the present-day Nepalese. Some of her designs

Designer Leila Hafzi

OTHER NOTABLE DESIGNERS: Katharine E. Hamnett, Linda Loudermilk, SANS, Commune

cross over to five or six distinct cultural groups. Some of the Nepalese, Tibetan, and Indian weavers collaborate with Norwegian and Iranian artists. Hand-knitted lace may come from a social project in Bangladesh, and then a Buddhist factory translates motifs into beautiful hand-painted silks.

"Nepal is so special," Leila explains. "Imagine such a poor country taking thousands of refugees from Bhutan and Tibet. They don't even have enough work for themselves, yet they still managed to adopt these newcomers who have a different culture and a different way of life, and they live in harmony, practically on top of one another. My idea was to create designs with each of these cultural groups and support the traditional techniques of each."

Becoming more reflective, Leila admits, "I know that trying to get kids off the streets, away from dope and pedophiliac tourists is one hell of a job. It is not the one I am most competent to do. Sometimes I look back on it and ask, 'Did I choose this, or did it choose me?' One thing is for certain: I am no longer a blind tourist." It's a curious statement because it carries so much meaning. One can even scratch out the word "tourist" and just make the statement, "I am no longer blind." The greatest part of being in Nepal for Leila has been her realization that, "Almost everyone has a choice. Even here. Helping people realize what is best for them, however, is a quest all on its own."

www.leila-hafzi.com

Hand-painted 100 percent silk Leila Hafzi dress
A silk-chiffon Leila Hafzi dress with horn-belt

Design Line: Noir

Peter Ingwersen worked at Levi Strauss for fifteen years before launching his über-sexy label, Noir, in 2005. Though Noir's sleek tailoring and sexy demeanor is a departure from the 501 environment, Peter incorporated into his line the idea of Corporate Social Responsibility, or CSR, something that he first learned about at Levi's. This is a concept whereby organizations consider the interests of society by taking responsibility for the impact of their activities on customers, employees, shareholders, communities, and the environment in all aspects of their operations.

"We want to be the brand that turns CSR sexy," Peter says. It's a bold statement, but it's not a stretch for this ultrachic Danish brand. Noir is liberating because it doesn't hold back its point of view. It is provocative, sensual, fearless, and even a little naughty. It oozes sex appeal. "You can't abolish the DNA of fashion," he attests. "It needs to be bona fide sexy for it to work."

Since Noir's launch, Peter has demonstrated that you can make commitments without compromise. "Our first collection was 45 percent certified, but now we are pushing 80 percent," he says. "You need to envision a plan—a 'wouldn't it be wonderful if . . . '—and then you work toward that commitment. Do it step-by-step."

One of Peter's "wouldn't-it-be-wonderful" goals was to help create the highest quality organic, fair-trade cotton in Africa and to be transparent every step of the way. "Many African nations are capable of producing quality cotton, but because other countries, like the United States, are highly subsidized [the government gives money to produce cotton], many African nations cannot compete in the global market," he explains.

Peter knew his team could help bring marketing and selling power to the table, but he would need partners that shared his vision and who would not compromise on quality, environmental standards, or ethics. He approached six sub-Saharan countries, including Kenya, Tanzania, and Uganda. The government of Uganda was the only one that responded. The Ugandan ambassador, eager to partner with Noir, said that the country was looking into cotton as one of its key development initiatives.

Peter Ingwersen, founder of Noir

Though it's taken a couple of years to get the quality fiber he was looking for, patience and a deep understanding of sustainable development have paid off. Peter has begun using the Ugandan-produced cotton (trademarked as Illuminati II) in his own line and has made it available to other luxury brands for purchase.

"It's not good enough to go to a dinner party and say you have the latest Balenciaga bag. It's about coming in with the latest sleek CSR product. That is the new prestige," he asserts. "You need to show that you care. You need to show you are involved, that you are part of the solution."

www-noir-illuminati2.com

A well-tailored, organic cotton-silk suit by Noir **www.noir-illuminati2.com**

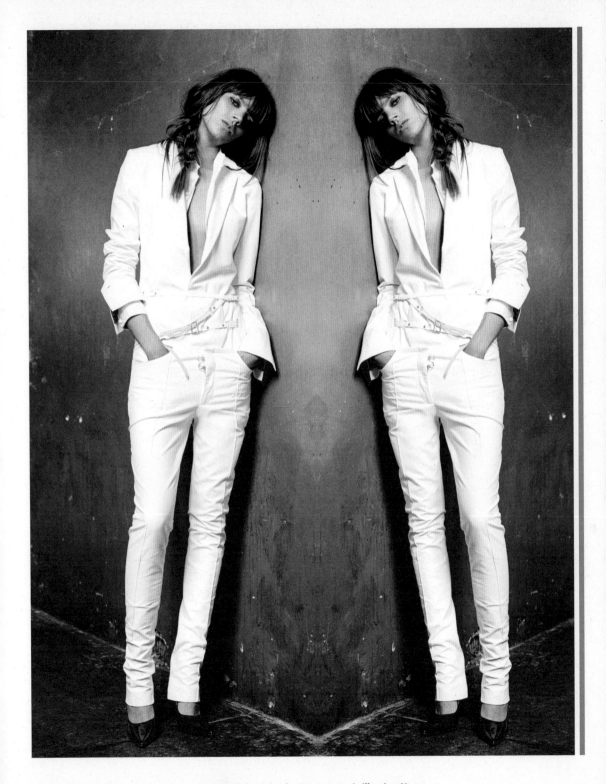

An organic cotton jean with men's -inspired dress shirt by Noir **www.noir-illuminati2.com**

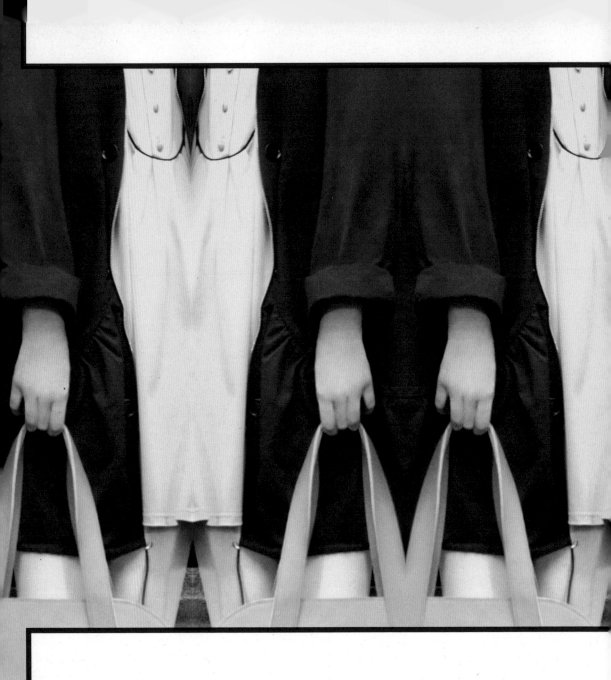

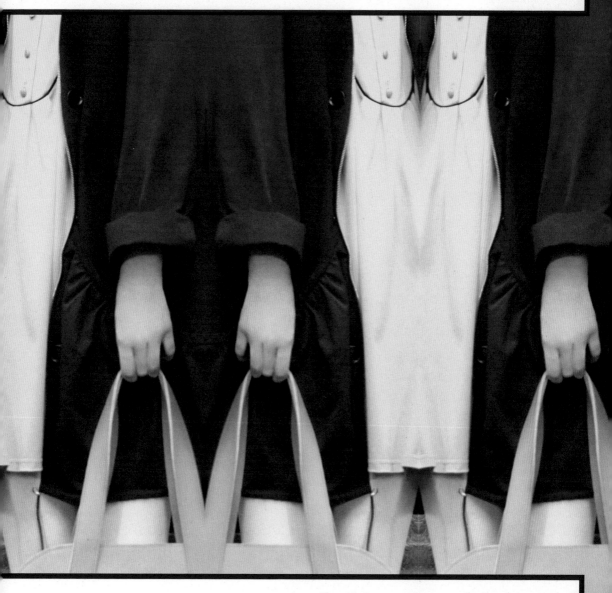

eco-fashion tips of the trade

"HOW MANY CARES ONE LOSES WHEN ONE
DECIDES NOT TO BE SOMETHING BUT TO BE SOMEONE."
—GABRIELLE "COCO" CHANEL, DESIGNER

Trade Tip #1: Smart Shopping

The market for sustainable products is rapidly growing, which means you'll find more options from designers and retailers. Unfortunately, you won't find many brick-and-mortar stores that exclusively sell sustainable style pieces, save for the occasional boutique or special section in a bigger retailer, though that is rapidly changing. Because the movement was born on the Internet, the Web remains one of the best places to find eco-brands. (See the next section, Look Online, for more information.)

If you're looking to update your wardrobe with some eco-fashion pieces, start by educating yourself on the brands dedicated to eco-conscious design. Well over 1,000 (and growing) noteworthy independent design labels, manufacturers, well-known retailers, and discount chain stores offer some form of eco-fashion, including items made from alternative fibers and recycled fabrics as well as sustainable accessory design.

LOOK ONLINE

As I mentioned above, the best place to look for eco-fashion is online. Googling may yield spotty results, so check out some online boutiques first to avoid becoming overwhelmed. Familiarize yourself with the designers sold on the sites. Retail Web sites are generally categorized by type of clothing, so it also helps to have in mind what you'd like to buy (e.g., a new cocktail dress, jeans, high heels, etc.).

Take a look at www.stylenaturally.com for an extensive list of designers and e-commerce stores. New ones are constantly being added; I've also included information about 30+ online shops in the Resources section to get you started.

If you find a specific designer that you like, check out his/her Web site for a listing of stores that sell the products—you may be lucky enough to find a store in your neighborhood. If not, see if you have the option of buying from the designer directly. When you do find a specific product that you want to purchase online, be sure to talk with a representative if you have any questions about fit and return policies. Once you get to know the fit and feel of your favorite design labels, it will become much easier to purchase products online.

LOOK FOR CERTIFICATION LABELS

There are certain certification labels on the market you should keep your eye on. Many clothing or accessory tags may just say "organic cotton" or "fair trade," while others may showcase logos to draw your attention to the label's environmental and social commitment. The apparel and accessories market has just recently adopted these logos to make it easier for the customer to spot, but don't be surprised if you don't see them all that much. They are still new.

Recently, I've seen a move in the industry toward total transparency in business practices, which means full disclosure of the entire supply chain. UK-based Historic Futures (www.historicfutures.com) provides software to track supply-chain accountability in the apparel sector but doesn't use any logo to call attention to the companies involved. MADE-BY (www.made-by.org), based in the Netherlands, helps document transparency while allowing apparel companies to use its logo. Nearly two dozen clothing companies have signed on to MADE-BY and thrown open the doors to their production process to show you where and by whom your garment was produced. Each clothing piece will have a MADE-BY "Check It Out" code. You can then log onto the designer's or MADE-BY's Web site, fill in the code, and voilà, you'll have the complete journey of your garment, from its origin to your closet, entirely at your fingertips.

In the Resources section, I've included a number of certification labels that you may come across in your quest for eco-fashion. Many are not yet used in the United States, but you will find them in several other countries.

LOOK AT THE TAG

If you're out shopping for eco-fashion but aren't yet familiar with eco-designers, the first thing you may want to take a look at is the tag.

Tags are notorious for not being very informative. However, checking them is at least a step toward

■ Marks and Spencer fair-trade organic tees **www.marksandspencer.com**

■ Marks and Spencer organic cotton socks **www.marksandspencer.com**

seeking out sustainable styles. Visit page 287 to learn about fibers and fabrics that are often associated with environmentally friendly clothes so you'll understand what you're seeing when you read the tag.

WHAT TO SHOP FOR

So now you're armed with some solid information about eco-conscious shopping, but how do you sift through all the brands out there? Where's a good place to begin? If you are new to the eco-fashion shopping circuit, consider the following strategies:

- Buy the Basics

- Accessorize

- Save for Something Special

Buy the Basics

Start with those items that you wear most regularly. We get the most mileage out of basics, which makes them a worthwhile investment. Socks and undergarments are the most basic of the basics. Companies like Gaiam offer functional, basic undergarments, and UK-based design label Enamore offers some very sexy intimates. Sam's Club, Target, Wal-Mart, and Victoria's Secret have also begun to integrate organic cotton into their basic lines. Once you have your organic cotton socks and

undies squared away, look for form-fitting tanks and tees that you can wear alone, layered, or under sweaters and sheer blouses. For basic sweaters and shirts, look for pieces that wear well and will work from season to season. Most of us consider jeans a basic staple, especially because they are so versatile and durable. Check out the list of eco-denim designers in the Resources section. If you are active, check out what eco-conscious companies are doing in the sportswear realm. You can find great sports bras, swimwear, running shorts, tanks, tees, yoga pants, and sweat suits through a number of outlets, including Ailin, Blue Canoe, Epona Clothing, Howies, Gaiam, Natural High Lifestyle, Nike, Of the Earth, Panda Snack, Patagonia, prAna, REI, Sahalie, Stella McCartney for Adidas, Timberland, Untouched World, Water Girl by Patagonia, and ZooZoo2, just to name a few.

Run, bunny, run! A simple basic tee, like this organic cotton Howies shirt, is great for layering over or under. **www.howies.co.uk**

Accessorize

Remember, you don't need to start big when shopping for sustainable style. Accessories—like shoes, sunglasses, purses, wallets, jewelry, and other small items—are a good place to start if you're looking to Green up your wardrobe.

Save for Something Special

Perhaps you've been lusting after a great pair of vegetable-tanned heels or a little black cocktail dress, but the price is more than you would usually shell out for a clothing item. Many eco-fashions tend to be on the high or competitively priced side, so you may find yourself saving up for one thing you really want and that you'll treasure for years. Being a smart shopper doesn't just mean thinking about what you buy; it also means spending your money wisely.

KEEP TRACK OF WHAT YOU LIKE AND SPREAD THE WORD

Make a checklist of the brands that you like the most. Oftentimes, stores and designer labels will have a mailing list that you can sign up for to be kept informed about the latest news and sales.

I wrote earlier that designers use the broad term eco-fashion to describe all sorts of environmentally and socially conscious fashions. Keep on the lookout for new brands through your network of friends, magazines, blogs (e.g., www.sprig.com; www.inhabitat.com; www.treehugger.com; www.sustainablestyle.org; www .stylewillsaveus.com; http://planetgreen.discovery.com; and www.grist.org;), and other forms of media.

▬▬▬ A recycled license plate journal, perfect for when you want to sketch or write on the go **www.haul.com.au**

▬▬▬ Slide your laptop into this striking billboard sleeve **www.haul.com.au**

▬▬▬ A pretty sweet hemp iPod case brought to you by the peeps at Fashionation **www.fashionationstyle.com**

▬▬▬ These sustainably harvested "eco" wood sunglasses are the perfect accessory for any outfit. **www.iwoodecodesign.com**

IF YOU ARE VEGAN

For many people, supporting animal rights and helping to prevent animal cruelty go hand in hand with environmentally and socially conscious fashion. This movement has largely been coined "vegan fashion," "cruelty-free fashion," or "compassionate fashion." When we think of vegan fashion, we often think of the absence of fur, but vegan fashion goes far beyond that.

Any product made without the use of animal products or without the exploitation of animals (e.g., testing) can be promoted as "vegan." Man-made fabrics, like synthetic suede, pleather, microfiber, upholstery, rubber, and raffia, are often used as substitutes for leather. Fur is often replaced with faux fur, made from synthetic fabric or organic cotton. (See below for a list of some vegan fibers.)

You may be surprised to learn that certain silks and wools are also considered un-vegan, if the silkworm or sheep were harmed in any way. Vegan fashion will often source "peace silk," in which the caterpillar is allowed to live instead of being boiled in water along with the silky cocoon. Vegan fashion also prevents sheep from undergoing a process called *museling*, which involves cutting the flesh of sheep. Just like being a vegan in the kitchen, being a vegan fashionista takes some serious thought and effort.

VEGAN FIBER ALTERNATIVES FOR SHOES AND BAGS

Faux Leather or Pleather

This material is made of polyurethane, or PU, a synthetic material. It is water-resistant, but not breathable, and can be hand-washed or wiped clean using a damp cloth.

Faux Suede or Suedette

Made from synthetic suede cloth and very soft to the touch, this can be treated with a spray-on waterproofer to increase water-resistance. (Note: This may darken some fabrics.) Clean with a damp cloth.

Stretch Fake Suede

This material is elasticized faux suede and is ultrasoft. It is breathable and very comfortable but not water-resistant. It can be treated with a spray-on waterproofer. (Note: This may darken some fabrics). Clean with warm soapy water and a cloth.

Satin

This is a tightly woven fabric that produces a beautiful sheen on one side. Most satin is man-made from materials such as polyester or rayon. Have satin professionally cleaned, as water may stain the fabric.

Microfiber

This lightweight fabric is tightly woven from a very fine polyester or nylon thread. Microfiber fabric is breathable and naturally water-repellent due to its construction process. When specially treated, it can also be waterproof. Wipe it clean using a damp cloth.

www.vegetarianshoesandbags.com

A vegan wallet by **www.veganqueen.com**

Trade Tip #2:
In with the Old—How to Buy Vintage

Choosing to dress vintage suggests a discerning eye for quality, craftsmanship, history, and design. Over the past decade, the pursuit for secondhand chic has become a worldwide craze, with no signs of waning. Boutique shops, consignment stores, eBay retailers, and underground shops have cropped up everywhere.

People often find different value in the same product. One woman's prized vintage may very well be another woman's thrift. Baseball caps, old Levi's, Patagonia jackets, and other vestiges of Americana that we clean from our closets are highly prized commodities in places like Japan.

Celebrities have also popularized vintage. I don't know if anyone will ever forget (or top) **Julia Roberts** accepting an Oscar at the 73rd Academy Awards in that classic black Valentino dress with white piping (see page 149). Many stars were quick to follow suit: **Kelly Clarkson** in vintage Travilla; **Jessica Biel** in Valentino and Hervé Léger; **Jacquetta Wheeler** in Vivienne Westwood; and **Sarah Jessica Parker** in Comme des Garçons. And though vintage can come with a hefty price tag, it's possible to come across fabulous finds with an equally fabulous price. Case in point: **Angelina Jolie's** black velvet dress that she bought for $26 at Wasteland on Melrose Avenue for the *A Mighty Heart* premiere.

> *Instead of purchasing name-brand designs or vintage pieces* that will break the bank, try renting. Web sites like www.blingyourself.com and www.bagborroworsteal.com loan out new or vintage designer pieces on a weekly, monthly, and yearly basis. Prada, Louis Vuitton, and Chanel bags, which often sell for thousands of dollars, rent for $100 to $250 per month.

GRANDMA KNOWS BEST

It takes a keen eye when it comes to shopping for vintage. My great-grandmother had that eye. She was quick, discerning, and knew what she liked. Secondhand vintage and flea-market finds were her specialty. And she wasn't afraid to bargain with the seller, especially if the piece had some sort of defect (e.g., broken zipper, missing button, small hole, stain). She gravitated toward luxe fabrics and silky drapes in rich jewel tones or shades of lavender and purple, which brightened her features. She always looked polished and put together, but never spent much on her wardrobe, which goes to show that you don't need to spend a fortune to look good.

Angelina Jolie at the *A Mighty Heart* premiere wearing her $26 vintage dress

My Style, Naturally: My great-grandmother had a small collection of vintage hats, which I have inherited and add to whenever I come across a great new piece. When I lived in Pennsylvania, my mother and I would go to estate shops in well-to-do neighborhoods—great places to find fabulous vintage chic! I was always on the look-out for classic hats from the 1920s through the 1960s, like toppers, cloches, and pillboxes. One time, I picked up three in one day for less than $30 total—a huge bargain for vintage hats in an urban area.

The beauty of shopping for vintage is that you never know what you'll find. You may set out to purchase a trench coat and bring home a handbag. Like any shopping experience, it's good to begin with an idea of what you're looking for. This helps you to be focused in your search, which is important; it's easy to get overwhelmed by the diversity and sheer volume of stuff in some stores. Vintage shopping, however, should never be too focused. It's the thrill of the hunt and the joy of uncertainty that makes shopping vintage such a worthwhile experience.

Vintage and secondhand chic often looks best when paired with some contemporary looks. Pair a silk evening or cocktail dress with a vintage clutch. Try an old rocker tee with the latest pair of trousers. Revitalize a long cardigan, shirtdress, or tunic with a vintage belt. Or pair your jeans with a vintage buttery-soft leather boot. That said, don't be afraid to layer on the vintage, especially if you have a great eye for what goes together. Some women happen to be vintage-style mavens.

Agyness Deyn has become a fierce style icon, often pairing thrift-market finds with designer clothes.

Julia Roberts at the 73rd Academy Awards, looking lovely in a vintage Valentino

Julia Gabella: Vintage Junkie
Marketing and press relations, Group SJR

It's a running joke in our office that Julia, a very stylish, fashion-forward young lady, owns nothing new. A frequent visitor to eBay and vintage and consignment shops, Julia guesses that she has purchased at least 20 pairs of vintage shoes, and more pieces on eBay than she can count. "Nobody can ever guess that I'm wearing all vintage," she says. "I know how to make it look contemporary."

Where are you from?
I grew up in New York City.

What are you wearing?

Look #1:

The black dress came from my next-door neighbor who never wore it. She inherited it from her ex-boyfriend's mother, who happened to be the former wife of a '70s rock star. I particularly like that dress because I know there was a fabulous story behind it. I'm sure that it has seen far better parties than I will ever see, but I've worn it to every fancy event for the last three years.

The purse is from Zachary's Smile, a vintage shop in New York. Everyone always comments on that bag. It's total eye candy.

The belt came from this little vintage shop in the Lower East Side. It was a replacement belt from one that I left in a hotel room. I know it's living on, though. Some French maid in Paris is probably wearing it now.

Look #2 (page 152):

The blue Diane von Furstenberg dress is my grandmother's. I was sneaking through her closet and found it. The $75 tag was still on it from Neiman Marcus. All I did was have it shortened. I bought the vintage boots for $62 and got heel taps put on them for $5 at the local cobbler. I wear them practically every day.

What are your favorite places to shop?

SOUTHERN UNITED STATES

Magazine Street in New Orleans pre-Katrina was fabulous, and I heard it dusted itself off pretty well.

The South is amazing for vintage because they have crazy estate sales. I once went on a cross-country trip and would rip out all the Vintage Shop listings in the Yellow Pages in every city that I hit. I found a phone book in Memphis that had all the vintage shops ripped out already!

LOS ANGELES

Decades in L.A. is great.

Denim Doctors is great, too. They take vintage Levi's and make them your style—whether you want flared or tight or skinny.

NEW YORK

I always go to the Barneys warehouse sale. I'm like an animal there. I bought a $4,000 dress for $300.

I shop at Century 21 to get all my underwear and gym clothes. I don't like paying full price for anything.

Tokio7 and Ina are really great vintage and consignment shops in New York.

GENERAL

All cities have good sample sales, which is when stuff would get thrown out otherwise.

What have been your best vintage finds?

A Gucci purse.

Also a pair of Italian leather Bally boots: I was bidding for a size-40 pair online. I knew they would be perfect and they were beautiful. There were a couple people bidding, and it was me and this other woman bidding down to the wire. She got them and I was so pissed! I sent the winner an e-mail and said, "You lucky b*tch. If for some reason they don't fit, e-mail me."

A month later, I got an e-mail from her saying, "I sprained my ankle and can't wear them." She told me that she would sell them to me for what she paid for them online, which was 100 bucks. Turns out, she lived in New York and told me to meet her down in SoHo. As I was waiting to meet her outside of Magnolia Bakery, she calls me from a cab and tells me the cab number. Sure enough, I see the Yellow Cab barreling down the road. I throw a wad of cash in the cab's open window, and she throws the boots out to me. It was worth it. I absolutely love them.

What are your rules of thumb when buying vintage online?

You can always try to buy a size bigger because vintage shoes tend to run small. I tend to wear a 9.5 shoe, but I will only buy a 10. If they are too big, you can add insoles. And make sure clothing measurements are given; read the measurements carefully, because vintage sizes are different from today's sizes.

What don't you buy vintage?

I have a problem buying vintage nightgowns and teddies, even though I own a few. I only buy vintage bathing suits if they are from dead stock, which is clothing supplies that have never been sold, direct from manufacturers. I found an old bikini at Amarcord, but it had never even been taken out of its original packaging.

What fashion pieces do you have to have?

I'm a bag girl. I like nice bags, but I don't own any that are new. Overall, I'm a big fan of accessories—not so much in the way of jewelry, but wallets, yes. I buy wallets at consignment shops.

I'm not really a jeans person. I'm particular about my shoes and pants. Pants have to be the right length for boots.

I love beaters: Little boys' X-large Hanes from Century 21 are essential to my wardrobe! They dress anything down just enough. I can wear that Diane von Furstenberg dress to the Lower East Side if I have a beater underneath it.

Which fashion era or icon do you love?

I would have to say the '50s; the clothes were classic and tailored better then.

As for fashion icons, Dita von Teese. I love her. I adore her. She's wild and still glamorous, which is a perfect mix. She is the definition of sexy. She's bad, dangerous, dainty, and sophisticated. That is the ultimate style challenge—to embody all of those different sides at once.

Take me through your closet.

It's just filled with all secondhand chic. Everything I own comes from a sample sale, a consignment shop, a flea market, eBay, or a friend. I don't own anything new. I'm also a firm believer in quality things. I'm not a label whore, but I'd rather spend my money on something that will last a long time and that is not disposable. It's worth it to get boots resoled. I think it's cool that a garment may have been worn by 15 people before me and still looks great. That's when you can tell it was made well.

Which fashion rules do you follow?

Hide your bad parts and never show too much. If you have the legs to pull off shorts, then pull off shorts, but don't go wearing a skimpy top, too. I'm a huge fan of shoulders and collarbones. Those are some of the sexiest parts of a woman's body.

What motto do you live by?

Nipples to the sky! My grandmother was a ballroom dancer and she would always say that. Posture is everything. Sit up straight, put your shoulders back, and walk in confidence. I find that if you stand up straight, it looks as if you've dropped 10 pounds.

Keep these tips in mind when shopping vintage:

LOCATE A STORE YOU LIKE

Look for shops in your area. I live in New York City—a city with no shortage of vintage stores. Don't get discouraged, however, if you live in a more rural area. When I lived in Pennsylvania, we traveled a few towns over to find the best vintage and estate stores. In fact, vintage shops located close to rural areas will often have better prices than those in urban centers, although they don't always have the selection. As I mentioned before, I bought mint-condition vintage hats for under $10 each! They were a total steal! I doubt I will ever find hats for that price here in NYC.

If you live in an area without a good vintage store, try shopping online. There are plenty of Web sites with a lot to offer. The downside to purchasing vintage pieces online, however, is that you can't try anything on or truly assess the quality of the item up close.

If you are looking for a specialty product, like a gown or a wedding dress, you might want to try antique and estate sales. If price isn't an issue, I would suggest contacting major design houses for their vintage collections. Searching in the affluent part of town for that key vintage piece can also yield good finds.

GET ACCLIMATED

I've seen vintage shops arranged by era, style, type of garment, size, and color. So when hitting a vintage shop, first take an initial scan of the store. Depending on the store's size and the volume of inventory, you may not get to see every item, which is why it makes sense to go in with a strategy. Then, if you are looking for a particular item, ask a salesperson to direct you to the right place.

WHAT TO LOOK OUT FOR

Vintage stores have a huge range of items. Sometimes it's tough to spot the real gems. Always look for designer names. Luxe fabrics, interesting stitching, beautiful embroidery or beading, snazzy buttons, nice paneling on the inside of garments, high-quality workmanship, timeless looks and shapes, of-the-moment looks (e.g., mod), selvedge denim with contrast stitching, and any other details that make the garment distinct are good things to keep your eye out for.

And note that I've gone to a few stores in Manhattan and found people trying to pass off relatively new, retro items as vintage. Though it is not common, be wary of "faux vintage" when shopping.

TRY GARMENTS ON

Always take the time to try on pieces, especially because vintage sizes differ from today's sizes. If you normally wear a size 4 or 6, you may wear a size 12 in a 1950s dress and a size 10 in a 1970s dress. Whatever you do, don't eyeball something and just decide it will fit you. I once bought a dress because I loved it so much, but I could barely get my hips into it. It wasn't a piece that could be tailored very easily so, in the end, it just sat on my shelf gathering dust.

If a piece doesn't fit quite right, the salesclerk may be able to tell you if it could be altered—and might also be able to suggest a good tailor. It is generally better to buy a piece that is a little bit too big than one that is a little bit too small. But if the seams can easily be taken out to be re-hemmed, then buying a smaller item may work.

GET A DEAL

If you are new to shopping vintage, it is sometimes difficult to tell whether or not you are getting a deal. I suggest perusing the Internet first for comparable items, just to get acclimated to prices. Always make sure that the craftsmanship and quality are up to par. Moreover, make sure you absolutely love the piece when you put it on.

In *Fashion Week Daily,* actress Shiva Rose says she'll be shopping vintage for a while: "Well, for years, I wore so many designer clothes, and then I wound up wearing the dresses that get passed around through the designers. Then I started buying vintage, and no one else was wearing it and it cost a lot less—so I'm sticking to vintage for a while. And it's more fun to shop for vintage."

Actress Pauley Perrette gives us a few tips for shopping secondhand: "Be consistent when you vintage shop, which is hard to do, but I try to hit my Goodwill and my Out of the Closet. Out of the Closet is fantastic. It benefits AIDS research. Whenever I have any time off, I try to be consistent and stop by a lot. Sometimes it gets to the point that I find stuff of mine because everything that I'm done with, I donate. I'm like, 'Wait, those are my shoes!' You really don't need to buy a $7,000 thing. You can support the Salvation Army, Goodwill, Out of the Closet. Five dollars goes a long way." (www.ecorazzi.com)

Trade Tip #3: Out with the Old

A big part of cleaning up our style is cleaning out our stuff. Living in New York, in a small apartment, and constantly being on the go forces me to simplify. Less is more, so the saying goes. I work on figuring out how to make less stuff work in more ways. I've learned that versatility is the key to having fewer clothes in my closet, saving money, and getting greater mileage out of the pieces I do have.

When your closet seems to be busting at the seams, it's time to give it a makeover.

Did You Know? The average American throws away 68 pounds of clothing and textiles per year.

Though it may be tempting to grab the trash bag when you clean out your closet—resist! There are much better ways to give our old trousers the boot. Only 48 percent of our stuff is recycled as secondhand clothing. Help eliminate waste and do good with your unwanted garb. Depending on your priorities and your style, consider the following options.

If You Don't Care about the Dough

THRIFT IT

It's crazy to think that less than half of postconsumer textile waste is recycled as secondhand clothing, but almost all of it (93 percent) can be recycled and kept out of the waste stream. I'm a frequent guest at the Salvation Army and local Goodwill retail shops. Of course, these shops are always good places to find unique pieces, but mainly they are quick-and-easy drop-off spots for your castoffs. My old winter jacket, still in fine condition, is in desperate need of a new home. Any interested parties should contact the Salvation Army on the corner of North 7th and Bedford Avenues in Brooklyn, NY.

Visit www.goodwill.org to find a drop-off location near you. If your old castoffs are worthy, they may end up on their e-commerce store at www.shopgoodwill.com. Revenue from all items fund education, job-training, and job-placement programs for people with disabilities and other disadvantages. This is just another reason why "thrifting it" is a good way to go.

Goodwill has recently launched William Good, a joint project with designer Nick Graham, founder of Joe Boxer. The William Good label repurposes and refashions secondhand clothes that don't initially sell off the racks. Clothes are altered or jazzed up with flashy appliqués to give them streetwise appeal. "We never know what's going to come in," Graham said in an interview with ABC News. "It's completely random." If the William Good brand does well, they will begin offering job-training courses for those particularly in need. The line includes men's and women's clothing and accessories at price points ranging from $20 to $100. Check them out in Goodwill's San Francisco stores or at **www.shopwilliamgood.com**.

GIVE IT

Donating clothing to charity is a fairly popular method of giving away the stuff we don't want any longer. Certain causes and associations have clothing charity drop-offs for fundraising purposes, such as the Multiple Sclerosis Association of America's (MSAA) Clothing Donation Program (www.msassociation.org/cloth.html).

Other organizations seek out clothes for specific causes. Dress for Success (www.dressforsuccess.org) helps disadvantaged women by providing professional attire, career tools, and network support. Each year, the organization reaches more than 40,000 women across the United States, Canada, the United Kingdom, and New Zealand. Similarly, the Princess Project (www.princessproject.org), the Glass Slipper Project (www.glassslipperproject.org), Fairy Godmothers (www.fairygodmothersinc.org), the Ruby Room (www.rubyroomseattle.org), and Operation Fairy Dust (www.operationfairydust.org) seek dresses, jewelry, shoes, and makeup to give to young girls who may not be able to afford them.

If you donate clothes to international or national causes (e.g., disaster relief, refugees), be sure to seek out charities that can assure the clothing goes directly to those in need.

Try to find local charities or clothing drives that are specifically equipped for doling out garments to needy populations. I remember both my church and local supermarket had a seasonal clothing-drop program for local families. Both were especially popular around Christmastime. If you have difficulty finding a program like this in your area, stop by a local store, mall, or church and inquire as to whether they can start one. The local Salvation Army may also be able to accommodate charity drop-offs. During national disasters and hurricane seasons, they usually set up specific times and places for such donations.

Style Spotlight

U'SAgain. U'SAgain is a for-profit commercial clothes-collection program. Local businesses sponsor the bins (at no cost), which act as drop-off areas for old or unwanted clothes. They recover almost half the clothes as secondhand clothing, with most of the products going to developing nations. They turn the rest of the clothes into wiping rags and fiber, and less than 10 percent winds up being discarded.

By diverting clothes from landfills, U'SAgain saves on space and provides a valuable service to many people.

www.usagain.com

If You Want to Make a Couple of Bucks

CONSIGN IT

Turn your castoffs into cold, hard cash. If your clothes are in particularly good shape, find a local consignment shop, or visit consignment-shop Web sites like www.consignmentshops.com for drop-off information.

Be sure to call and/or visit the place where you plan to sell your items before dropping them off. Don't forget to ask about store policies. Ask how long they will keep your clothes, if they will buy them on the spot, and what percentage you will get from the sale. Also, ask what type of clothes they are looking for. In the middle of the summer, chances are they will not take any winter gear. Some consignment stores may also be pickier than others—it really just depends on the store. Be aware that if your pieces don't sell, you may have to pick them up from the shop. The clothes that seem to do best are vintage pieces and brand-name products in good condition, though this varies by store and location.

Style Spotlight

Tokio7
Location: East Village, NYC

Tokio7 is one of the most sought-after secondhand consignment shops in Manhattan. They have built their reputation on being highly selective, which is why the place is so popular among Brandanistas (name-brand lovers) looking for a bargain. The store has a great lineup of Japanese designers, as well as vintage and last-season pieces by a number of other designer labels from around the world.

FLEA IT

If you don't mind spending some time peddling your old duds, you might want to consider getting a space at a local flea market. You'll usually have to pay a booth fee, but the benefit of a flea market over a consignment shop is that you will reap all of your profits with no middleman. Visit the National Flea Market Association's Web site to find a market near you (www.fleamarkets.org). Also on their Web site, you'll find a handy "flea finder." Alternate sites with information and forums on flea markets around the country include www.fleamarketguide.com and www.keysfleamarket.com.

PARK IT

In a garage, on a sidewalk, or in your yard . . . wherever you are, if you get a lot of traffic in your area and you don't mind spending some time in the sun, "parking it" is a great way to make some money. But if your next-door-neighbor lives in the next county, this may not be the best option.

It's always fun to set up some sort of lemonade stand while you sell your pieces. I know it sounds really grade-school, but it's a great way to lure customers, especially if it's sweltering outside. Plus, if you don't sell any clothes, at least you'll make some greenbacks by doling out $1 icy beverages to parched people. If you don't like the idea of selling clothes by yourself, talk a few of your girlfriends into setting up shop with you for half a day. There's no question that your friends have pieces they're dying to get rid of. Plus, with the extra money you make, you can have a girls' night to reward yourselves for braving the sun.

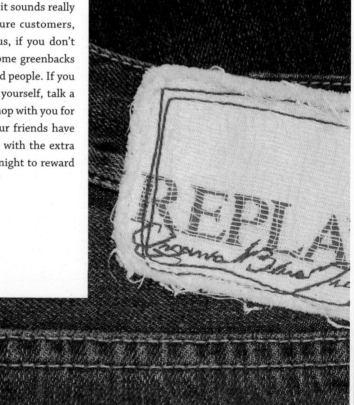

▬ Replay label **www.replay.it**
▬ Organic blue jeans with leather buttons **www.replay.it**

EBAY IT

If you just don't have the time on your hands to flea it or park it, do what thousands of Internet entrepreneurs do, and eBay your stuff away.

If You Want to Have Some Fun

ALTER IT

Though altering may not work for all the items you want to get rid of, it makes sense for some things. With a little creativity and a good local designer, you could transform your trousers into a funky purse or your old tees into cute little boy shorts. Though you may not be the best designer, sketch your vision for the project, make a few calls, and take your pieces in. Doctoring your duds is just another way of taking out the old and bringing in the new.

Style Spotlight

Recycle Your Jeans
Location: Cumbria, England

Recycle Your Jeans is part of a company called Softwalker, Ltd., in Cumbria, England. They take the jeans that you don't want and turn them into a pair of recycled denim sandals. If you don't have jeans to give them, you can buy a recycled pair "off the rack."

www.recycleyourjeans.com

Jill Danyelle: Do-It-Yourselfer Artist (*www.danyelle.org*)
Crafter; therapist; writer

Jill popped onto the sustainable-style scene with her first blog, fiftyRX3. It was a fun day-to-day photo documentary of what she wore, with a goal of averaging 50 percent of reused, reduced, or recycled garments (hence the name). She explored the greater relationship we have to our clothing and was not shy to ask others what her style said about her. Now she's embarking on a new project that centers around her relationship with her possessions, evaluating whether possessions enrich our lives through utility and beauty to an extent that is balanced by what they may cost us in time, money, and space.

Where are you from?

I grew up in Woodstock, NY, spent some time in the Midwest, and moved to NYC to attend Columbia University. Aside from a brief stint living in Barcelona, I haven't left.

What are you wearing?

Look #1:

The piece is called anti-pattern, because it was all done with draping and sewing that was not very premeditated. . . . It is recycled from cashmere sweaters and is super soft and comfortable. The shoes are by Chie Mihara. She has a quality line that I feel is timeless. . . . The organic cotton T-shirt underneath is by John Patrick Organic, which has a great line of sustainable separates.

Look #2 (page 163):

This second outfit is a dress that I made out of broken umbrellas collected from the streets of NYC following a thunderstorm. It was the first in a series of pieces made as part of the fiftyRX3 project. The belt is vintage as is the ring. The bracelet is made of small silver beads and was a gift from my sister many years ago. The Escama bag was made by a Brazilian craft cooperative out of recycled pull tabs. It came in a swag bag at the first SANS show. The shoes are an amazing pair of vintage Charles Jourdan pumps. I love their shape.

Did you always make your own clothes?

No, I started out studying fine art and was always dabbling in creative things, but aside from some pretty bad hand-sewn attempts and a crocheted sweater vest, I never really made anything to wear. Finally, I bought a sewing machine, started playing around with it, and eventually signed up for some classes at Parsons, then later the Fashion Institute of Technology, to learn how to make patterns and sew properly.

What do you like about it?

As with anything creative, the sense of accomplishment and self-expression is very fulfilling. Wearing something you have made for yourself is a fantastic feeling. I have a real reverence for the craft of a well-constructed garment. After learning how to make clothes, I have newfound respect for everything in my closet. It can be quite tedious from start to finish. Sometimes, I don't have the patience and would rather design all the elements and let someone else put it together; other times, I revel in the process.

What are your favorite places to shop?

I really do not shop that much. My closet is already quite full, and I am trying to focus more on enjoying and wearing what I already own. However, I will never turn down a good flea market. I just love the

history of things and always wonder about where they came from.

Are there any fashion pieces that you have to have?

No, I really do not believe in that. I do feel fashion can be driven by the need for change, and I am as interested in that as the next person. Yet, for me, this could be pulling things out I haven't worn in a while or mixing things in different ways. I may add in a trend-driven item here or there, but I think true style is just believing in yourself and pulling things together well. It isn't about the must-have item or brand-name "it" bag.

What fashion era or icon do you love?

I like vintage clothing, but I don't want to look too contrived or feel I am in costume, as dressing all from one era might make me feel. I tend to mix different decades together with contemporary pieces. However, if I had to choose, I suppose I'd be a flapper or a hippie. Maybe I just like loose dresses or the nonconformity that was happening in those eras. . . . As for icons, I think Lisa Eisner is interesting. I mean, anyone who pulls off wearing Sammy Davis Jr.'s old suits has to be confident. And that is what style is really about after all, less what you wear and more how you wear it. So in that regard, I see people every day just walking around the city who interest me more than anything in fashion magazines. Who I find most fascinating are those so clearly outside the reaches of any fashion dictate or style conformity. I wonder what compels them.

Take me through your closet.

Well, living in NYC, thankfully, has kept it edited, as I don't have a lot of space here.

I have two small closets in the hallway. One is devoted to dresses; they are so comfortable and easy to wear. That is also where my recycled collection for fiftyRX3 lives. Among the contemporary pieces, the closet includes vintage wool-jersey and dead-stock crocheted dresses that I have collected over the years, along with a handful of formal gowns. The other small closet is devoted to coats and jackets. The typical variety one might expect for the full range of seasons we get here in NYC.

The main closet would probably be divided. First there are the everyday jeans, T-shirts, and sweaters. I have jeans in all shapes and sizes. My T-shirts tend to be about the fabric and cut. Generally, I don't like designs on my T-shirts, with some exceptions, including two beautiful batik T-shirts from Bali that I have had for about 20 years. I tend to get cold easily, so I have a variety of sweaters and wraps for all seasons. Then I suppose there is the typical range of skirts, pants, and woven tops. Within each category, there are some special pieces and things that I have collected. I have some nice Oscar de la Renta and Yves St. Laurent vintage pieces but also a lot of obscure stuff that is equally loved. In terms of things that aren't vintage, I have added in organic T-shirts and jeans. I think John Patrick Organic is great for everyday style. I also have invested in some designer pieces that I will hang on to forever. I am a fan of Maria Cornejo and have several pieces, including a skirt from her collection where she utilized a woven bamboo fabric.

My shoes and bags reflect my clothing. I try not to be redundant or excessive, but have a variety of bags in the necessary sizes and colors to get me through the demands of living in a city where you need to carry your stuff with you. I tend to like pared down designs without a lot of embellishment. I have several pairs of vintage Ferragamo boots that wear like iron. I also have a few pairs of shoes by Chie Mihara, who I discovered when I was in Barcelona. Her shoes are well crafted, timeless, and unique, yet accessible. I bought a pair of boots from one of her first collections and still wear them as much as the heels I bought last summer. I am currently wearing a pair of Nike running shoes that I have had for ten years; they have been washed and mended over the years, but are currently missing part of the tread. When I give up on them, I will send them back to the company, and they will grind up the rubber soles to use in playgrounds that they build in underserved communities.

Which fashion rules do you follow?

I dress for myself. Basically, I want to feel good about what I am wearing and where it came from, but this can manifest itself in many ways. There are a variety of things that influence what I put on everyday, just like for everybody, but I never take it too seriously or become a slave to it. There is plenty in my closet to have fun with when the mood and occasion strike; other times I find a simple comfort in austere uniformity.

What motivates you?

I am motivated by the need to express myself creatively and the desire to feel good about the work that I am doing.

EXCHANGE IT

Exchanging clothes is very similar to swapping (see below), but you have a little more choice. Depending on what you are in the mood for, you can trade in your castaways for cash or other clothes at designated clothing-exchange shops.

Style Spotlight

Buffalo Exchange. Buffalo Exchange buys, sells, and trades clothing and accessories. You can bring in your former favorites for trade or cash on the spot. Each store's inventory constantly rotates, and they have a good selection of designer wear, vintage, jeans, and one-of-a-kind items. (See Resources for store locations.)

www.buffaloexchange.com

SWAP IT

You and your girlfriends swap everything—from secrets to boys—so why not swap your clothes, too? You can either go to a community swap or hold one of your own. A community swap makes for a good way to get people together and to reuse and recycle clothes. Swaporamarama.org has information on swap centers in your area and great step-by-step instructions on how you can start your own. The gist of it is this: Bring your clothes to the swap center and then find something there that you like. If it doesn't quite fit, there are seamstresses, designers, and do-it-yourselfers on hand to sew your new garment for you on the spot.

Online sites dedicated to swapping and selling are popping up all over the place. Swapstyle.com opens the closets of people around the world for a free-for-all of swapping, selling, and buying clothes, jewelry, shoes, bags, and cosmetics. And if you want to see how you can bring the swap party to your pad, try a weekend Swap Soiree with your pals.

How to Have a Swap Soiree. Here is the recipe for a great girls'-night-in:

Invite your friends over to your place. I suggest a group of five to twenty (the more the merrier, really).

I always like to pair the Swap Soiree with good food and drinks. Listen to some great music, rent a couple of good movies, or watch reruns of *Sex and the City* to unwind and get ready for your swap session.

For the clothing swap itself, everyone should bring a pile of clean clothing, accessories, hats, shoes, and other wearables to swap.

As long as you bring something to swap, you can take as much home as you want. The trick, though, is not to take home more than you brought. The point of a clothing swap is to get rid of your old stuff to make room for "new" stuff. Showing up with four articles of clothing and leaving with forty is a recipe for clutter and closet chaos.

If you are feeling crafty, I suggest adding a little DIY workshop to the soiree. Look in the Resources section for some excellent craft-book suggestions.

When the swap is over, you can either ask that the leftover clothes go home with their original owners, or you can keep the leftover clothing and donate it, recycle it, or have a side-walk sale.

Lots of teens and twenty-somethings head to Buffalo Exchange for great deals. Stores like Buffalo Exchange see an upswing of buyers during downturns in the economy.

Esosa Edosomwan: Swap Artist (www.sosae.com)

Multidisciplinary artist; entertainer

I met Esosa back in college, where she was studying Textiles and Fashion Design, making her own clothes, producing her own films, and acting in the local theater. Now that we've both graduated, it was great to catch up with her and see how her style and work have evolved. Keep an eye out for her upcoming film.

Where are you from?

I grew up in Virginia. My parents are from Nigeria. They were born there and came to America for school. Nigeria is a strong heritage—very driven people and very gifted. That has really formed who I am.

What are you wearing?

Look #1:

The armband and necklace are by Ambiguous Jewelry Art (www.ambiguousjewelryart.com). She lives in Brooklyn, and all her pieces are one-of-a-kind and made from found materials. The armband and necklace are called Afro Punk and are made from old jeans, suede ties, and belt buckles. The earrings are all beaded. It's wearable art, which is totally cool.

The shirt and sweater I got at a clothing swap. I started swapping a lot because you can get together with your friends and get rid of stuff that you don't want. I usually give away my stuff to Goodwill or do a clothing swap. I had this bright-pink pair of Gucci pants that I was never going to wear and my friend Crystal took them.

My pants are Gucci. I got them from a friend who owns a styling agency.

My shoes are from Payless. They have really great styles at affordable prices.

Look #2 (page 168):

The earring is from Ambiguous Jewelry Art.

The necklace was used on one of my film sets. I loved it so much, I asked if I could take it home.

I got this jacket and the shirt from a clothing swap.

I don't remember where I picked up these boots, but I've had them for a while.

What are your favorite places to shop?

Portobello Market (London) is great. You can walk around, and all the designers could be couturiers selling samples for like thirty pounds.

Vintage stores in Paris are completely amazing. It's European vintage, so I find it to be more interesting than what we have here in America.

Harriet's Alter Ego is a shop on Flatbush in Brooklyn (www.harrietsalteregoonline.com). The woman who runs it is Nigerian. They make everything in the store, so it's all one-of-a-kind.

Why do you swap?

I don't like shopping so much; I love swapping because I don't need to spend any more money. I just get together with a good group of my girlfriends and swap.

Who are your favorite designers?

I'm not into the brand thing. I'm into what I like and what makes me feel good. Ambiguous Jewelry Art is different and simply amazing. Idyllic Couture is cool (www.idyllic4u.etsy.com). She makes clothes

out of remnants from the fashion district and puts faces on it, like of Frida Kahlo. John Ashford's shoes (www.johnashford.ws) are all hand-painted. He paints faces of people like Bob Marley and Jimi Hendrix. They have high, high heels though. That's for when you want to look badass. I'm flat-footed though, so I have to get him to make me a pair of flats. Ron-N-Ron (www.ron-n-ron.com) does all menswear, but I think they are genius. I love their colors and vintage references and want to look like the fabulous woman's complement to their menswear.

What fashion era or icon do you love?

I am obsessed with the '60s and '70s, especially because of the political climate. Politics and fashion are inseparable. It's interesting to me to see how street fashion comes out of a specific time or culture.

I love how Tamara Dobson, who played Cleopatra Jones, dressed. She was this special agent and would kick someone's ass but looked amazing every time. I love that stuff.

Janelle Monáe, too! That chick is out of this world. Her music is heaven to me and her style is amazing.

Take me through your closet.

It's a rainbow-colored hodgepodge of craziness! I'm not afraid of color. Purple and red are fabulous. I can pile color on color. I have a lot of vintage clothes, too. Most stuff in my closet that I will never give away is from London or Paris. They just have better stuff over there.

What are your favorite pieces from your wardrobe?

One of my favorite pieces is a vintage-fabric jacket with big sleeves. I like it because I made it for myself, and I still wear it a lot.

There is this sweater dress from Harriet's Alter Ego with gray stripes on ivory that is tight on the body, but has giant sleeves. There is no way that you can't make a statement in that.

What motivates you?

Since I embarked on making my last film, it's really become my mission to fill a void in the entertainment industry. I see and know from getting to meet some of the greatest black female filmmakers of today in Los Angeles that it is still "a struggle" for black female and just plain female directors in Hollywood. Apparently, only 1 percent of the Director's Guild of America is comprised of black females. When I set out to make my short film, I wrote, acted, and directed, which many men have done, like Spike Lee and Woody Allen. When I really thought about it, I couldn't think of any visible black females with a body of work as an actress-writer-director. My vision is to fill that void, and in creating that possibility for myself, I am committed to inspiring other young women that it is possible. My motto really has become to live a life beyond limits—breaking through limits I have created for myself or that society has created for me, which I choose not to accept!

What motto do you live by?

Use the talents that you have been given and always encourage other people to use their talents. I believe in a higher power, and if you have vision, you can make it happen. I stay very focused in a spiritual sense. I wake up every single day and try to be grateful and to value where I am as a human—and to continue challenging myself.

My family is really important to me. I've always been driven, but during college, I had a crisis where I lost a close friend. I still went after what I wanted, but I put the people in my life as a priority. The important part is the connection that you have with people. You can't just run around and push without making any connections. Life is too precious.

Trade Tip #4: Come Clean

Throughout this book, I've highlighted cool companies, outlined creative advice on how to clean out your closet, and offered advice on finding eco-stylish fashion. But now it's time to talk about something that we do every month, if not every week—washing our clothes. Quite frankly, washing clothes is a dirty job, and we all have to do it. But I'm sad to say, washing and drying your clothes is a lot dirtier than many of us even realize!

Between 80 and 85 percent of the energy used to wash clothes comes from heating the water.

WHAT CAN YOU DO?

Use cool water instead of hot: It'll save you money, save on energy, and reduce CO_2 emissions by 500 pounds each year.

Conventional detergents contain organic chemicals (compounds made up of carbon) that are known to be toxic and act as endocrine-disruptors and estrogen-mimics.

WHAT CAN YOU DO?

Use eco-friendly detergents and alternatives in place of the chemically intensive ones. Look for cleaners like Ecover, Seventh Generation, and Mrs. Meyer's, among others. A non-detergent alternative: EcoBalls, which hail from the UK. EcoBalls have minerals on the inside, formulated to ionize the oxygen in the water to remove dirt from the fiber more effectively.

Washing a small load of clothes wastes water.

WHAT CAN YOU DO?

Fill her up! Washers are most efficient when operated at their maximum capacity, so wash only full loads. If your clothes aren't really dirty, don't just throw them in the laundry basket. Wear them again until you truly have to clean them.

———— Line drying helps save energy because, guess what? Wind is free!

———— Most environmental damage comes from caring for our clothes. Be sure to choose a more eco-friendly detergent like ECOS

All washer systems were not created equal.

WHAT CAN YOU DO?

If you are in the market for a new washing machine, look for an Energy Star model. These washers clean your clothes using half as much energy and only 18 to 25 gallons of water per load (compared to the 40 gallons used by a standard machine).

Dryers all use around the same amount of energy, but you can line dry whenever possible. You could save up to $75 annually and 700 pounds of CO_2 from entering the air when you line dry your clothes for six months out of the year.

Dry cleaning isn't good for the environment.

WHAT CAN YOU DO?

It is estimated that 80 percent of commercial dry-cleaning businesses in the United States used perchloroethylene (perc) as a solvent. Short-term exposure creates all sorts of adverse health effects, including eye, skin, and nose irritation, and it is even identified as a probable human carcinogen. The Environmental Protection Agency (EPA) also lists it as a hazardous air- and water-pollutant.

Try wet cleaning. Wet cleaning uses water as its solvent and is approved by the EPA as environmentally preferable. In order to find a wet cleaner near you, visit http://earth911.org. Do a search for "wet cleaning" alongside your zip code, and the nearest business will be located.

Eco-friendly and Green cleaners will often use wet-cleaning processes. Sometimes they will also use a cleaning technology that involves liquid carbon dioxide. The carbon gas is captured from existing emissions, pressure is applied, and the gas becomes a liquid and a very effective solvent. Check to see if your dry cleaner is using one of these two processes and if not, use Earth911 to find another cleaner.

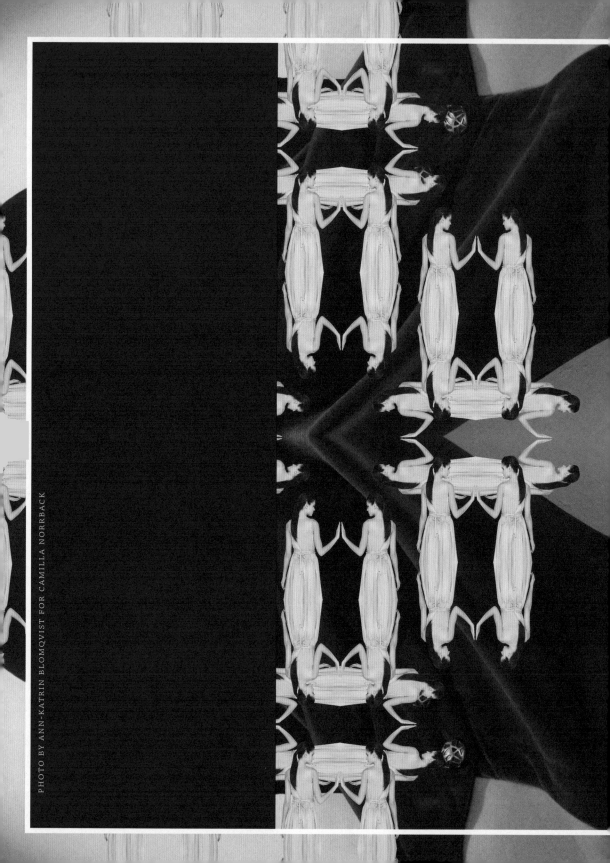

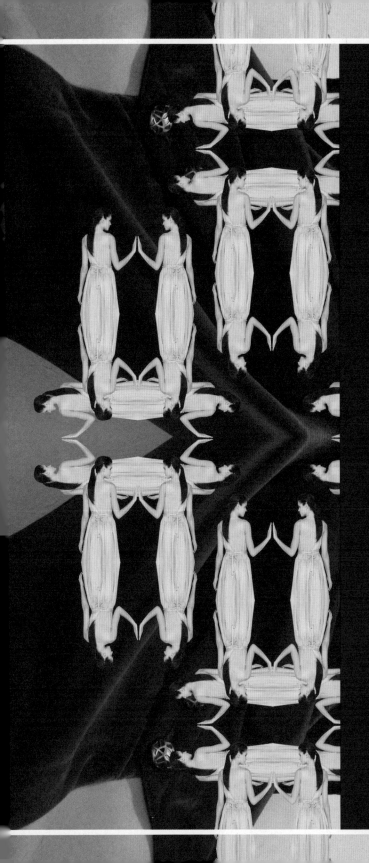

eco-beauty

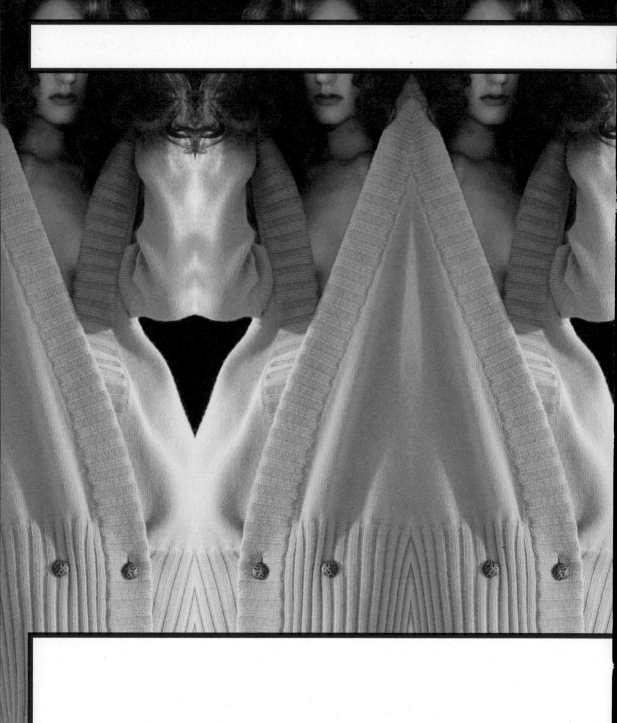

PHOTO BY ANN-KATRIN BLOMQVIST FOR CAMILLA NORRBACK

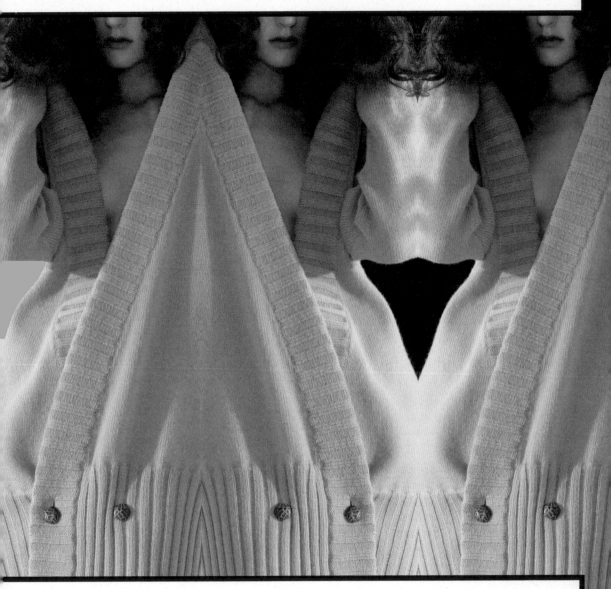

eco-beauty 101

"BY ASKING A NOVEL QUESTION THAT YOU DON'T KNOW THE ANSWER TO, YOU DISCOVER
WHETHER YOU CAN FORMULATE A WAY OF FINDING THE ANSWER, AND YOU STRETCH YOUR OWN MIND, AND
VERY OFTEN YOU LEARN SOMETHING NEW."
—WALTER GILBERT, 1980 WINNER OF THE NOBEL PRIZE IN CHEMISTRY

Beauty Basics: Back to Your Roots

Sustainable beauty, like sustainable fashion, developed at a grassroots level in all corners of the globe. Early adopters like Weleda (1921), Dr. Bronner (1948), and Dr. Hauschka (1967) were steeped in rich, healthy, and, in some cases, biodynamic ingredients from the start. Anita Roddick's The Body Shop was founded in 1976 and sources many of its ingredients from local community and fair-trade groups. Many other brands, such as organic-certified Miessence (1992) and Stella McCartney's Care line (2007), emerged as a response to the synthetic chemicals found in our everyday cosmetics. Up until recently, not many visible brands occupied the space, and very few outwardly advertised Green principles. That has changed dramatically in the past few years. The natural and organic segment of personal care is now the fastest growing in North America, with an increase of 20 percent each year. Great brands now appear in supermarkets, drugstores, mail-order catalogs, online stores, and high-end stores, such as Fred Segal and Barneys.

Some brands have even embraced exploring "sustainability" beyond the ingredients. Estée Lauder–owned Aveda, though not a 100 percent organic line, largely focuses on community-development partnerships with the indigenous peoples with whom they source materials. In the fall of 2006, they switched their primary manufacturing facility in Blaine, Minnesota, to 100-percent wind energy, which is a good start for any company given the enormity of global warming. Origins, another Estée Lauder–owned brand, recently signed on with Community Energy to offset 100 percent of their carbon emissions from their North American retail stores and U.S. manufacturing facilities with renewable energy certificates. And Ted Gibson's high-profile salon in New York City's Flatiron District offsets all its carbon emissions through wind energy and tree planting. Still other companies look to reduce waste in product packaging. Aveda, Origins, Pangea Organics, and Osea use postconsumer recycled-waste containers or glass containers, which can easily be recycled.

TREND FORECAST

Julie Gilhart, *senior vice president and fashion director of Barneys New York*

"Cosmetics is definitely the place where it is going to happen faster than fashion. We carry Stella McCartney's Care line, Nude, WEN, Jurlique, and Josie Maran's cosmetics line, which have all been positively received. Tracie Martyn is also someone we have carried for a long time. Cosmetics are more like food; people want products that are natural and that have no synthetic chemicals."

The core of sustainable beauty is the ingredients. It's no accident that many of the best eco-conscious brands got their start with ingredients grown in their backyards: fresh-scented chamomile (*Anthemis nobilis*) for hair rinses and skin fresheners; the strong piney scent of rosemary (*Rosmarinus officinalis*) for hair tonics and skin treatments; marshmallow root (*Althea officinalis*) for chapped hands and lips; and zesty lemon (*Citrus limon*) for shiny hair, to name just a few. Today, sourcing

Some of the best products for our skin come straight from the earth. Pictured here is Astara violet flame enzyme mask. **www.astaraskincare.com**

is more sophisticated—gathering oils, scents, and restorative nutrients from plants, algae, and minerals from the depths of the Arctic Ocean to the dry deserts of Australia to the deep rain forests of the Amazon. The "backyard" of most brands may have grown, but the idea remains the same: use the freshest, purest, most nutritious, naturally derived ingredients from the earth.

It takes care and expense to create these products. So it's no surprise that many of the brands that we rely on haven't chosen to go the natural route. It's becoming increasingly apparent with glaring headlines in the news such as:

- "Lead in Lipstick"

- "Cosmetics Can Cause Infections"

- "New Laws Include Mercury Ban in Cosmetics"

- "Non-Science Used to Market Cosmetics"

"What—mercury in cosmetics?!?"

"We have a mercury cleanup in aisle 1. A lady has spilled her mascara."

In case you missed any of these headlines, I'll break it down for you:

There are dangerous ingredients in your cosmetics.

There, I said it. Someone had to sooner or later. And better sooner than later, considering that there is so much unnecessary, unhealthy stuff lurking inside the herbal-fresh scents of your shampoos and body washes, the red lacquer sheen of your fingernail polish, and the lusciously gooey shine of your cherry blossom–flavored lip gloss. (Don't worry: I'll dish all the dirty little secrets Perez Hilton–style in just a few.)

The idea is quite simple, really, according to Horst Rechelbacher, founder of Aveda and new food-grade cosmetics company, Intelligent Nutrients: "If you wouldn't put it in your body, why would you put it on your body?" That sounds a little silly since you won't be drinking shampoo with your dinner, but it starts making sense when studies show that up to 60 percent of what we apply to our skin is absorbed into our bloodstream. I don't know about you, but those are statistics I don't want to play beauty roulette with.

Did You Know? How many products do you use on a daily basis, including shampoo, deodorant, toothpaste, lotion, and makeup? The average woman uses a dozen personal-care products every day, totaling 168 chemical ingredients.

When it comes to the products we put on our bodies, we must get back to our roots (and perhaps that means your natural hair color, too). Look for products that responsibly source the cleanest, purest, naturally derived ingredients that also perform their jobs well—from clearing up acne and cleaning our hair to making our kisser kissable and fingernails fabulous.

Spin the Bottle

Read the ingredient list. That's the best way to get acquainted with the products you use. Don't pretend that what you use on your body is good for you just because a pretty spokesmodel or celebrity said so in a commercial. You need more information than that to make a good decision.

Did You Know? Only 11 percent of the 10,500 ingredients documented in personal-care products have been evaluated for safety.

Ingredient lists can be a nightmare to decipher. We may know what rosemary is, since we cook with it, but trying to decode something like imidazolidinyl urea or diethanolamine (DEA) is next to impossible without doing a little research. You may not be surprised to hear that these are synthetic chemicals that we would be wise to steer clear of. The best advice to follow is: Simplify. Look for simpler ingredient lists with recognizable ingredients and fewer or no synthetics.

I would also suggest you start to shop for your beauty products the same way you shop for your groceries. Some of the healthiest, purest products are nutrient-rich, food-grade formulas that have a shelf life. It may seem odd to buy personal-care products with a "Use by" date, but it makes sense when you think about it: We know the most nutritious foods for our bodies are made with fresh ingredients, not ones that are packaged in plastic and pumped with synthetic preservatives. Something that is made to last forever can't be good for our bodies and surely isn't good for the earth. Yet most of our personal-care products have been embalmed with synthetic preservatives, such as formaldehyde and parabens, and can last for years, if not, dare I say, decades.

In the long run, your body won't benefit from a concoction of synthetic compounds devised by a chemist. Granted, some of these chemicals are included in small amounts, but think about how many products we apply to our bodies daily, and think about how all the ingredients in each of those products may be reacting with one another.

And let's be clear: Most of those synthetics find their way into our beauty products because they are cheap, quick, and easy. Most of the brands we see advertised in magazines and on supermarket shelves spend very little in the way of ingredients and far more on marketing their products. Sure, I love looking at the glossy ads, but when it comes to my body, I want fabulous products that are pure, safe, and effective. Fresh, naturally derived, organically certified ingredients may rightly fetch higher prices, but at least I know that these companies have me, their customer, in mind when sourcing ingredients.

It's Not Mainstream until the Makeup Artist Sings

While the industry is indeed beginning to create cleaner products, you won't yet find these products lining drugstore shelves or behind most cosmetics counters. They haven't quite hit the mainstream yet. And here's how we know: Everyone knows that makeup and hair stylists are some of the most pleasantly chatty people in the world. For over seven years, I've been getting my hair primped, pulled, and curled and my face moisturized, glossed, and powdered, but I can count on one hand the number of times eco-conscious cosmetics and safer alternatives have been brought up in conversation.

The silence is not an intentional omission; people just don't know. The celebrities and models that grace the glossies are usually at the mercy of whoever did their makeup and hair, and the artists are at the mercy of the companies that give them products to use or what company they train under. (Hair and makeup artists are always getting free and discounted products to experiment with.) I'm positive, however, that if makeup and hair artists found out what was in their pretty little products, it would be the talk of the town!

My revelation came in 2001, when I was researching the health effects of land-applying sewage sludge. In short, everything that gets washed off our streets or farm fields, down our sinks, drains, and toilets makes its way to the treatment plant. The resulting "sludge" is then reapplied to our land. Sounds like a far cry from the makeup chair. . . . or is it? Turns out, the balancing act I was doing between sludge research and eco-modeling was more closely related than I thought! People often find it difficult to believe when I tell them that my sewage sludge research has everything to do with style. The following conversation usually results.

Person: "What on earth are you talking about?"

Me: "Take a look at the ingredient list on the back of that hair spray. Turns out that some of the cosmetics ingredients that we wash down our shower drains, like benzyl alcohol, triclosan, toluene, xylene, phenol, phthalates, alkyl benzyl sulfonates, tricresyl phosphate, and nitrosamines, are turning up in sludges. It's a potent chemical concoction."

Person: "Doesn't it just go into a landfill or something?"

Me: "Over 60 percent of sewage sludge gets reapplied to our land and can find its way back into what we eat and drink. Those chemicals just don't 'go away.' In fact, there is no 'away.' We're not only putting them on our bodies on a daily basis, we're recycling them in our very environment."

So, did you expect to hear the words "sewage sludge" mentioned in a style book? Probably not. But then again, did you ever think embalming fluid was in your body wash?

Beauty and Balance

Bringing balance to your beauty regime doesn't start with fancy products. It starts with these simple strategies:

Hydrate responsibly

You want to know how you get that salon shine? I'll let you in on a little secret: It's in the water. You want to know how Brazilians have such perfectly shaped behinds? (You wish the secret was in the water, but I digress.) Do yourself the biggest beauty favor and get a water filter for your shower and your kitchen sink. Water filters remove all the unwanted chlorine and heavy metals that can make our skin and hair feel dull, limp, and lifeless. Filters also help ensure that we are drinking the purest water possible, eliminating the need to buy bottled water. Keeping that in mind, drink more water. At least 70 percent of our skin's blemish- and wrinkle-fighting ability comes from the water we drink.

Go naked

Use less makeup or no makeup at all. This will not only allow your skin to breathe, but will begin to make you feel comfortable with the woman "behind the mask."

Simplify

Use fewer products with fewer or no unwanted chemicals or synthetic additives. This ensures you get the best products for your body with a minimal amount of effort, giving you more time in the day.

Play dress up

Wear clothes that make you feel good about yourself, accentuate your figure, and bring out your natural color. When you put together a wardrobe that works for you, you may find that you don't even need that much makeup.

Love the Skin You're In

Your dermis is one of the most resilient, yet sensitive, organs of your body. It is the canvas that connects your outside world to your inside world. Think of it less as an impenetrable force field and more as a gateway. What we put into our bodies is reflected on the outside and what we put onto our bodies gets in. The rich omega-3 fatty acids of grilled salmon at dinner do in fact give us the smoothest skin, shiniest hair, and strongest nails. Conversely, the ingredients in the lotion we apply to our body after a hot morning shower seep through our skin into our system.

Many of us tend to look at our skin in real time. How many times have you said: "Why does this pimple have to show up now?!" It's not a question of why; it's a question of what and when. What triggered it and when? What is your body telling you? Instead of taking a proactive approach to beauty—paying attention to what we put into and on our bodies—we do the opposite and become reactive. We dab that benzoyl

cosmetic junkie (as so many of us are), try to go a few days a week with just a base moisturizer or SPF cream and a little lip balm. Before you go to bed, splash a little water on your face with a dab of balancing cleanser. Use a little toner if your skin is oily or a light moisturizer if your skin is dry. Try to intervene less. Your skin will thank you, as will your hair and your nails, which are an extension of your lovely dermis.

Biggest Beauty Boo-Boos

I don't think there would be as much damage done, both to women and to the environment, if the cosmetics industry either:

1. Paid more attention to science, or

2. Abided by the natural and organic food-grade standards.

If one or both of the above happened, we'd have fewer nasty synthetics in our products and more nutrient-rich ingredients. Due to loopholes in federal law, however, companies can put virtually any ingredient into our personal-care products (and they do). Even worse is that the government does not require any tests to make sure the product is safe before it is placed on store shelves. Forget, for a moment, the little bunny that signifies "No testing on animals." We too are lab rats. The products we use are tested on us every day.

peroxide onto the blemish, but in the process make our skin crack and peel, eliminating our natural antiaging oils. So many of us wage war on our skin by slathering it with an arsenal of "beauty" products: body washes, lotions, masks, makeup, serums, and antiaging creams. Your skin already has to work hard to process what happens inside your body. So give it a break.

Embrace your beautiful self in the morning before you apply product. Love your natural state and don't let your product-obsession take control. Take charge of your beauty regime and learn to listen to what your body needs before muffling it with expensive makeup and creams. If you are a self-confessed chronic

Eco-Stylephile: CAMPAIGN FOR SAFE COSMETICS

Campaign for Safe Cosmetics' Challenge: Raise awareness for nontoxic personal-care products.

The Campaign for Safe Cosmetics was formed in 2002 after the release of a report called, "Not Too Pretty: Phthalates, Beauty Products, and the FDA." The report tested 72 name-brand beauty products for phthalates, a chemical linked to birth defects. An independent laboratory found phthalates in nearly three-quarters of the products tested, even though the chemicals were not listed on any of the labels. The concentrations in the products ranged from trace amounts to nearly 3 percent of the product formulation.

Campaign for Safe Cosmetics' Solution: Research toxins in our beauty products, write reports, and produce consumer-awareness campaigns to inform the public.

The Campaign for Safe Cosmetics has come out with a number of reports, shedding light on potential safety issues in our cosmetics. The organization has also developed a pledge, called the Compact for Safe Cosmetics, which is a first step for companies to take when moving toward using safer ingredients. Today, more than 600 companies have signed this compact.

www.safecosmetics.org

What Can You Do?

▬ Join the Campaign for Safe Cosmetics, or sign up for updates at **www.safecosmetics.org**.

▬ Use safer cosmetics. Read on, and to learn also visit **www.cosmeticsdatabase.com**.

▬ Ask your store to carry organic and naturally derived personal-care products and cosmetics.

▬ Contact your favorite brands to get them to go Greener.

▬ Get a group of friends together and host an eco-conscious spa or salon at your house or in your community; try out the latest home-beauty recipes; or take a look at the Cosmetics and Personal Care section (page 191) for examples of companies and products that abide by cleaner principles, and then pamper yourselves to see what brands work the best for you and your girlfriends. For more information, check out **www.safecosmetics.org/action/houseparty.cfm.**

It's mind-boggling to think about what goes into the products we use every day. Worse, up to 80 percent of personal-care products on the market today may contain one or more hazardous ingredients that aren't even listed on the labels, which may not be an intentional omission. Substances such as lead, 1,4-dioxane, and nitrosamines can sometimes be a by-product or contaminant from the manufacturing process, as you will find out below.

Did You Know? Women absorb up to 5 pounds of damaging chemicals from their personal-care products every year.

Animal Parts

Using beauty products with animal-derived ingredients is a big no-no for Veganistas, but even omnivores may feel a bit queasy about slathering fat from a bird or furry beast on their face. If this sounds like you, steer clear of mink, emu oil, and tallow, which can be found in anything from nail hardeners, facial creams, skin lotions, and conditioning agents. They may not be terribly damaging to your hide, but they certainly are damaging to our furry little friends. The oils contain very similar physical properties to human sebum, but there are great botanical alternatives, like macadamia-nut oil and sea-buckthorn oil.

Also listed as: oil, emu; emu oil; mustele oil; oil of mink; mink oil; sodium tallowate; tallow; sodium salt; sodium salt tallow; fatty acids

Butyl Acetate

Have you ever stepped into a nail salon and felt as if you should be wearing a hazmat suit? There's a place in Brooklyn where I like to get a cheap little mani from time to time, but the ladies all sport MJ-style face masks because the chemical stench is so foul.

Butyl acetate is one of the many fumes you are probably inadvertently inhaling. It is used in perfumes, nail polish, and nail-polish remover. Continuous, repeated exposure can cause skin dryness and cracking. Vapors may induce dizziness and are narcotic in high concentrations. Over time, people working in poorly ventilated nail salons can develop a condition known as "painter's syndrome," a permanent condition that causes walking problems, speech impediments, and memory loss.

Also listed as: acetic acid, butyl ester; 1-acetoxybutane; butyl ethanoate; butyl ester acetic acid; butyl ester, acetic acid; n-butyl acetate

Butylated Hydroxytoluene (BHT)

This is a preservative and antioxidant that helps slow the rate of color change in cosmetics. It can be found in a wide range of beauty products. In addition to our cosmetics, it's a common ingredient in pharmaceuticals, jet fuels, rubber, petroleum products, and embalming fluid—yes, to help preserve corpses. It is now banned as a food additive in many countries due to adverse health affects, but it is still used in the United States. When we apply it topically, it can cause eye irritation, contact dermatitis, and other allergic reactions.

Also listed as: BHT; DBPC

Coal Tar *

Make sure you read the fine print on those antidandruff shampoos, hair dyes, and topical treatments for psoriasis and skin rashes. Coal tar, a thick liquid or semisolid obtained from bituminous coal, is often listed as one of the ingredients. And most of the synthetic colors and dyes found in our cosmetics are derived from coal tar. There is now sufficient evidence that coal tars are carcinogenic for humans. The EU banned them from cosmetics in 2004. The United States still allows their use.

Also listed as: tar, coal; coal tar solution
* Side effects may include cancer.

Diazolidinyl Urea and Imidazolidinyl Urea

These two chemicals are common preservatives and can be found in a range of products, from baby shampoos to sunscreens, soaps to makeup. Imidazolidinyl urea is the second-most-identified cosmetic preservative causing contact dermatitis, according to the American Academy of Dermatology.

Both diazolidinyl and imidazolidinyl urea have contamination potential. They may release formaldehyde, which is a suspected human carcinogen and a skin and eye irritant. And sure, "urea" sounds a lot like "urine"—because it is! Though the ingredient is most commonly derived through a synthetic process, it is the same chemical composition as animal urine.

Also listed as: N- [1,3-Bis (Hydroxymethyl) -2,4-Dioxo-4-Imidazolidinyl]–N; N'-Bis (Hydroxymethyl) Urea; Urea; N,N"-Methylenebis [N'- [1-(Hydroxymethyl) -2,5-Dioxo-4-Imidazolidinyl] Urea]

Ethanolamines: DEA, MEA, TEA

This group of compounds includes harmless-sounding three-letter abbreviations, like MEA (monoethanolamine), DEA (diethanolamine), and TEA (triethanolamine). They are widely used as detergents in hand soaps, lotions, shaving creams, shampoos, and bath powders. DEA is a colorless liquid made from soybeans or coconut oils and is often listed as oleamide DEA, lauramide DEA, or cocamide DEA. Given that these are derived from fruits and veggies, they may not sound dangerous, but they are processed in a way that makes them extremely hazardous. The compounds can cause allergic reactions, eye irritation, and dryness of skin and hair. More importantly, all ethanolamines may form nitrosamines, which are among the most potent cancer-causing ingredients found.

Also listed as: 2-aminoethanol; ethanol, 2-amino-; 2-hydroxyethylamine; monoethanolamine; 2-amino-ethanol; ethanol, 2 amino; MEA; ethanol, 2,2',2"-nitrilotris-; 2,2,2"-nitrilotris [ethanol]; TEA; trolamine; 2,2',2"-nitrilotriethanol; ethanol, 2,2,2 nitrilotris; amides, coco, N,N-bis (2-hydroxyethyl)-; coco fatty acid amide; coco amides; coconut diethanolamide; coconut fatty acid diethanolamide; cocoyl diethanolamide; lauramide; lauric diethanolamide; lauryl diethanolamide

Ethyl Acetate

Here is a good example of a naturally occurring substance that has been bastardized by synthetic manufacturing processes. This colorless liquid with a fruity odor naturally occurs in wines and other naturally fermented products. The chemical, often used to decaffeinate coffee, can be naturally derived from fruits, but is usually derived synthetically and can be harmful if ingested.

It is often found in nail enamels and nail-polish removers, as well as mascaras, perfumes, and tooth-whitening treatments. It is a mild eye and skin irritant and central-nervous-system depressant. The vapors are irritating, and prolonged inhalation may cause damage.

Also listed as: acetic acid, ethyl ester; ethyl ester acetic acid; acetic acid ethyl ester

Formaldehyde

Yup, this is the same stuff used to preserve those frogs you had to dissect in junior high biology. It's a common chemical used as a disinfectant, germicide, fungicide, and preservative. It can be found in a range of cosmetics, including nail polish, nail hardeners, deodorants, and shaving cream. Diazolidinyl and imidazolidinyl urea are two chemicals that may release formaldehyde as a by-product.

Formaldehyde vapors are intensely irritating and can trigger asthma. Skin reactions after exposure to it are very common because the chemical can be both irritating and allergy producing. It is a highly reactive chemical, which means it can team up with other chemicals to produce mutagenic and carcinogenic effects. Its use in cosmetics is banned in Japan and Sweden.

Also listed as: formalin; formic aldehyde; mer-thaldehyde; methanal; methyl aldehyde; oxomethane; oxymethylene

Fragrance

Fragrance is one of those ubiquitous words on almost any ingredient list. It can be found in everything, including perfumes, lotions, shampoos, body washes, and deodorants. Companies are not required to list what chemicals make up fragrances because this information is considered a trade secret. So, essentially, fragrances can include any number of nasty chemicals and neurotoxins, which may cause a range of symptoms from headaches, rashes, and dizziness to, yes, allergies. Fragrances are also one of the top five allergens in the world.

Also listed as: parfum

Hydroquinone

Skin lighteners, suntan lotions, freckle creams, hair colorings, and nail treatments may all contain hydroquinone. The bleaching chemical can cause a skin disease with disfiguring and irreversible blue-black lesions. The EU banned the use of hydroquinone in skin lighteners.

Also listed as: 1,4-benzenediol; 1,4-dihydroxy-benzene; P-dioxybenzene; 4-hydroxyphenol; P-hydroxyphenol; 1,4 benzenediol

Lead

Lead and lead acetate haven't only been found in toys recently, but also in our cosmetics, such as hair dye, topical astringents, and more commonly, lipstick. According to *Women's Health* magazine, the average woman inadvertently eats between 4 to 9 pounds of lip gloss and lipstick in a lifetime. Ick. Lead is toxic in all forms, can build up in the body, and is a proven carcinogen. In young children, it can cause brain damage. Research has shown that no level of lead is harmless.

Lead is not always intentionally added to products; it is a by-product of manufacturing, so you often won't find it on ingredient lists. This makes it tricky to figure out which products are lead-free. The only answer is to get involved: write to companies and see what www.safecosmetics.org has to say.

Also listed as: Acetic acid, lead salt; lead diacetate; plumbous acetate; lead salt acetic acid

Mercury

Mercury has been widely banned because it is potentially dangerous through all portals of entry, including the skin. It had once been used in bleaching creams, but was banned after it was shown to cause mercury buildup in the body, which leads to chronic symptoms like inflammation, nervousness, fever, and rash. Even if it is ingested in small amounts, it can be fatal. Mercury is still found in some eye preparations and cosmetics, like mascara, as a preservative called thimerosal.

Also listed as: HG; mercury, dissolved; mercury, total; thiomersal; thimerosal; mercurochrome; merthiolate

Nanoparticles

Not technically a "substance," the term *nanoparticles* refers to the size of certain substance particles. Nanotechnology uses particles 80,000 times smaller than the width of a human hair, which means some of these particles can penetrate cells and tissues much more readily. You can now find nanoparticles in shampoos to carry ingredients deeper into the hair shaft, in antiaging materials to reduce signs of wrinkles, and in skin and sun creams. Research on the health effects of these particles hasn't been able to keep up with the technology, though recent studies show that they can cause brain damage in fish. Nanoparticles are not included on ingredient lists. Berkeley, California, became the first city to regulate nanotechnology. It requires companies and research labs to disclose nanoparticles in products to the city government and to provide information about known health or safety risks. Organic organizations, like Soil Association in the UK, were the first to prohibit man-made nanoparticles in cosmetics. Gundula Azeez, Soil Association policy manager, has said, "There should be an immediate freeze on the commercial release of nanomaterials until there is a sound body of scientific research into all the health impacts."

Parabens (Methyl-, Ethyl-, Propyl-, Butyl-)

Methyl-, ethyl-, propyl-, and butyl-parabens may sound like your great-aunt's bridge-playing buddies, but they are in fact a group of chemicals that is widely used as preservatives in cosmetics. An estimated 75 to 90 percent of cosmetics use them, including shampoos, makeup, lotions, and deodorants. In 2004, a study published in the *Journal of Applied Toxicology* said that they are a cause for concern after a study found traces of parabens in twenty women who had breast tumors. Parabens are believed to be estrogen-mimics, which can cause some women to develop breast cancer.

Also listed as: 4-hydroxybenzoic acid; benzoic acid, 4-hydroxy-; methylparaben, sodium salt; benzoic acid, 4-hydroxy-, butyl ester; P-hydroxybenzoic acid, butyl ester; benzoic acid, 4-hydroxy-, propyl ester; propyl 4-hydro-xybenzoate

Petrolatum

What's Tyra Banks's biggest beauty secret—the one she calls her "eye and anything cream"? Answer: Vaseline. Tsk-tsk. Hasn't anyone told her that petroleum jelly has no health benefits? This may come as a surprise, considering that the iconic yellow-blue jar of goo is a fixture in many households' cosmetics cabinets. Even though mineral oil and petrolatum, otherwise known as petroleum jelly, have no fragrance or other funky ingredients, they are highly processed hydrocarbons, derived from petroleum, which does not break down in the environment or on our skin. They have absolutely zero nutrient value for the skin, and they block sebum and the body's natural ability to regulate moisture, which can lead to dryness and chapping over time.

Also listed as: mineral jelly; petrolatum amber; petrolatum white; petroleum jelly; yellow petrolatum; mineral grease (petrolatum)

Phthalates

Pronounced "thal-ates," these are gender-bending chemical compounds. Recent studies show them to be mutagenic, cancer-causing, and especially harmful to the developing male reproductive tract. Companies use them not only in cosmetics, but also in plastics, packages, and plant pesticides. Diethylhexyl phthalate (DEHP) and dibutyl phthalate (DBP) are on California's list of potential cancer-causing agents. In 2004, the EU banned them in nail polish. They are still widely used in the United States, including in our nail polish, deodorant, products with "fragrance" listed on the bottle, hair spray, lotion, and hair gels. Pregnant women should avoid products, like nail polish, with phthalates.

Also listed as: 1,2-benzenedicarboxylic acid, dibutyl ester; dibutyl 1,2-benzenedicarboxylate; di-n-butylphthalate; DBP; 1,2-benzenedicarboxylic acid, diethyl ester; diethyl 1,2-benzenedicarboxylate; DEP; diocytl phthalate; bis (2-ethylhexyl) phthalate; DEHP

Placenta

You're probably reading the word *placenta* above and wondering, "What the?!?" Yes, some products, like anti-wrinkle and damaged-hair treatments, actually contain placenta, the mucous lining of the mammalian womb that is expelled after birth. The placenta in cosmetics is often derived from the uteruses of slaughtered animals.

According to *In Touch* magazine, Eva Longoria uses a placental-based cream on her face to get a "baby-faced" look. The American Medical Association has found no evidence that it is a wrinkle-remover. More important, the Campaign for Safe Cosmetics cites a number of case studies showing that placental extracts may give the body a spike of hormones significant enough to spur breast growth in babies.

Also listed as: placental protein; placental extract

Propylene Glycol

This chemical can actually be derived from natural sources (vegetable glycerin mixed with grain alcohol), but more often cosmetic companies use a cheaper, synthetic version derived from petroleum. It's the most common moisture-carrying ingredient, which sounds harmless, but that means it penetrates deep into the skin and can weaken protein and cellular structure and allow other chemicals to reach our bloodstream. The ingredient, found in everything from deodorant to liquid foundation, can also cause allergic reactions, hives, and eczema. Also watch out for PEG (polyethylene glycol) or PPG (polypropylene glycol) on the label because they are related substances.

Also listed as: 1,2-dihydroxypropane; 2-hydroxypropanol; methylethyl glycol; 1,2-propanediol; propane-1,2-diol

Sodium Laureth Sulfate and Sodium Lauryl Sulfate

This is the commonly used substance that makes things soapy. As a result, you'll often find it on the ingredient list for bubble baths, cream depilatories, toothpastes, body washes, and shampoos. Many brands will substitute sodium lauryl sulfate for sodium laureth sulfate because it is purportedly "gentler." Lauryl is converted to laureth by adding the petroleum-derived chemical ethylene oxide, which in the process creates the contaminant 1,4-dioxane, a known animal, and likely human, carcinogen.

Also listed as: sodium dodecyl sulfate; sulfuric acid, monododecyl ester, sodium salt; sodium salt sulfuric acid, monododecyl ester; dodecyl sodium sulfate; PEG- (1,4) lauryl ether sulfate, sodium salt; polyethylene glycol (1,4) lauryl ether sulfate, sodium salt; sodium PEG lauryl ether sulfate

Synthetic Colors

The bright, jewel-toned colors of many body washes and shampoos, as well as dyes you find in hair rinses, hair color, and cosmetics, are most often derived from coal tar (see page 184), which can cause cancer in humans. You can pinpoint synthetic colors by finding FD&C or D&C, followed by a color and a number on the ingredient list. Examples include: FD&C Red No. 4; D&C Blue No. 1 Aluminum Lake.

Talc

Talc is a finely powdered mineral that is the primary ingredient in many blushes, powders, eye shadows, deodorants, bar soaps, and foundations. Cosmetic-grade talc is a proven carcinogen, and studies show that it can increase the risk of ovarian cancer. Prolonged inhalation can also cause lung problems because it is so similar in chemical composition to asbestos.

Also listed as: cosmetic talc; French chalk; talc $(MG3H2 (SIO3) 4)$

Toluene

Derived from petroleum, toluene may cause liver damage, fetal development damage, and skin and respiratory tract irritation. Nail polish is composed of up to 50 percent toluene.

Also listed as: benzen, methyl-; methylbenzene; toluol; methyl-benzene; benzene, methyl

Before you apply, spin the bottle and check the list of ingredients.

PHOTO BY ANN-KATRIN BLOMQVIST FOR CAMILLA NORRBACK

cosmetics *and* **personal care**

"LET'S INTRODUCE AN ERA BASED NOT ON WHAT WE CAN EXTRACT FROM NATURE, BUT ON WHAT WE CAN LEARN FROM HER. . . . WE CAN DISCOVER WHAT WORKS IN THE NATURAL WORLD, AND MORE IMPORTANT, WHAT LASTS. AFTER 3.8 BILLION YEARS OF RESEARCH AND DEVELOPMENT, FAILURES ARE FOSSILS, AND WHAT SURROUNDS US IS THE SECRET TO SURVIVAL. THE MORE OUR WORLD LOOKS AND FUNCTIONS LIKE THIS NATURAL WORLD, THE MORE LIKELY WE ARE TO BE ACCEPTED ON THIS HOME THAT IS OURS, BUT NOT OURS ALONE."
—JANINE BENYUS, AUTHOR OF *BIOMIMICRY*

Beauty—More than Skin Deep

Our beauty regimen—what we apply to our bodies on a daily basis—differs from fashion in the sense that it is what we do when no one is looking. But that doesn't mean that its effects are invisible. The same goes for skin care and makeup. We might not get as many compliments on our flawless foundation as we do on our fabulous high heels, but you'll be rewarded with health and beauty by choosing responsible products that are right for both you and the world in which we live.

This section will discuss wonderful eco-conscious alternatives, covering head to toe. Divided into Hair; Face; Makeup; Body; and Hands, Feet, and Nails, with different subsections under each category, this section will give you information about some of the products on the market today. I've literally spent months scouring the world for some of the finest products, many of which are highlighted here. My initial search started with the ingredient lists, overall company ethos, organic and fair-trade certification, and, of course, product performance. In most cases, I have tried the products and am happy that I can share my insights here, but I encourage you to try the products for yourself to see what works for you. Read on to find not only the above-mentioned information, but also profiles of inspiring people, product histories, and personal vignettes.

Check the ingredients before you apply.

HAIR: LOVE YOUR LOCKS

Did you ever stop and think about the relationship you have with your hairdresser? If you're like me, it's someone that you see quite regularly and trust enough to alter your look—sometimes dramatically. That goes to show that we put a lot of faith in healthy tresses and good haircuts, so why not get savvy on the healthiest, most nutritious products for lovely locks.

Care for Your Hair

For strong, shiny, healthy hair, choose a nourishing shampoo and conditioner, like the ones in this section. And don't fret if these brands don't suds up like drugstore brands. Contrary to popular belief, we do not need to have all those suds in our shampoo for it to actually work. Additionally, be gentle when washing your hair—whether it is curly, wavy, or straight. That squeaky sound your hair makes when it's being washed is a cry for help as your hair's life-force is being sucked out of it. Hair doesn't want to be squeaky clean. If, one day, you find yourself in the salon chair, having your hair washed to the point of squeakiness, kindly tell your stylist to quit it.

There's no need to wash your hair every day, especially if it's long. Overwashing makes hair dry, brittle, and listless. Let your natural oils work their way down the cuticles to the hair shaft. Because of all the time I spend in the gym and all the goop stylists put in my hair, I tend to wash it every other day. If you must wash your hair daily or every other day, here's what to do: Skip the shampoo from time to time, especially if your hair is stiff from too much hair spray or gel. Go straight for the conditioner or a conditioning shampoo. Let it sit on your hair and comb through. Wash it out after a few minutes. That will help moisturize, condition, and clean your hair, without overdrying it. If you feel the need to shampoo, apply a little to the scalp and wash it out after you condition your hair.

Shiny Hair au Vinaigre: To give a healthy shine to dull, lifeless hair, I use an apple cider–vinegar rinse just after I shampoo. Vinegar is known to restore your hair's natural pH, remove buildup, and help prevent dandruff and itchy scalp.

Dissolve ½ to 1 tablespoon of vinegar in a cup of cool water, and place the mixture in a spray bottle. Shake. Spray or rinse generously and thoroughly throughout hair. You can either leave the mixture on or rinse with cold water afterward. Use up to twice a week.

L'Huile d'Olive for Dry Hair: I remember one December I was desperately scanning the supermarket shelves for something that would bring my tired, dull hair back to life. I stopped and picked up an Alberto VO5 hot-oil treatment. I think it was about $5 or $6 for two tubes. What a waste! I've learned that olive oil is far safer and better for your hair. The VO5 oil had added fragrance (mystery chemicals), parabens (can cause irritation and allergies), and octoxynol-9 (endocrine-disrupting).

Cold-pressed, extra-virgin olive oil, as well as many other naturally derived oils, such as jojoba and argan, is very similar in composition to our sebum, our body's natural oil. It absorbs readily, locking in moisture, especially if our skin and hair are dry. Olive oil is also particularly good for us because it contains high levels of antioxidants.

For a hot-oil hair treatment, put one-half cup of extra-virgin olive oil in a glass jar. Run the closed jar under hot water for 30 to 60 seconds to heat the oil. (Alternatively, you could

Use natural oils to restore health, vitality, and shininess to your hair

microwave it in a microwave-safe container, but remember that microwaves heat quickly, so test the oil first to avoid burning yourself.) Open the jar and place a little olive oil on your palms and fingers. Massage gently through dry hair, paying special attention to your ends and any brittle portions. Wrap your hair in plastic wrap or wear a shower cap for 15 to 30 minutes. (Note: You could also leave it on overnight.) After you are finished, remove the plastic wrap, get in the shower, and wash your hair thoroughly with a gentle shampoo, making sure you remove any residue. You may also want to finish up with a Shiny Hair au Vinaigre rinse post-shampoo.

A light conditioning detangler that has a lovely aroma. It's great for all hair types and safe to use on color-treated hair. **www.johnmasters.com**

A deep-colored shampoo that is gentle on the hair and particularly good for those of us who have dry or brittle locks **www.johnmasters.com**

This lovely mixture of organic apple-cider vinegar and herbs helps eliminate nasty buildup and restore pH levels to the scalp. Try our version on page 194. **www.johnmasters.com**

shampoos and conditioners

I got to test out the range of Sexy Hair Organics products before it hit the market. This is a lovely nourishing formula of shampoo that replenishes dull, lifeless hair. Sexy Hair even has its own recycling awards program. **www.sexyhair.com**

I normally don't use leave-in conditioner, but it's a terrific companion when you're spending a lot of time in the sun, on the beach, or in some other place that is harsh on your hair. The fruity aroma and lightweight spray are lovely after a cool shower. **www.druide.ca**

A lovely scented shampoo that clarifies the hair and leaves it quite shiny **www.desertessence.com**

Like many eco-friendly shampoos, WEN doesn't lather, which means it doesn't have a lot of the harsh, stripping formulas of conventional shampoos. I live a very active lifestyle, so I am always washing my hair. I love this shampoo formula because I can use it every day, if needed, without drying out my hair. **www.wenhaircare.com**

I was first introduced to this shampoo through one of my guy friends. I really like the light lather and slightly sweet smell. **www.shikai.com**

I was really impressed with the fresh, lively scent of the Timothy Han formulas, and the lemongrass gives it a nice kick. **www.timothyhan.com**

Timothy Han conditioner is a nice follow-up to the shampoo. **www.timothyhan.com**

This is another one of those great conditioning washes that I can use on my hair every day. **www.hamadibeauty.com**

Yes, Giovanni has some of the coolest packaging, but they also have some great products. This shampoo has a light lather and invigorating tea tree, which helps eliminate oil and buildup and leaves your scalp feeling clean and fresh. **www.giovannicosmetics.com**

After using Max Green shampoo and conditioner, my hair was quite shiny. The shampoo had a nice, light, woody botanical scent. **www.maxgreenalchemy.com**

Intelligent Nutrients and Aveda

Horst Rechelbacher says his environmental activism led him to where he is today. The son of an herbalist mother and shoemaking father, Horst began a three-year apprenticeship in the beauty and salon industry at the age of fourteen, which later gave way to his pioneering studies in plant-based care and aromatherapy. Horst, who founded Aveda in 1978, laid the founding principles of the company, including the idea to use organic, plant-based materials and to support and work closely with indigenous peoples throughout the world. At the end of 1997, Horst sold Aveda to Estée Lauder, and a new chapter in his life began.

In the summer of 2008, he officially launched Intelligent Nutrients (IN), a new line of food-grade personal-care products. "Even when I had Aveda," he says, "I always tried to be ecologically supportive." Now, Horst says, he's taking it to a brand new level of awareness. "For the longest time, I understood that petrochemicals in our consumer products were not the way to go. Manufacturers do not make the raw materials. They buy them from the chemical companies that simply make the materials, like surfactants (e.g., sodium lauryl and laureth sulfates) in shampoos."

Horst acknowledges that he had to completely reinvent himself and found chemists who would start from scratch. "People say it cannot be done, but it can. We do it in food."

"The USDA should never compromise its standard on organics," he says resolutely. "So many manufacturers are coming in looking to dilute the standards and add chemicals to our products. I say, 'Why are we going backward? Why are we compromising the organic certification to benefit manufacturers?'"

Horst says he will be very active in the organic sphere and will continue to uphold the idea that products we put on our body need to be healthy and nourishing. "Don't put anything on your body that you can't digest," he explains.

Much of Horst's activism is done through his eponymous foundation and through Intelligent Nutrients. Though it's a start-up company, IN will support different groups in countries where they do sourcing, particularly Africa, where there is a wealth of seed oils. "Seed oils are a whole new chemistry that has been introduced to us," says Horst. "We are working with the medical community at the University of Minnesota. They've become disciples of seed oils because of their anti-nucleic activities." In fact, if there is one thing Horst has accomplished through the years, it's generating a growing cast of followers who look up to him for guidance in sound ecological practices.

www.intelligentnutrients.com

Horst Rechelbacher of Intelligent Nutrients

This has a nice subtle smell and will give you a perfect head of shiny hair. I suggest applying it like you would perfume. Spray into the air and "walk" your head into it. Don't spot-spray the hair too close-up or you risk looking greasy. **www.giovannicosmetics.com**

A nice gel that helps condition, style, and add body to your hair **www.giovannicosmetics.com**

Place a small amount of this gel in your damp hair, and comb it through. It will condition and help seal split ends—and it really pumps up the volume after a blow-dry. **www.giovannicosmetics.com**

styling gels, sprays, and mousses

This natural mousse works well with thick hair to give it a natural hold during the day. **www.giovannicosmetics.com**

Try this hair spritz if you're looking to tame your tresses, keep the shine, and get a great hold. I particularly like this product because it comes out easily in the shower. **www.giovannicosmetics.com**

This styling product is great for any guys or gals with short hair. **www.giovannicosmetics.com**

▬▬▬▬ I'm not a big fan of the rosemary scent, but this product is a godsend. After a lot of tugging and pulling on my hair, this product helps restore luster, eliminate frizz, and soothe the scalp. **www.usa.weleda.com**

▬▬▬▬ This product is especially loved by my girlfriends with curly and kinky hair. **www.maxgreenalchemy.com**

▬▬▬▬ Did you ever find that after swimming in the ocean you have the loveliest beach-wavy hair? In the hair chair, it can take up to an hour to get those perfect beach tresses. John Masters's sea mist spray helps cut down on the time it takes to get lovely sea locks. **www.johnmasters.com**

▬▬▬▬ I've used this with both dry and damp hair, and it really helps give silky body to the hair. It contains no alcohol, so it doesn't have that drying effect of many conventional products. **www.johnmasters.com**

A great texture paste that brings out natural definition without any greasiness **www.maxgreenalchemy.com**

This gel applies smoothly and does not leave hair sticky, tacky, or greasy. **www.maxgreenalchemy.com**

I like traveling with this defrizzer, particularly in hot climates. Just rub the oil on your palms and through your hair to tame flyaways. **www.johnmasters.com**

FACE

Faces are a thing of beauty: They come in all shapes, sizes, and shades—and that is what makes them so intriguing. And let's face it—your pretty little mug is the first thing people notice, so why not make a great first impression by taking care of what you've been given.

—— This is a light astringent with a lovely rose aroma that really refreshes my face after cleansing. **www.usa.weleda.com**

—— Shake this bottle well and then spray for a lovely hydrating mist. I particularly like to spray it over a light foundation to give myself a lovely dewy glow. **www.burtsbees.com**

—— This is one of the yummiest smelling products. It's hard for me not to want to eat it. That being said, it's a great product that leaves a subtle, smooth finish to the face, giving you a radiant glow. I found it to be exceptional when my skin was feeling parched or after multiple days of heavy makeup use. **www.burtsbees.com**

—— This is a great product for combination skin. I spray it onto my face and then moisturize. **www.astaraskincare.com**

cleansers, toners, mists, and scrubs

I love Jurlique's spritzers. I don't know which I like more—the rosewater balancing mist or the citrus purifying mist. Both rehydrate the skin and provide instant uplift. Perfect during the hot summer months or the stuffy winter months. **www.jurlique.com**

Great botanical-based cleanser that leaves skin rejuvenated **www.chocolatesun.net**

Many facial toners contain alcohol, which dries the skin. Druide's products don't contain any alcohol and help re-moisturize the skin. **www.druide.ca**

This dual moisturizer and toner has an unbelievable scent. . . . Of course, I'm a sucker for citrus. **www.alqvimia.com**

To foam or not to foam? Duchess Marden has two types of cleansers: crème and foam. Both are lovely, so you'll just have to see which suits your style (and your skin). **www.duchessmarden.com**

A lush, creamy cleanser, certified organic by the Soil Association, that wipes away with a damp cloth and leaves your skin feeling smooth and supple **www.essential-care.co.uk**

A light exfoliator that is very enriching to the skin **www.porticospa.com**

A yummy, honey facial cleanser **www.luckyduckonline.com**

I especially love toners that don't contain alcohol or glycerin, and this one steers clear of both. It's formulated with cold-pressed plant extracts to give your skin the best nutrients. **www.luvalla.com**

This cleanser has a lovely natural scent and is soft on the face. **www.luvalla.com**

I found that this hydrating mist works well over makeup. Just spritz a couple of times to give your skin a nice dewy glow. **www.juicebeauty.com**

This cleanser gently exfoliates the skin while it cleanses. **www.mychelleusa.com**

This is one of my favorite beauty products in the world. The sweet, subtle scent combined with the consistency and cleansing properties make this a must try. **www.miessenceproducts.com**

Zia's toner is very refreshing and gives your skin a moisture boost. The rose, aloe vera, and seaweed extracts give it a pleasant scent and terrific healing properties. I love these sprays after a long plane ride or on cold windy days. **www.zianatural.com**

▬▬▬ I love this cleanser to remove any makeup or pesky residue from the day, plus you can't go wrong with the scent.
www.pangeaorganics.com

▬▬▬ I have to congratulate Origins on their foray into organics. This is a gentle gel that foams lightly and feels good against the skin.
www.origins.com

▬▬▬ I'm not usually one for facial scrubs, but Pangea's version is very nice. I mix the cleanser and facial scrub on heavy makeup days.
Yes, this is a godsend! **www.pangeaorganics.com**

▬▬▬ I took Osea products with me to the dry deserts of Africa. What a good move! The red algae and safflower extracts give the
formula a terrific moisture boost. People with skin allergies will particularly like this product. **www.oseaskin.com**

Osea

Jenefer Palmer didn't really think of her past connection to the sea when developing her seaweed-based skincare line, Osea, until recently. "I will never forget," she says. "I was doing a training with 25 people and I had this 'Aha!' moment."

"I was telling a story about my grandmother, Elsa, who was one of the first female chiropractors. When she was in her forties, she injured herself, but kept walking and working. One night, she dreamt that the ocean would heal her. She sat up and said to my grandfather: 'Pick me up, carry me to the beach, and put me in the water.' Not too unusual of a request for my grandmother, who was a strong-willed woman," Jenefer says assuredly, "except for the fact that it was the middle of December in New York!"

"She and my grandfather started a movement very similar to the Polar Bear Club. She found the cold water and its minerals to be very fortifying. The sea was a source of healing."

In 1981, Jenefer became spa director of the Murrieta Hot Springs in California. She found some Tuli root, a mineral-absorbing plant that the indigenous people of the area once used as a compress for inflammation, growing near the mud-bath buildings. "We got seaweed and volcanic ash and grew the Tuli root in the mud," she says. "We then cut it into blocks and sun-dried it. When I added powdered seaweed to it, I realized how great the stuff was as a treatment."

As a spa director, Jenefer found that beauty salespeople pushed their products on her all the time. "I picked up the bottles and read their ingredients. I was horrified. I noticed two things. One—it was all synthetic, and two—it was all the same stuff; the only difference was the sales pitch and the outer packaging.

"I felt women were being lied to, especially since there is transdermal absorption of our cosmetics," she says. That wasn't well-known back in the '80s when Jenefer was working at the spa. "Now with birth control and nicotine patches," she says, "women understand how easily substances can pass through their skin."

And she is a stickler when it comes to labeling ingredients correctly. For her own products, she follows International Nomenclature for Cosmetic Ingredients (INCI) standards, which is a system for naming cosmetic ingredients based on the Latin language. "For example, vitamin E is not an INCI name," she says. "Instead it is tocopherol, and there are many variations of tocopherol; some are naturally derived and others are 100 percent synthetic. And the correct terminology is naturally derived instead of natural. It's like saying wine is 'natural.' It's not. It's naturally derived. Unfortunately, wine doesn't grow in the wild."

It took Jenefer eleven years to create Osea, and her first account was with Fred Segal, eight years ago, where she remains to this day. She sources seaweed and algae directly from Iceland, Hawaii, Indonesia, Patagonia in Argentina, and île de Molène—a UNESCO biosphere reserve off of Brittany. "The colder the water, the more mineral content in the seaweed," she says. "I used a supplier at one point, but found that I could get higher quality seaweed by going direct. To meet the people and see it harvested—watch it collected on the

Jenefer Palmer

shoreline when it comes in and laid out to dry—really deepened it for me."

Once Osea was established, Jenefer was the first to sign the Campaign for Safe Cosmetics, a coalition working to eliminate harmful chemicals from our beauty products. "I guess people were hesitant to sign on, but being a Sagittarius, I jumped right in. It was a no-brainer for me, and now there are over 600 companies that have signed up!"

www.oseaskin.com

masks

A highly effective mask that helps clear the skin and leaves your face supple **www.pangeaorganics.com**

A soothing mineral mask **www.miessenceproducts.com**

Burt's makes a terrific mask that can be mixed with other products. I call it kitchen-cosmetics: mix with avocado, banana, yogurt, or other yummy nourishing foods to make a great face food. **www.burtsbees.com**

Astara is a true leader in making highly effective masks that help refine pores and give skin new life. **www.astaraskincare.com**

A deeply cooling and regenerative moisturizer made with red algae **www.oseaskin.com**

This is another phenomenal product from Astara—deeply moisturizing and perfect after a facial mask. **www.astaraskincare.com**

I grew up in northeastern Pennsylvania with dreamy, sweet-smelling lilacs and forsythia bushes. The minute I opened the tube to Kiss My Face's Obsessively Organic Under Age moisturizer, all of those scents came back to me. This has easily become one of my favorite facial moisturizers. **www.kissmyface.com**

facial moisturizers, creams, and serums

This creamy moisturizer makes your skin feel super silky. **www.luvalla.com**

I started using this cream in the winter months when my skin was cracking. It worked exceptionally well! **www.drhauschka.com**

A little of this floral-scented gel goes a long way. It feels cool and refreshing, and readily absorbs into the skin. **www.jurlique.com**

I use Kiss My Face tinted moisturizer almost exclusively as my foundation, sunscreen, and face lotion. It's light and provides just enough coverage for the redder parts of my face. **www.kissmyface.com**

Avocado is known to be restorative to the face. Essential Care's formula is more manageable, less messy, and very effective. **www.essential-care.co.uk**

This lotion is good when my skin is at its oiliest. **www.jurlique.com**

I may be too young to enjoy the full effects of this anti-aging serum, but it did make my face feel very soft. **www.johnmasters.com**

This product has a refreshing aroma that sinks right into the skin. **www.juicebeauty.com**

This moisturizer has a lovely scent and doubles as a sunscreen. **www.juicebeauty.com**

If you don't mind natural oils on your skin, I highly recommend this product. It has a lovely, nutty scent and feels particularly good when skin is thirsty. I squirt two drops in my palms, rub together, and gently apply over my face and neck at night. **www.mambinoorganics.com**

Keys Eye Butter is rich, thick, and particularly good around the edges of the eyes. It was also very effective on my elbows and knuckles. **www.keys-soap.com**

Duchess Marden makes this exotic serum and lotion treatment for the face, neck, and décolleté. **www.duchessmarden.com**

Spray this interesting and effective product into your hands and rub thoroughly over your face and neck. It provides a good base for foundation or tinted moisturizer and has a positive synergistic effect when used together with the face oil. **www.kimia.co.uk**

For all the ladies looking for a terrific under-eye cream, look no further. MyChelle's version gave my eyes a smooth lift, especially in the mornings. Dab a bit on your fingertips and apply gently under the eyes. **www.mychelleusa.com**

▬▬ I know some of the ladies out there are looking for a great antiwrinkle serum. Try this one: It contains five peptides to help support collagen and elastin production. **www.mychelleusa.com**

▬▬ This product is well suited to help heal hyperpigmentation from the sun and to soothe acne or blemish scars. **www.kimberlysayer.com**

▬▬ This lovely moisturizer strengthens skin. For those of us who are concerned with wrinkles, this will help contract collagen fibers. **www.kimberlysayer.com**

▬▬ This nice, lightweight cream has a soothing scent and absorbs easily into the skin. **www.pangeaorganics.com**

▬▬ This great serum really locked in moisture. I didn't even need to reapply. **www.nudeskincare.com**

This is a perfect cream that you can apply to your face, neck, and décolleté before going to bed. **www.oberoncosmetics.com**

I love this product! If you can't tell, I'm into multifunctional products. This is a 3-in-1 deal. You get a moisturizer, a foundation, and a sunscreen all in one. **www.sukicolor.com**

This soothing cream absorbs quickly into the skin. I like to add a bit of facial oil to the cream when my skin is feeling a tad dry. **www.usa.weleda.com**

This lotion has a deep herbal scent and absorbs readily into the skin. It's especially good in dry weather. **www.origins.com**

It's sometimes difficult to find a moisturizer that is light and airy on the skin while providing ample protection against the sun. Kimberly Sayer provides a terrific solution with this facial lotion. It is particularly good for those of us who are prone to breakouts. **www.kimberlysayer.com**

At one point, I was using pure tea tree oil on my blemishes, but that can have a drying effect. Burt's herbal blemish stick has just the right amount to spot-treat pimples. **www.burtsbees.com**

This blemish stick contains a little alcohol to help dry out pimples, but also contains great herbal extracts to help treat breakouts. You can use this as much as you need to. **www.burtsbees.com**

blemish treatments

During certain times of the month, my hormones go all in a tizzy and I tend to break out.
I was often duped into buying conventional drying agents until I discovered that they
hinder more than help. I found each of these products to be highly effective.

■■■■ This product helps exfoliate and rejuvenate skin for those who are prone to breakouts. **www.skinceuticals.com**

■■■■ This is a perfect cream for zit spot-treatments. Just use a pin-sized dot on anything that is about to flare up. What I love about this formula is that it doesn't dry or flake the skin like conventional blemish treatments. **www.jurlique.com**

■■■■ This is a highly effective product. The peppermint scent took me a while to get used to, but it did help reduce breakouts. **www.kissmyface.com**

■■■■ A plant-based skin treatment that soothes and restores your skin while keeping blemishes at bay **www.therawise.com**

Eco-Stylephile: AFRICA NATURALLY LIMITADA

Africa Naturally Limitada Challenge: Restore land and help empower indigenous peoples in Africa.

Over 75 percent of Mozambique's native forestland has been cut down; leaving a land that is far less fertile than it originally was. Those living on the land have been challenged with restoring it, while making a living. Allan Schwarz, of the a.d. schwarz label, helped diversify jobs in this area by teaching native Mozambicans about the secret of tree and seed oils.

Africa Naturally Limitada Solution: Create a tea tree and sustainable forestry cooperative to extract oils.

Tea tree, or melaleuca, oil is an essential oil distilled from a tree species native to the northeastern coast of Australia. The oil is used in many cosmetic products, particularly in body washes, toothpastes, hair rinses, and in blemish control. Though tea tree isn't native to Mozambique, Allan found—after a ten-year trial period—that the plants actually grow well on degraded soil, and there is no risk of tea tree becoming an invasive species (spreading outside the planting area and taking over indigenous plants). On a ten-acre test plot, Allan has set up a tea tree oil distillation cooperative to help make use of a piece of land that has undergone drastic deforestation. Each member of the cooperative, native Mozambicans, owns a share in the company and participates in the entire process. Every single component of tea tree is used in the process. Tea trees are

harvested when mature and sprout up again without any replanting. The logs and larger branches are used to fire the distillation process. Small twigs and leaves are distilled. Oil is distilled twice, and the purified water from the distillation is used to water seedlings. The high-quality oil is then sold to companies like the Body Shop, who use it to create personal-care products.

What Can You Do?

- Look for cosmetic products that specifically work with fair-trade groups or have a history of working with indigenous peoples.

- Encourage your favorite brands to give back to the places they source.

Tea tree branches are distilled to extract the tea tree oil. It takes about a ton of branches and leaves to make 13 to 22 pounds of tea tree oil.

Man carrying tea tree for distillation preparation.

Every part of the tea tree plant is used. Here, women carry tea tree trunks for light construction.

Tea tree goes through two distillation processes. The 100 percent pure oil is sold, as well as the last distilled water.

Tea tree plants are cut down and will resprout after eight months without any replanting.

MAKEUP

Attention all makeup junkies: According to the *Daily Mail*, women spend close to $16,800 on cosmetics over their lifetime! Now I don't know if this section will help you simplify your medicine cabinets and makeup bags or get you to explore the marvelous world of eco-conscious makeup. Whatever the case, this section introduces you to a number of choices to make your eyes eye-catching, your pout pretty, and your cheeks flush.

▬ A mineral-based foundation, bronzer, and setting powder from Oberon **www.oberoncosmetics.com**

▬ A mineral-based corrector powder that helps offset red or sallow skin tones or cover imperfections, blemishes, or reddened areas **www.beautemineral.com**

▬ A mineral-based foundation powder from Alima **www.alimacosmetics.com**

▬ Jurlique Citrus Silk Finishing Powder can be lightly dusted over foundation to help reduce shine. **www.jurlique.com**

▬ Colorescience makes this no-fuss brush to apply mineral foundation with minimal mess. Highly recommended. **www.colorescience.com**

cover-ups, foundations, and setting powders

This loose finishing powder will help wick away moisture and keep a glossy face at bay. **www.janeiredale.com**

Jane Iredale's no-mess compact finishing powder is perfect for last-minute touch-ups. **www.janeiredale.com**

Lavera loose mineral powder **www.lavera.com**

Larenim's loose mineral foundation powder **www.larenim.com**

A fluid foundation that goes on naturally and feels lightweight **www.lavera.com**

This is a pretty cool foundation, and the coverage is absolutely flawless. Basically, the bottle is designed to be an airless pump. The beads contain a number of active ingredients that are released onto the skin as soon as it is applied. Try it for yourself. **www.janeiredale.com**

Nvey has a light coverage that feels surprisingly refreshing on the skin. **www.nveymakeup.com**

A terrific little compact with no-fuss mineral foundation powder **www.mineralogie.biz**

Joppa's blushers and bronzers come in a variety of alluring shades with the coolest names. Try Blushing Bride, Desert Night, or Bahama Bronzer. Better yet, check out their Web site and name your own! **www.joppaminerals.com**

A perfect little bronzer compact for when you're on the go **www.larenim.com**

Real flakes of 24-karat gold result in a sexy shimmer and a natural glow. **www.janeiredale.com**

A liquid crystal serum with algae extract that helps tighten fine lines around the eyes. You don't need much, so when you apply, use sparingly. **www.colorescience.com**

Brush a soft pink hue to your cheeks with Lavera's compact. **www.lavera.com**

A convenient and stylish compact for when you need a little extra blush or bronzer **www.beautywithoutcruelty.com**

bronzers and blushers

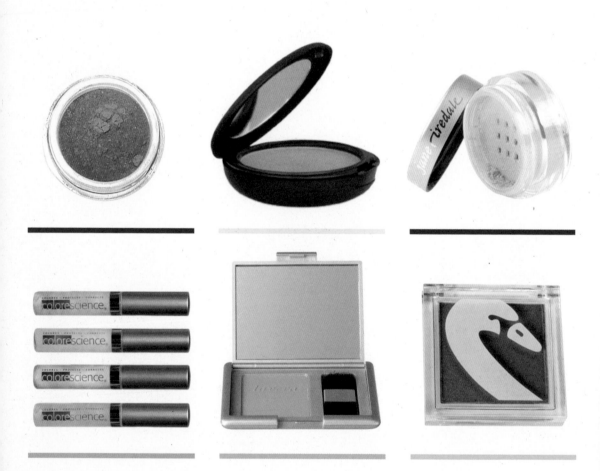

- Oberon has a strong range of foundations, bronzers, blushers, and eye shadows. **www.oberoncosmetics.com**
- Perfect for when you want a brush-on tan. Use it on your face, décolleté, shoulders, and arms. **www.mineralogie.biz**
- Nvey's handy little bronzer compact **www.nveymakeup.com**
- Miessence mineral-based blushers and powders **www.miessenceproducts.com**

■ A dark mascara that truly brings out your lashes **www.drhauschka.com**

▨ A Mineralogie eyeshadow compact **www.mineralogie.biz**

▨ Nvey's lovely selection of color eye shadow **www.nveymakeup.com**

▨ Suki's mascara helps lengthen and strengthen lashes. **www.sukicolor.com**

eyes

Nvey black eyeliners bring out your sensuous side. **www.nveymakeup.com**

A totally fun eye glitter stick for when you want to glam up your look **www.lavera.com**

Lavera eyeshadow **www.lavera.com**

Pencil Me In natural pencil eyeliners. Great for outlining eyes and playing up color **www.pencilmeincosmetics.com**

Oberon has a number of brightly colored, mineral-based eye shadows for girls who love to experiment with color. **www.oberoncosmetics.com**

Creamy eyeliners that go on so smoothly **www.janeiredale.com**

Afterglow's black mascara is perfect for bringing out your lashes. **www.afterglowcosmetics.com**

Eye accent pencils from Pencil Me In **www.pencilmeincosmetics.com**

A playful variety of eye shadows from Alima **www.alimacosmetics.com**

A deep-black liquid eyeliner, perfect for bringing out your eyes **www.beautywithoutcruelty.com**

Larenim's mineral-based blue eye shadow **www.larenim.com**

Mineralogie's deep-black eyeliner **www.mineralogie.biz**

It's the color of cotton candy, but tastes more minty fresh. Goes on smoothly and not sticky **www.janeiredale.com**

A yummy honey lip balm to quench your parched lips. Both my guy and girlfriends love this product. **www.burtsbees.com**

Lip Drink has a subtle citrusy taste and is perfect for chapped lips. **www.janeiredale.com**

Ecco Bella's red lip crayon for when you want ravishing red lips **www.eccobella.com**

lips

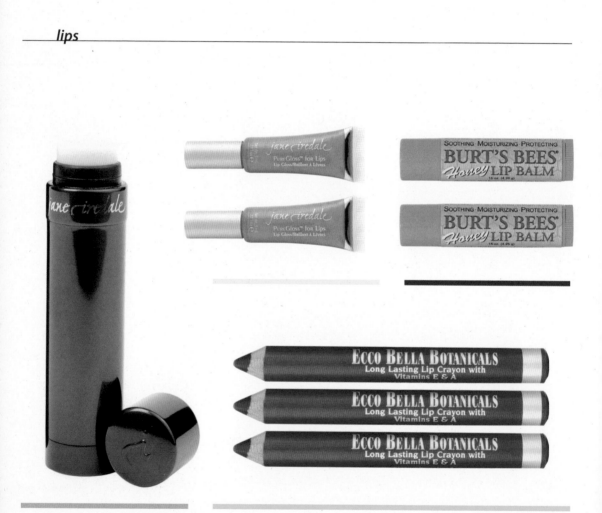

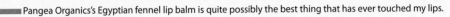

Pangea Organics's Egyptian fennel lip balm is quite possibly the best thing that has ever touched my lips. **www.pangeaorganics.com**

A lustrous pink lip gloss and moisturizer **www.nveymakeup.com**

A perfect lip balm with SPF for when you are out in the sun or skiing **www.lavera.com**

Colorescience's lip serums help maintain moisture in your lips while giving an iridescent, prismatic effect to your lips. **www.colorescience.com**

Lovely lip glosses in a variety of shades **www.eccobella.com**

I like Ecco Bella's lip smoothers because you can use them over or under your lipstick, or just on their own. **www.eccobella.com**

Ecotints lip balm goes on smoothly and has a lustrous sheen without being sticky. **www.ecolips.com**

Jane Iredale's PureGloss has a wonderful shimmer and wears well throughout the day. **www.janeiredale.com**

Colorescience creates some really amazing "lip glazes" that stay on well, without any tacky or sticky feeling. **www.colorescience.com**

Dr. Bronner's yummy organic lip balm **www.drbronners.com**

BODY

Many of us wouldn't consider our skin an organ, but that is precisely what it is. Not to mention it being the largest organ of our body, it sure merits some good loving from us. Be kind to your body; protect it from the sun; and lather it with luscious, good-for-the-earth lotions to make it smooth, soft, and supple.

This TheraNeem mouthwash has a pretty impressive taste that really wakes up your mouth. **www.organixsouth.com**

A refreshingly yummy spray that fits in your purse for when you need a burst of freshness **www.miessenceproducts.com**

An invigorating herbal toothpaste **www.auromere.com**

A lively mix of clove, eucalyptus, peppermint, sage, ratanhia, and myrrh. Just add a few drops of this highly concentrated solution to a glass of water. **www.usa.weleda.com**

toothpastes and mouthwashes

■ A minty fresh toothpaste by Green People **www.greenpeople.co.uk**

■ Neem is often known as the "Toothbrush Tree" because it helps maintain healthy teeth and gums. **www.organixsouth.com**

■ This is a great natural alternative to all the conventional toothpastes out on the market. Minty taste and no fluoride or sodium lauryl sulfate **www.tomsofmaine.com**

soaps

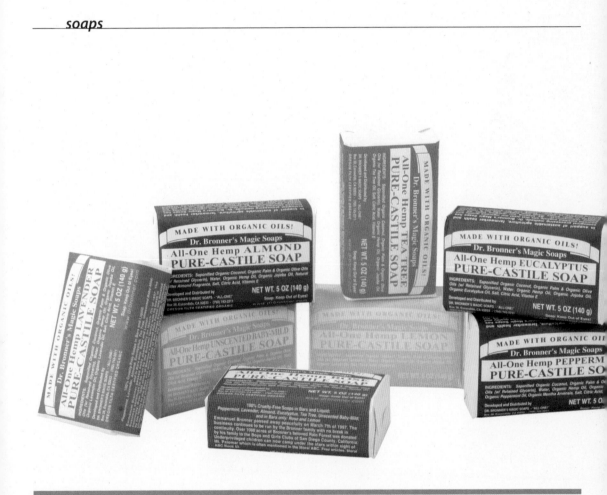

These yummy soaps have the most unbelievable scents! I love the grapefruit bar and the lemon verbena. **www.hugonaturals.com**

An all-organic, fair-trade soap that you can feel good about **www.drbronners.com**

Pomegranate is not just great in a juice, it's also great in soap. **www.pomega5.com**

Dr. Bronner's makes this multipurpose soap, which I love to use not only in the shower, but also for washing delicate garments, like stockings, bras, panties, and silks. **www.drbronners.com**

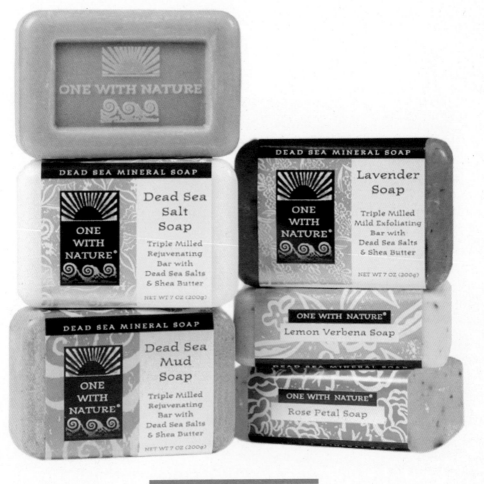

When I was younger and would get sore muscles from running, my mother would send me into the bathtub with Epsom salts. Biggs and Featherbelle has created a very effective soak that includes different types of salts, tapioca starch, sandalwood, and a unique blend of essential oils to soothe your muscles and your mind. **www.biggsandfeather.com**

A revitalizing soap, made by the Canadian vanguards of clean **www.druide.ca**

I love this exfoliating salt scrub. It leaves my skin super soft and silky. **www.astaraskincare.com**

You can make your own sugar body scrub or dip your fingers into this sugary concoction. **www.kissmyface.com**

bath salts, scrubs, and body washes

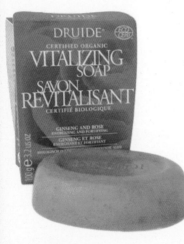

Holy Willy Wonka and the Chocolate Factory! For any woman who loves chocolate, Giovanni's Hot Chocolate Sugar Scrub is a must! This decadent treat will satiate all of your body needs (just don't try to eat it). **www.giovannicosmetics.com**

Dip into some Cool Mint Lemonade. This exfoliating scrub is very refreshing in a cool shower in the summer. **www.giovannicosmetics.com**

Superfresh and aromatic body wash, fit for a queen **www.giovannicosmetics.com**

CLEANSE
moisturizing
body wash
savon hydratant
pour le corps

Pure Organic Technology™

Cucumber
Song
Ode au
Concombre

giovanni ®
ORGANIC BODY CARE
10.5 fl oz ℮ 310mL

HOT CHOCOLATE™
sugar scrub

Pure Organic Technology™

with crushed cocoa beans

giovanni ®
ORGANIC BODY CARE
Net wt 9 oz ℮ 260 g

COOL MINT LEMONADE™
salt scrub

Pure Organic Technology™

with crushed mint leaves

giovanni ®
ORGANIC BODY CARE
Net wt 9 oz ℮ 260 g

I love using Pangea's facial scrub on both my face and body when I need a gentler exfoliator. **www.pangeaorganics.com**

Jo Wood's Usiku Organic Bath Oil is heavenly. The aroma alone will make you want to stay in the tub for hours. **www.jowoodorganics.com**

A wonderful shower gel with a soft woody scent **www.druide.ca**

▬▬▬▬▬▬ Pangea's shower gels are very concentrated, so a little goes a long way. **www.pangeaorganics.com**

▬▬▬▬▬ A creamy formula with a citrusy sweetness that leaves your body silky smooth **www.essential-care.co.uk**

Shea butter can be on the greasy side, but it is an incredible emollient that I love right after a hot shower. Hugo is a master at luscious aromas, and this body butter scent really stays with you throughout the day. **www.hugonaturals.com**

This product is highly suggested for women who are going through pregnancy, weight gain, or weight loss. The natural oils, including almond, hazelnut, rose hip, and wheat germ, help maintain the skin's elasticity and minimize stretch lines. **www.alqvimia.com**

This product will moisturize your skin and give you a healthy, tanned glow. **www.chocolatesun.net**

A favorite treat for expecting mothers (just ask Heidi Klum)! **www.biggsandfeather.com**

body lotions and oils

A perfect organic lotion treat for the entire body. It absorbs readily and has a nice floral scent. **www.drbronners.com**

An incredible enriching moisturizer that contains royal jelly, the honey bee secretion that is used to feed queen bees as well as larvae in the first few days of their growth. This lotion also has a little mica in it, which gives your skin a nice shimmer. **www.burtsbees.com**

Enfusia creates these nice light moisturizers that glide on easily, absorb readily, and smell tasty. **www.enfusia.com**

I was on a *Lucky* magazine shoot, and all the girls on the set could not stop putting on Giovanni's grapefruit lotion! It's lightweight with the most scrumptious grapefruity scent. **www.giovannicosmetics.com**

A velvety organic body lotion that feels heavenly on the skin **www.terressentials.com**

Amka is Swahili for "to wake"—and that is exactly what this enlivening, refreshing moisturizer will do. **www.jowoodorganics.com**

This is a great balm to use after a stressful day. Just rub it on your muscles and breathe in the herbal aroma. **www.kathys-family.com**

This handcrafted lotion has a soothing scent and is good for your face, hands, and body. **www.pangeaorganics.com**

I love that you can turn this bottle upside down and all-the-way-around to get some hard to reach spots. Spritz on after a hot shower and rub it in. **www.origins.com**

A delicate moisturizing formula that leaves your skin feeling soft and supple **www.porticospa.com**

If I'm planning to wear a shorter skirt or dress, I'll rub this Perfect Organics product on my legs to give them a natural glow. **www.perfectorganics.com**

Miessence

Australian native and mother of three, Narelle Chenery's first successful product sale was to her uncle. "He's Greek and he had a terrible time with his shaving rash," she laughs. "He asked me if I could make something for him to try."

Narelle accepted her uncle's challenge, researching the best ingredients. She came up with an aftershave balm of mints, coriander, lemon, orange peels, marshmallow, burdock root, and a host of other herbs that she had planted in her garden. She used vodka to preserve the formula and let the concoction sit on her kitchen windowsill for 4 weeks, turning it every day. "It cured his rash!" she exclaims. "We sold the rest to his hairdresser because he was raving about it so much."

That was 15 years ago. Prior to that, Narelle was selling another range of beauty products in the United States. "Like most women, I trusted the brand, which claimed to be all-natural and organic. Then one day, I picked up a cosmetic ingredient dictionary. Needless to say, I was pretty shocked that the ingredients were not just unnatural, but unsafe. It got me thinking," she says. "If this brand isn't what they claim to be, then what others aren't?"

Narelle turned into what she calls an "ingredient freak" and found only a few brands that didn't use synthetic ingredients in their formulas. "I began writing articles to educate women and making products in my kitchen," she says. "I'm not a trained chemist so I didn't have any preconceived notions to use harsh chemicals in my products."

"The key issues in making beauty products are emulsifying and processing. That's where a lot of brands like to add chemicals, but there is no need because you can preserve and emulsify products naturally. Mayonnaise is a great example; it's naturally emulsified. Milk is also naturally homogenized."

Miessence is certified organic through Australian Certified Organic (ACO) and the U.S. Department of Agriculture (USDA) and is now sold in more than 60 countries. "We make 'living products,'" Narelle says. "The nutrients that make up our formulas are very active. Their shelf life is about 6 months from the opening of the product and 30 months in unopened conditions. We actually make our products every two months to ensure we get the freshest products for our customers."

www.miessenceproducts.com

Vodka Is Not Potatoes: It drives Narelle crazy to see other companies call their products "all-natural." "Cocamide DEA is a great example," she explains. "Lots of companies will put parentheses after the ingredient that says (made from coconuts). Sounds harmless, right? Well, it's like saying vodka has the nutritional value of potatoes. When you think of coconut, it is pure and from the earth, but this version of coconut is not the same. The manufacturing process contaminates it and it is no longer pure coconut oil." The contamination that she speaks of can form nitrosamines, which, as we learned earlier, are some of the most potent cancer-causing ingredients.

The Environmental Working Group's Report on Sunscreens shows that Badger is one of the safest and most effective sunscreens on the market. It has a mild lavender scent, and is fairly waterproof and broad spectrum. It is a tad on the oily side, which doesn't react well with my face, so I like to put it on the rest of my body, especially my back, chest, and shoulders—and put a different one on my face. **www.badgerbalm.com**

Key's Solar Rx Sunblock is a chemical-free, UVA and UVB broad-spectrum sunscreen. It is an emollient as well as a sunscreen, so your skin will feel moisturized. It has a tendency to feel a little greasy at times. **www.keys-soap.com**

A very nice sunscreen that goes on smoothly and works well without leaving any white residue **www.desertessence.com**

sunscreens and after-sun lotions

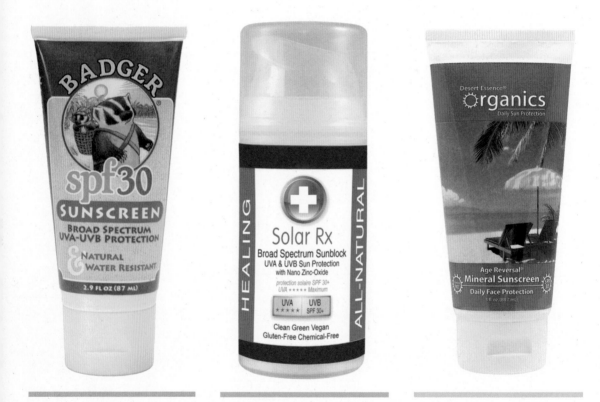

This is a refreshingly cool sun soother that absorbs readily in the skin and has a pleasant, fresh scent. I often use it just as a regular lotion for the face, hands, and legs. **www.burtsbees.com**

A very protective spray for you and the young ones **www.lavera.com**

A broad-spectrum sunscreen with shea butter **www.chocolatesun.net**

Juice Beauty does a nice sun-protection cream that works really well on the face and neck. **www.juicebeauty.com**

I'm really into the application of this sunscreen. The rollerball is perfect for rolling all over the body. **www.colorescience.com**

A chemical-free mineral sunblock **www.mychelleusa.com**

A cool, soothing lotion with vitamin E and jojoba that absorbs readily into the skin **www.lavera.com**

A quick-absorbing sunscreen that is perfect for face, neck, and chest **www.lavera.com**

A quick-absorbing sunscreen that is light and effective **www.luvalla.com**

A high-performance sunscreen, perfect for those sunny days **www.uvnaturalusa.com**

A highly effective cream if your skin gets sun- or wind-burned **www.maxgreenalchemy.com**

The Tom's of Maine line of shaving products is quite nice for both men and women. **www.tomsofmaine.com**

I'm a huge fan of Pacific's All Natural Shaving Oil. I take it on trips with me, especially wilderness or outdoor excursions. It lasts forever and has the nicest scent. All my guy friends are in love with this product. They're not used to shaving with an oil (as opposed to a foam), but once they find out how amazing it feels, they're totally converted. **www.pacificshaving.com**

shaving

STYLE, NATURALLY

Dr. Bronner's Shaving Soap Gel has a wonderful glide to help prevent any nicks or cuts. **www.drbronners.com**

For all the special men in your life, check out Oberon's organic Meadowfoam Shaving Gel. **www.oberoncosmetics.com**

I absolutely love the soft scent and feel of The Art of Shaving products. The Pre-Shave Oil is especially good for areas that you may nick or cut. As a side note, they make wonderful shave kits for men. **www.theartofshaving.com**

An invisible, unscented deodorant. The stick is dry, so I found it best to apply right after you get out of the shower. If you like a roll-on or spray, they have that, too. **www.thecrystal.com**

If you're into a light lavender scent, this is a good choice. I found that it didn't last after heavy workout days, so you may need to reapply. **www.kissmyface.com**

A ton of my guy friends use Tom's of Maine, so I thought I'd give it a shot. I bought the unscented version because some of the other scents were more masculine. It worked really well, and I didn't need to reapply. **www.tomsofmaine.com**

deodorants and antiperspirants

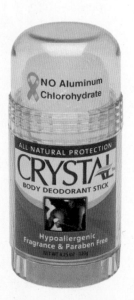

STYLE, NATURALLY

I initially bought this fruity blend because "Asian Pear" sounded yummy. I ended up liking it a lot but don't normally wear it during heavy workout days. **www.natures-gate.com**

A refreshing, 84 percent certified organic deodorant with a subtle scent **www.greenpeople.co.uk**

This is a great product that truly lasts for the whole day. **www.miessenceproducts.com**

I prefer a dry deodorant, but the Weleda citrus spray deodorant was nice and perfect after a long workout and shower or on a hot summer day. **www.usa.weleda.com**

I gave Terressentials Spice Deodorant to one of my guy friends and he absolutely loved it. It held up through heavy sweats and long days. I'm not into the spiced smell for myself, but I tried it out and it held up nicely. **www.terressentials.com**

■ The sweet, succulent scent of vanilla **www.eccobella.com**

■ Tsi La fragrances are filled with botanical essences and exotic spices and are enriching and sensuous. **www.tsilaorganics.com**

■ Aftelier does an impressive array of custom botanical perfumes that will really trigger your senses. **www.aftelier.com**

perfumes and fragrances

My friends always ask me what scent I'm wearing. This is it. **www.essenceofvali.com**

An array of soft, sophisticated scents by Valerie Bennis, the founder of Essence of Vali and a certified aromatherapist **www.essenceofvali.com**

This is a light and refreshing body spritz, with aloe to leave your skin feeling hydrated. **www.luckyduckonline.com**

An incredible organic blend of bergamot and vanilla makes this a sumptuous treat. **www.patyka.com**

HANDS, FEET, AND NAILS

Our pretty peds and fingers are constantly on the go, but are probably the things that get the least amount of pampering. Why not treat our feet and fingers to some Personal Care Rx?

Nails: Buffed, Shined, and Polished

As I mentioned earlier, your hair and nails are just an extension of your skin, so naturally your French-manicured tootsies react to outside forces in much the same way as the rest of you. Nails can become brittle, thin, discolored, and cracked if we do not care for them properly. Be sure to moisturize your nails frequently. You can do this with your regular hand lotion or with cuticle oil; check out the products outlined in this section.

 I like going to the salon or spa to get my nails done, but at one point they were becoming cracked and brittle. Constant use of nail polish and nail-polish remover was doing them in. But don't fret, you don't need to forgo manis and pedis altogether. You can always get them oiled and buffed, but if you are going to get polished, too, then try to bring your own nail lacquer and a non-acetone polish remover. Chances are, the polish your salon is using includes harmful chemicals, like formaldehyde, toluene, xylene, dibutyl phthalate, and synthetic colors. (See the Beauty Blacklist on page 183 for more information about these ingredients.)

Here is a safe, effective, and quick tip, straight from Beyoncé's nail technician at the Paint Shop in Beverly Hills. Take a vitamin E capsule, break it open, and massage the oil into your nails and cuticles. The vitamin E lubricates and moisturizes nails. Popular nail oils that you can buy in the store will often have naturally derived vitamin E, otherwise known as tocopherol, which is different from tocopherol acetate.

Treat your feet right with nourishing treatments.

▬ Manicures and pedicures can be too much of a good thing, wearing out and weakening nails. This nail-strengthening cream is an incredible fix when used daily. **www.barielle.com**

▬ A great scrub for tired, worn-out feet **www.kissmyface.com**

▬ A yummy hand cream with the spicy citrus scents of bergamot and grapefruit **www.kissmyface.com**

hand and foot lotions, cuticle care, and nail polishes

■■■■ This fortifying, protein-based coat glides on easily and gives your nails an incredible luster. **www.barielle.com**

░░░░ This wonderful nail firmer helps restore natural oils that have been stripped from your fingers and cuticles. **www.barielle.com**

■■■■ A great deodorizer and cool mist to refresh tired, aching tootsies **www.aromafloria.com**

■■■■ Spa Foot Balm helps alleviate tired legs and cracked skin. A perfect follow-up to the foot scrub **www.aromafloria.com**

■■■■ Wearing heels all day or being active outdoors can take a toll on your feet. This gentle exfoliator will help soften and heal the bottoms of your feet. **www.aromafloria.com**

Finally, there is a nourishing alternative to conventional nail-polish removers! It may take just a tad more scrubbing, but I love using this Suncoat nail-polish remover. It's like giving my fingers a moisturizing oil treatment. **www.suncoatproducts.com**

I take my Anise nail colors with me almost every time I get a manicure. The manicurist doesn't seem bothered that I like to bring my own. **www.nailaidworks.com**

A decadent dessert for tired toes **www.desertessence.com**

A nourishing nail pen that you can keep in your purse for emergency hangnails **www.drhauschka.com**

I tend to nibble on the side of my finger when I'm deep in thought. I keep this product by the side of my desk to slather on my nails to help renew and heal the cuticles and skin. **www.badgerbalm.com**

A lovely French manicure set **www.suncoatproducts.com**

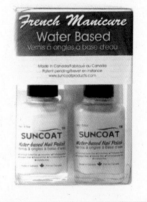

Aromafloria's Honey Papaya Soothing Hand Crème is as yummy as it sounds. **www.aromafloria.com**

A zesty wax that is perfect for when your fingers or cuticles are feeling a bit dry **www.burtsbees.com**

Max Green Alchemy Cuticle Rescue is an all-natural oil-based nail treatment that helps strengthen dry, cracked cuticles or discolored nails. **www.maxgreenalchemy.com**

Peacekeeper gives all of its distributable profits to help fund women's health advocacy and human rights issues. **www.iamapeacekeeper.com**

This product is perfect for chapped hands, cuticles, heels, and elbows. **www.badgerbalm.com**

A 100 percent natural and 85 percent organic, talc-free, herb and cornstarch powder that helps deodorize, absorb moisture, and refresh the feet. **www.kathys-family.com**

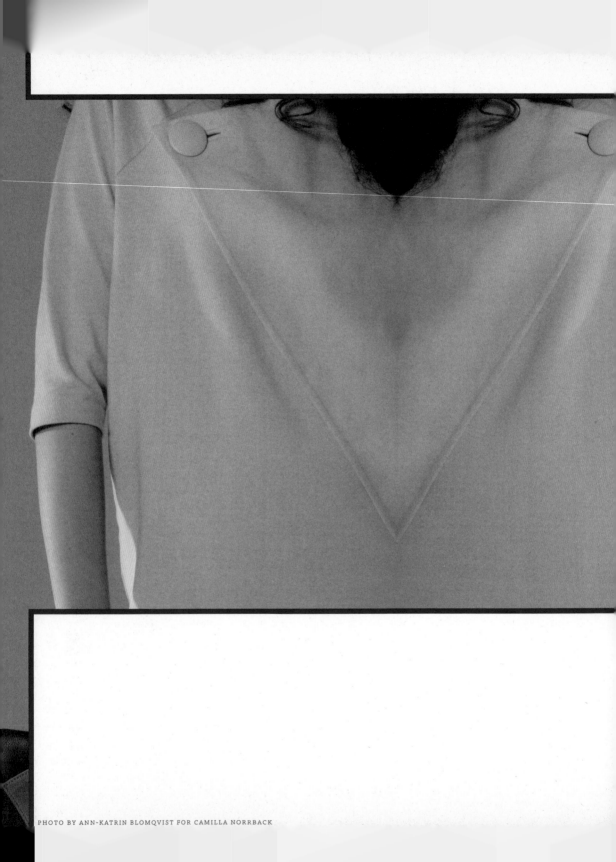

CHAPTER 06

eco-beauty tips of the trade

IT TAKES PATIENCE AND A KEEN EYE TO MAKE SURE YOU ARE GETTING THE HIGH-QUALITY BEAUTY PRODUCTS THAT YOUR BODY DESERVES. NOW THAT YOU'RE ARMED WITH SOME OVERALL INFORMATION ABOUT THE INDUSTRY, AND YOU ALSO HAVE LISTS OF NOTABLE BRANDS, I'M GOING TO SHARE A FEW TIPS TO HELP YOU FIND WHAT YOU'RE LOOKING FOR.

"WHEN WE HEAL THE EARTH, WE HEAL OURSELVES."
—DAVID ORR, ENVIRONMENTAL EDUCATOR

Trade Tip #1: Smart Shopping

WHERE TO SHOP

These days, environmentally and socially conscious personal-care products are more accessible than eco-fashions. If you have a local natural- or organic-food market in your area, take a look at the personal-care products they carry. You'll often spot great brands that have been around for a while, like Weleda and Dr. Hauschka. (Note: Don't always rely on popular brand names to give you the best product or the best results. Always check the back of the ingredient label, ask questions, and if you can, sample the product). Larger cosmetics companies naturally have more products in more accessible places, such as supermarkets, drugstores, cosmetics counters, and spas. Estée Lauder's product lines include Origins Organics, which is certified organic by the USDA, and Aveda, known for its sourcing partnerships with indigenous peoples around the world. Burt's Bees, now owned by Clorox, can be found in many of the same places as Origins Organics and in Target. Another brand that is fairly easy to come by is Tom's of Maine, now owned by Colgate-Palmolive.

Dozens of worthy personal-care brands turn up in the marketplace every year. Follow the same steps that I outlined in the fashion section: educate yourself on the brands dedicated to eco-beauty, and then experiment to determine what works for you.

LOOK ONLINE

Turn to the Internet if you strike out at your local stores. The stores listed in the Resources section will give you a place to start. You can do a search online for "organic beauty products" or "eco beauty products," but again, anyone can tag their brand as such. Using the tips outlined in this book will help you develop a discerning eye for what is and what isn't authentic.

Skin Deep, www.cosmeticsdatabase.com, is the largest database of and safety guide to cosmetics and personal-care products. This site, an initiative by the Environmental Working Group, rates tens of thousands of cosmetics products and gives them a toxicity score: 0–2 is a low hazard; 3–6 is a moderate hazard; and 7–10 denotes a high hazard. It's really easy to use and addictive once you start. Just type in the product, brand, ingredient, or the ingredient list if the product is not listed, and find out what they have to say about products you use or those you're considering trying. They've also recently added a review/comment function to the site, which is nice because sometimes it's good to get other opinions before making a purchase. I used this feature when researching some of the products that I use, including Miessence Balancing Cleanser and Kiss My Face 3WayColor. Keep in mind, however, that even though this is the most comprehensive consumer-accessible information available on the Internet, there still are data gaps, so approach this as a guide rather than as the be-all-end-all of eco-beauty.

LOOK FOR CERTIFICATION LABELS

Since the FDA does not require cosmetics companies to test their products for safety before we use them, more companies are looking to certify their products through third-party organizations, such as the USDA, Natural Products Association, or ECOCERT, out of France. Each certifying body has different criteria in order to give their "certified-organic" or "natural" seal, and the Resources section will help elucidate what some of the more popular of these labels mean. Please keep in mind, though, that certification can be quite expensive. As a result, many small upstart companies that are actually organic may not be able to afford a third-party organic or natural label. I would encourage you to support these upstart companies, but never be afraid to ask them questions.

In addition to organic or natural certification, there are other labels you may see, including "Vegan" and "Not tested on animals." Turn to Resources (page 289), to familiarize yourself with these labels.

LOOK AT THE INGREDIENTS

I can't stress the importance of this one enough. The ingredients label is your best friend when it comes to buying beauty products. If you ever have a question about an unfamiliar ingredient, check it out at www.cosmeticsdatabase.com, do a search for it online, or refer to an ingredients dictionary, such as *A Consumer's Dictionary of Cosmetic Ingredients*.

WHAT TO LOOK FOR WHEN SHOPPING

Knowing where to begin when shopping for personal-care products can be a challenge. Keep in mind that you'll want to eventually switch over to healthier products, but it's not always feasible to do this right away. Keep these strategies in mind:

- Buy What You Reapply
- Be Sensitive
- Indulge

Buy What Your Reapply

This is a valuable rule of thumb to follow. Start with items that you use more than twice a day—toothpaste, soap, lotion, lip balm, lip gloss or lipstick, foundation, and powder. Then look at what you use on a daily basis, like shampoos and conditioners. Because you expose yourself to these products more often, it's important that they be both safe and effective.

Be Sensitive

Use healthful and nourishing products, particularly around sensitive areas where skin may be thinner or more prone to breakouts. Such areas may include around the eyes, under the arms, and the bikini area.

Indulge

Sometimes you just need to spoil yourself with that one decadent beauty treat. Perhaps it will be a day at an organic spa or an expensive facial cream that you absolutely love or maybe something as simple as a mineral-bath soak. Whatever your indulgence, be sure to pamper yourself appropriately.

Spread the Word

Beauty secrets are meant to be shared. If you find a great new product, don't keep it to yourself. According to a Mintel consumer report, 64 percent of women aged 18 to 65+ said they are more likely to buy new products if a friend recommends them.

Trade Tip #2: How to Have Fun in the Sun

WEAR SUNSCREEN

If there is one thing from childhood that I always remember, it is my mother's gentle abetments to: "Chew with your mouth closed, sit up straight, and wear your sunscreen." All are appropriate words of advice to ensure that a young girl doesn't grow into a gum-smacking hunchback with sun-spots—an image that I'm sure none of us relishes.

At a glance, all of the above advice seems like it would be so easy to follow, but even something as obvious as using sunscreen every day can be confusing. First the uncomplicated part: Sunscreen is one of the ultimate, easy-to-apply, antiaging, antiwrinkle, anti-sun-spot-development, skin-cancer-prevention beauty treatments. Use it. You can have fun in the sun, like snooze-fests on the beach, without all the long-term dermal nightmares that can accompany too much of a good thing. Tan lines can be okay, but not when you look like a candy cane.

Ever since I was young, I've applied (at least) SPF 15 sunblock, and in recent years, I've upped that to SPF 30, with reapplication every couple of hours. I've thankfully eschewed sunburn with my mother's sound advice. What she didn't tell me was that, even though I was applying precisely what the back of the bottle called for, I still wasn't fully protecting myself from the sun.

Here comes the complicated part: The "All-day protection, broad-spectrum, chemical-free, waterproof, sweatproof," sure-this-stuff-is-foolproof claims are not always what they may seem. A recent study by the Environmental Working Group shows that a whopping 84 percent of 891 sunscreen products on the market offer inadequate protection from the sun or contain ingredients that can compromise our health. The report shows that 13 percent of sunscreens with a 30 SPF and higher protect only from sunburn, which is caused by UVB radiation. The formulas unfortunately don't contain any ingredients that protect our sensitive skin from UVA radiation, which is what causes aging, skin damage, and skin cancers.

This next point may seem paradoxical, but bear with me: More than half of sunscreens are so unstable that they actually break down in the sun relatively quickly. They first absorb the sun's energy so it doesn't penetrate our skin, but then they release the captured energy by breaking apart, reacting with other chemicals in the sunscreen, and sometimes causing a chain reaction of free radicals. It's like a series of kamikaze fighter jets crashing inside your body at the cellular level.

Free Yourself of Free Radicals: It took me a long time to understand the concept of free radicals. Let's be honest, it sounds like the name of a great jam band, not something we should be mindful of when applying makeup. It's an important concept to understand, however, especially because it's directly linked to cellular health and aging.

Our body is made up of tiny units called atoms. Electrons occupy the layers around the atom. It is the number of electrons in the outer shell of the atom that determines the stability and behavior of the atom. Unpaired electrons are like your best friend after a bad breakup with her boyfriend: unstable, frenzied, and bouncing around from relationship to relationship, probably breaking every single heart along the way. These unpaired electrons are called free radicals, and they go from atom to atom, stealing electrons and turning *them* into free radicals. As a result, there is a deleterious cascade effect that can affect every atom in the vicinity.

Our bodies are normally able to handle free radicals, but if we constantly introduce stressors on our body or do not get an appropriate amount of antioxidants, the free radicals will cause damage. That is why it is particularly important for us to protect our skin from sun damage and steer clear of any unstable chemicals in our sunscreens, both of which induce free radicals.

The EU is leaps and bounds ahead of the United States when it comes to improving sunscreen formulas. Of the brands available in the United States, only 16 percent of the 891 formulas surveyed are both safe and effective, blocking both UVA and UVB radiation, remaining stable in sunlight, and containing very few ingredients that can be hazardous to our health. If you're curious to see where the top-selling brands fall on the sun protection and safety meter, or if you'd like to see where the brand you use ranks, I'd encourage you to check out Skin Deep at www.cosmeticsdatabase.com.

PROTECT YOURSELF FROM THE SUN

It's a myth that you can only get badly sunburned in the summer months. Sunscreen should be worn year-round, especially if you are a winter sports junkie. If you've ever seen someone come back from a ski trip with a sunburn, it's because UVA rays reflect off snow. UVA rays are also more damaging at higher elevations, so be sure to apply sunscreen. Keep the following words in mind when shopping for or applying sunscreen:

- Pre-Apply
- Broad Spectrum
- SPF
- Reapply
- UPF

Pre-Apply

Make sure you apply sunscreen 20 to 30 minutes before you head outside. It takes a while for the sunscreen to settle on your skin and become effective.

Broad Spectrum

Truly broad-spectrum sunscreen helps block both UVA and UVB rays. Check www.cosmeticdatabase.com and the previous chapter to find out which brands are the best.

SPF

These letters stand for Sun Protection Factor, which measures the amount of time it takes for skin exposed to sun to redden. For instance, if your skin begins to flush after ten minutes, a product with SPF 30 would keep you from burning for 300 minutes. SPF 15 absorbs about 93 percent of the sun's rays, and SPF 30 absorbs 97 percent. Sunscreens over SPF 30 don't supply much more protection and usually include unnecessary ingredients that can especially irritate those with sensitive skin.

Reapply

Sunscreens, even if they are advertised as "waterproof," still need to be reapplied. Try doing so every one to two hours.

UPF

If it makes sense, wear protective clothing. Clothes, including hats and shirts, inherently protect us from the sun, even without a layer of sunscreen underneath. Just as sunscreens are measured with SPF, clothes can have a "UPF" rating. UPF stands for Ultraviolet Protection Factor, which indicates how much of the sun's UV radiation is absorbed. According to www.skincancer.org, a fabric with a rating of 50 will allow only one-fiftieth of the sun's UV rays to pass through. Darker clothes with tighter weaves offer skin the best protection from the sun. Lighter, looser fabrics do not protect as well. Do a light test to see if your clothes are suitable for the sun: Hold your shirt up to a light. If you can see through it, then the sun's rays will penetrate it. Also keep an eye out for UPF-rated clothes, which you will often find in outdoor and sports shops.

PHOTO BY ANN-KATRIN BLOMQVIST FOR CAMILLA NORRBACK

CONCLUSION

Style is deeply enmeshed in who you are. It also, in many ways, is reflective of our culture and our perception of the times. As the world changes, so does our style. (The correlation between the economy and hemlines comes to mind.) And so it's no surprise that climate change, fair trade, poverty, and ecosystem restoration—once material for the evening news and political debates—have found their way onto the pages of lifestyle and fashion magazines. Style helps us to connect with these otherwise daunting issues. By raising awareness in an approachable way, sustainable style gets more people involved and helps us figure out how to make caring for the environment a part of our busy lives. We begin to realize that our choices, no matter how small, can resonate in the sphere of influence. That is empowering.

As Julie Gilhart has said, the fashion industry discusses trends, and not necessarily movements. But that's just what we're involved in right now: a movement. One that is like a gathering storm on the horizon, fueled by each and every one of us. Whether you recognize it or not, you are a part of this movement. Reading this book places you there. Asking how you can style your world better makes you a part of it. Just as we bring our own unique flavor to an outfit— whether with a patent red heel or a juicy pink lip—we bring our own distinct style to the movement.

This movement is yet young. People are still trying to boil down such complex global issues as fair trade and climate change to make them fit digestible headlines: "Top 10 Eco Looks for Spring" and "Green Tips for the Home." But eventually we will move beyond this. Eco and Green will become invisible, and the headlines will simply read: "Top 10 Looks for Spring" and "Tips for the Home"—and yet we'll know that these articles are full of environmentally friendly products and information. Not only that, but I've already seen magazines and other forms of media digging deeper into the issues—tackling carbon footprints of clothing and debating what fiber is more sustainable than the next. This will have become the standard, the default, the norm. And as we change, so will the language.

Now that you've read this book, I hope you expect more from your clothes, your products, and the world around you. I hope you are inspired to make this part of your lifestyle. I encourage you to be curious, to learn, and to enrich your life by staying involved. Make it a part of who you are. Make it a movement you can call your own.

That is *Style, Naturally*.

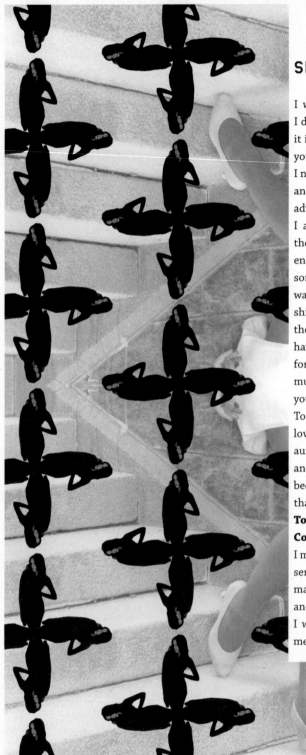

SHOUT-OUTS

I want to give a shout-out to **Shawn McDonald**. I dedicate this book to you. I may never have started it if it weren't for the dinner we had that night when you told me to "just start writing a little every day." I never thought I would one day have a finished book, and you probably never thought I would take your advice. To **Don:** A wonderful kindred spirit whom I am so happy to have met. Thank you for being there when the people closest to me couldn't be. You enabled me to move forward with my dreams during some of the roughest hours. I will never forget it and want you to know that I deeply cherish our friendship. To **Tom:** This is to our night of Jon Stewart and the beautiful relationship that night led to. Did you have any idea what you were getting into? Thank you for never doubting me, but most of all thank you so much for your unconditional love and support and your beautiful, beautiful soul. I love you so much. To my parents, **Bob** and **Diane**, and the rest of my loving family—my brother, **Travis**, grandparents, aunts and uncles—who never hindered my creative and environmental pursuits or tried to stop me from becoming the person I endeavored to be. Warmest thanks to my professors and mentors—**Tom Eisner**, **Tom Gavin**, **Barbara Bedford**, **Bobbi Peckarsky**, **Cole Gilbert**, **Ellen Harrison**, and anyone else I may have left out. You are like my second family and serve as a continuous source of inspiration. You all made my time at Cornell so extremely worthwhile and have helped fulfill a dream that I've had since I was a young girl. Thank you for keeping up with me and for believing in my wildest ideas. This book is also for all the teachers in my life who've helped bring out my creative writing juices, starting in the fourth grade. Thank you all! Please keep in touch. I miss all of you.

A big thank you to my housemate: **Silvani Cruz**, for being so cool during nights when I would have to work late on the book. Thanks to **Tory Hoen**, who pre-edited my book, and to **Julia Gabella**, who helped with work on my myriad projects, even when she was busy, busy, busy. A special thank you to all my friends and those closest in my life: Thank you for keeping up with me and for staying close, even when I am far away. I know my nomadic existence can be difficult on all of you. Thank you for being patient with me and for understanding my burning passion.

A special thanks to **Alex**, who not only supports me wholeheartedly in my crazy endeavors but challenges me to be better every day. I don't think there's any other person that I talk to more—morning, noon, or night, you always seem to find time. You are the truest of friends and I am blessed that you are in my life. To **Robert:** the book agent who never gave up. Of course, Robert, you are more than a book agent. You are a great supporter and friend who believed in me from the beginning. To my editors, **Jodi Warshaw** and **Kate Prouty:** You are the bomb! Thank you for your constant enthusiasm and your guidance throughout the writing process. You made the entire book-writing process a pleasant one. A special thank you to my copy editor **Brenda Modliszewski** and my graphic designer **Jay Peter Salvas**, both of whom had the monumental task of helping put the book in order. And, of course, I'd like to say a big thank you to the entire team at Chronicle Books! A special shout-out to all the participants in this book who allowed me to have them photographed: **Julia Gabella, Esosa Edosomwan, Benita Singh, Tiffany Brown, Pamela Daniels, Natalie Chanin, Bahar Shahpar, Peter Ingwersen, Leila Hafzi, Scott Hahn, Safia Minney, Blake Mycoskie, Galahad Clark, Monique Péan**, and **Karine Rodriguez**. A huge thank you to all my wonderful photographers: **Jon Moe, Henrik Adamsen, Zabou Carrière, Richard Burns, David Black**, and **Akira Yamada**. Thanks also to **Erica Gray** who helped do some of the hair and makeup. A big thank you to **Niko Courtelis** and **Isabelle** who have been so wonderful throughout the book process—this is dedicated to you!

A special thanks to my brothers and sisters over at **Energy Action** and **Green for All** who inspire me every day to speak up and take action for a clean, just future. This is our time to rise up. May we do so together. Lastly, I thank all the fearless visionaries in this space who breathe life into this movement every day of their lives. Your energy, integrity, and compassion do not go unnoticed. I want you all to know that I am your #1 fan. It is a privilege to know and work with you all. And a very special thank you to all of the designers, brands, retailers, and tireless activists who supported my work over the years—in so many different ways. May we all stay true to our vision and roots and forge ahead with great speed and efficacy.

Resources

Eco-Fashion Retail Web Sites

www.adili.com

www.argostyle.com

www.beklina.com

www.bettyandbabs.com

www.bohmo.com

www.BTCelements.com

www.cocosshoppe.com

www.devidoll.com

www.ecocitizenonline.com

www.ecogirl.com.au

www.exclusiveroots.com

www.fairtradeboutique.co.uk

www.fashion-conscience.com

www.fashionethic.com

www.gominyc.com

www.green-balance.dk

www.hipandzen.com

www.kaightnyc.com

www.mintandvintage.com

www.nimli.com

www.nusdansleschanvres.com

www.organicavenue.com

www.shopenvi.com

www.shopequita.com

www.shopmodify.com

www.shopsetchi.com/home.htm

www.sodafine.com

www.swedenorganics.com

www.terramar.co.uk

www.thegreenloop.com

www.thenaturalstore.co.uk

www.tigerlilyludlow.co.uk

www.tobi.com

www.worldofgood.com

www.xtremegreen.com.hk

www.zanisa.com

Eco-Beauty Retail Web Sites

www.beautynaturals.com

www.edenorganicx.com

www.futurenatural.com

www.lovelula.com

www.puresha.com

Vegan Fashion Retailers

www.alternativeoutfitters.com

www.beyondskin.co.uk

www.charmoneshoes.com

www.earth.us

www.mattandnat.com

www.minkshoes.com

www.mooshoes.com

www.novacas.com

www.stellamccartney.com

www.vegetarian-shoes.co.uk

www.vegetarianshoesandbags.com

Eco-Denim Designers

www.annacohen.com

www.aokijeans.com

www.arne-carlos.com

www.ascensionclothing.co.uk

www.breaddenim.com

www.camillanorrback.com

www.covetthis.com
www.delforte.com
www.earnestsewn.com
www.edun.ie
www.elsom.com.au
www.fairindigo.com
www.goindigojeans.com
www.gracecello.com
www.howies.co.uk
www.hug.co.uk
www.kohzo.ch
www.komodo.co.uk
www.kuyichi.com
www.les-racines-du-ciel.com
www.levi.com
www.lifegate.it
www.lindaloudermilk.com
www.lookatryann.com
www.loomstate.org
www.machja.com
www.mavi.com
www.missionplayground.com
www.nautica.com
www.oqoqo.com
www.replaybluejeans.com
www.ricalewis.fr
www.roganNYC.com
www.serfontaine.com
www.sharkahchakra.com
www.slingandstones.com
www.stellamccartney.com
www.volcom.com

Organizations Supporting Organic Initiatives

Anti-Apathy: a nonprofit organization, based out of the UK, that supports people who take creative approaches to social and environmental issues. Fashion is one of Anti-Apathy's main focal points. www.antiapathy.org

Better Cotton Initiative: an organization and global initiative to encourage adoption of better management practices in cotton cultivation in order to achieve measurable reductions in key environmental impacts, while improving social and economic benefits for farmers. www.bettercotton.org

Co-Op America: a national nonprofit consumer organization that uses the strength of consumers, investors, businesses, and the marketplace to work toward creating a socially just and environmentally sustainable society. www.coopamerica.org

Environmental Justice Foundation (EJF): a nonprofit organization that works to promote organic cotton initiatives throughout the world. www.ejfoundation.org

Ethical Fashion Forum (EFF): a network of designers, businesses, and organizations focusing on social and environmental sustainability in the fashion industry. www.ethicalfashionforum.com

International Federation of Organic Agriculture Movements (IFOAM): an organization helping to lead, unite, and support the organic movement throughout the world. It brings together more than 750 member organizations across 108 countries. www.ifoam.org

Organic Consumers Association (OCA): a grassroots, nonprofit, public-interest group that deals with issues of food safety, industrial agriculture, genetic modification of plants and animals, corporate accountability, and environmental sustainability. Check out their "Coming Clean" petition aimed at strengthening standards for organic cosmetics; the "GE Free" petition to ban genetically modified crops; and the "Clothes for a Change" petition to encourage apparel companies to use organic cotton and fair labor standards. www.organicconsumers.org

Organic Exchange: a nonprofit organization committed to expanding organic agriculture, with a specific focus on fiber crops like organic cotton. www.organicexchange.org

Organic Trade Association (OTA): a membership-based business association that focuses on the organic business community in North America. Its mission is to promote and protect the growth of organic trade to benefit the environment, farmers, the public, and the economy. www.ota.com

Pesticide Action Network (PAN): a network of more than 600 NGOs, institutions, and individuals in more than 60 countries that works to replace the use of hazardous pesticides with ecologically sound alternatives. www.pan-international.org

Sustainable Cotton Project (SCP): an organization focused on educating farmers, consumers, and manufacturers about the impact of conventional cotton. They work with farmers on other methods of farming (such as organic Biological Agricultural Systems in Cotton (BASIC) and transitional cotton, or cotton that is being converted from conventional to organic). www.sustainablecotton.org

Sustainable Style Foundation (SSF): one of the first nonprofit organizatons to link style with sustainability. The organization is known for the SSF Best Dressed Environmentalist List, the OSSA Awards—ten industry awards that epitomize style and sustainablility—and *SASS Magazine*. www.sustainablestyle.org

Eco-Fashion and Ethical-Fashion Shows

Note: Eco- and ethical-fashion shows are held throughout the world every season. Past shows have taken place in Berlin, Oslo, Paris, London, São Paulo, Rio de Janeiro, Miami, New York, Toronto, Vancouver, Los Angeles, Seattle, Portland, and San Francisco.

All Things Organic (held in Chicago): an exclusive organic trade show. www.organicexpo.com

Designers & Agents (D&A): an independent, international alternative marketplace for more than 1,000 designers and retailers. The organization even has its own "Green Market" featuring the hottest designers who do the eco thing. www.designersandagents.com

Estethica (held in London): a large, organic and ethical-fashion bazaar, held during London Fashion Week. www.londonfashionweek.co.uk

Ethical Fashion Show: Held in Paris and Rio de Janeiro, this foremost international fashion and trade event is dedicated to ethical and sustainable apparel and accessories. The Ethical Fashion Show is held in Paris every year. A second show debuted in Rio de Janeiro in November 2008. www.ethicalfashionshow.com

Future Fashion: Held in New York City, this premier fashion event, coordinated by Barneys New York and Earth Pledge, brings top-name American and European designers into the sustainable fashion fold. Designers like Marc Jacobs, Ralph Lauren, Calvin Klein, and others develop one-of-a-kind pieces made out of sustainable fabrics, which are then showcased during Fashion Week. http://earthpledge.org

Green Festival: Held in Chicago, Washington DC, and San Francisco, this event created by Global Exchange and Co-Op America, brings together local and national socially responsible businesses and environmental, social justice, and community organizations. www.greenfestivals.org

Prêt à Porter Paris: a premiere salon featuring a wide selection of fashion and accessories from around the world—from the most contemporary to the most cutting-edge. It is also one of the best places to see great ethical fashion brands. www.pretparis.com/en/

Eco-Friendly Fibers

The following materials are often associated with environmentally friendly clothes.

Note: Just because a designer uses one or more of the following fabrics in their products does not mean that they are committed to sustainable design, fair treatment of their workers, or socially conscious practices throughout their company.

ANIMAL FIBER

Alpaca: these cute little llama-like creatures yield some of the finest fiber on earth. The fiber is silkier and lighter in weight than wool and contains no lanolin. Better yet, the animals tread more lightly on the earth than other grazers.

Angora: bunny fur that is clipped from long-haired rabbits. Soft, smooth, and very luxurious.

Cashmere: the fine fiber from a furry goat. It is principally sourced from China, Mongolia, Iran, Afghanistan, Turkey, New Zealand, and Australia. There can be considerable differences in how goats are treated, so sometimes it's important to know where the designer has sourced material.

Chitin: fiber derived from the shells of sea crustaceans, such as crabs and lobsters.

Felt: this may be one of the oldest fibers in the world. It is generally created by wetting and matting wool or wool-like fibers (such as alpaca).

Merino: a popular sheep's wool that is tight and springy. Wool often undergoes a chemical-scouring process, making it a not-very-Green choice. However, more and more companies are bringing organic wool, or o-wool, and sustainable wool, or i-merino, to the market.

Milk: here is a relatively new idea: Dewater milk and then bioengineer it to create a soft fabric that is often spun with silk, wool, cotton, or ramie.

Mohair: a fiber made from the hair of the Angora goat. Mohair is removed by shearing the animal, as with wool, has a high luster, and is useful as an alternative to fur.

Wool (organic): a general term that refers to all types of fiber from sheep, goats, alpacas, and other related four-legged creatures. As mentioned under Merino, wool generally goes through intense chemical-scouring processes, but organic wool uses a much cleaner process.

PLANT FIBER

Note: Some plant fibers, like bamboo, may be processed using rayon-type techniques, which combine heat and chemicals to help break down the material into a fiber. This is not considered an organic process.

Bamboo: Moso bamboo is most commonly used in housing materials, but it became quite a hit on the fashion scene about six years ago. Bamboo is a grass, so it grows back without deliberate replanting. (If you are lucky enough to have a lawn, you know what I mean.) It also doesn't require many, if any, chemical inputs to grow, so many are touting this as a sustainable alternative to petroleum-based fabrics, like nylon and polyester.

Cotton: Fifty percent of our fiber needs are fulfilled by cotton, which is conventionally made using pesticides. In fact, the manufacturing of cotton uses 25 percent of the world's pesticides! As a result, there has been a move toward "cleaner" cotton, which involves BASIC, organic, and transitional cotton, the latter referring to cotton that has not yet reached the three-year certification mark for growing without pesticides.

Hemp: This plant has been given an unwarranted bad wrap due to its psychoactive counterpart. (I think you know what I mean.) But hemp is strong and grows quickly without much, if any, chemical use. However, due to its coarse-feeling fiber, it is best when blended with other fibers, like cotton and silk.

Jusi and Piña: *Jusi* is the fiber of abaca, or banana silk. *Piña* is made from pineapple leaves. Both yield nice fabrics, especially when combined with silk. Jusi is usually mechanically woven, and piña is generally handwoven on a loom. These fabrics were originally used in the Philippines to make *barongs*, the native dress of Filipinos.

Kenaf: a type of hibiscus, principally grown in Asia and parts of Africa. It feels very similar to hemp or jute fiber and is best when blended because of its coarse nature.

Linen: a fabric derived from the flax plant. It is a stiffer fabric, so it won't stick to the skin, and it generally dries quickly.

Lyocell: generally a soft fiber made from wood pulp through a rayon process (meaning it is somewhat chemical intensive); it has many cottonlike characteristics. It is often called Tencel, Seacell (using seaweed), or Modal (beech-wood pulp).

Ramie: a flowering plant of the nettle family that has been used as a fiber for a long time. It is nicest when blended with cotton or wool and is similar to linen.

Sasawashi: an interesting fabric from Japan that is produced by mixing *kumazaa*, a wide-leafed bamboo, with rice paper—the same stuff used for wrapping sushi.

SYNTHETIC FIBER

Polyethylene terephthalate (PET): a fiber made from recycled plastic bottles or old polyester clothes. The products are recycled and later turned into new clothes.

NATURAL, BUT MAN-MADE FIBER (USING MANUFACTURING TECHNIQUES TO CREATE FIBERS DERIVED FROM NATURAL MATERIALS

Ingeo: the first fiber made from renewable resources, such as corn and soy. It is often called PLA or polylactic acid fiber. It is not always considered organic, because some of the plants used to make the fiber may be genetically modified, which means foreign genes are inserted into the plant's DNA.

PROTEIN FIBER

Silk: a natural protein fiber obtained from the cocoons of silkworms, which are actually caterpillars. Most silk is cultivated before the silkworm turns into a moth, and thus the caterpillar is killed. With "wild silk," or "peace silk," the silkworm is allowed to emerge from its cocoon. Silk organza is often created from silk, but do not assume this always to be true: some organza is made from synthetic materials, like nylon.

Clothing Certification Labels

1% for the Planet is an alliance of corporations that donates 1 percent of their sales to environmental organizations worldwide. Some apparel and accessory companies that are members include: aGaiN NYC, Anna Cohen, Autumn Teneyl Designs, BTC Elements, the GreenLoop, Muumuu Heaven, Not Just Pretty, Plain Jane Creates, the Battalion, Red Camper, Stewart and Brown, and of course, this book! To learn about other companies that contribute, visit the "Members" section at www.onepercentfortheplanet.org.

The **Agriculture Biologique** logo is used in the EU. Products may qualify to use the logo if they contain more than 95 percent organic components, were produced or processed within the EU, and were certified by an independent inspection body. www.agencebio.com

The **BASIC** or **Cleaner Cotton** logo stands for Biological Agriculture Systems in Cotton. Products with this logo are made with cotton created using a combination of Integrated Pest Management, sustainable-farming techniques, and a minimal amount of pesticides. The goal is to save farmers money while reducing and eliminating certain farm chemicals, such as insecticides, pesticides, fertilizers, and water consumption. American Apparel and prAna have started purchasing certified Cleaner Cotton to incorporate into their apparel lines. www.sustainablecotton.org

The **Carbon Neutral Clothing (CNC)** logo establishes an "ecological footprint" for a garment. The ecological footprint is a calculation that accounts for emissions generated along the supply chain. Funds from each certified product are sold and allocated in matching amounts to programs such as reforestation, conversion to organic farming, or renewable energy investment. www.carbonneutralclothing.com

Cradle to Cradle (C2C) certification is used in the textile industry, mainly for home furnishings, but is not yet being used extensively in the fashion arena. C2C certification signifies that a company has achieved a credible amount of improvement in the environmental design arena and is therefore helping customers purchase products that define a broader definition of quality. The certification scheme, developed by McDonough Braungart Design Chemistry, analyzes the following: materials; design for material utilization, such as recycling and composting; the use of renewable energy and energy efficiency; efficient use of water; and strategies for social responsibility. www.mbdc.com

The **European Eco-Label** logo has been used for more than 10 years in European countries. Products that bear the "flower" have been checked by independent bodies for compliance following a set of strict ecological and performance criteria. www.eco-label.com

The **Fair Trade** logo is most commonly seen in the food industry, but is slowly making its way into the apparel and accessories market. Keep in mind that a fair-trade product will not always have a certified logo, so it is good to contact companies to ask about their purchasing guidelines and practices. TransFair is the third-party certification organization that issues the Fair Trade logo primarily for food products; the International Fair Trade Association endorses organizations that produce non-food fair-trade products, including fashion and crafts. www.ifat.org

The **Organic Cotton** logo may occasionally be found on organic cotton products, but more often than not, the clothing and hang tags will just say "organic cotton." www.organicexchange.org

Made-By was started by a foundation in the Netherlands to provide transparency in the apparel sector and to promote fair trade, social standards, the use of environmentally friendly cotton, and other sustainable textile-processing practices. There are currently close to two dozen labels that carry the Made-By logo, including Rianne de Witte, Edun, Kuyichi, Intoxica, and iNTi Knitwear. www.made-by.org

Cosmetic Certification Labels

Australian Certified Organic (ACO) is one of Australia's largest certifiers for organic and biodynamic produce and has more than 1,500 operators within its certification system. ACO provides certification services to operators from all sectors of the organic industry, including cosmetics companies. Certification ensures compliance with national production standards and allows tracing of all products back to their origin. www.australianorganic.com.au

German-based **BDIH** was the first organization to launch a certification for natural cosmetics in 1986. In order to be certified, cosmetic products must comply with a list of general principles and are also prohibited from including certain substances, such as genetically modified organisms (GMOs), synthetic dyes, synthetic fragrances, ethoxylated raw materials, animal-based products, silicones, paraffins, and other petroleum products. Testing on animals is not allowed. www.kontrollierte-naturkosmetik.de

ECOCERT is a French company that has created its own criteria for both natural (ECOCERT Naturkosmetik) and organic (Cosmébio) cosmetics standards. ECOCERT is the main certifier in Europe and started to certify cosmetic products in 2003.

The ECOCERT Naturkosmetik label standards are as follows:

- 95 percent minimum of the ingredients must be natural or from natural origin.

- 50 percent minimum of the vegetable ingredients must be certified organic.

- 5 percent minimum of the ingredients composing the finished product must be certified organic.

The **Cosmébio,** or **"Bio,"** label is stricter. Its parameters are as follows:

- 95 percent minimum of the ingredients must be natural or from natural origin.

- 95 percent minimum of the vegetable ingredients must be certified organic.

- 10 percent minimum of the ingredients composing the finished product must be certified organic.

www.ecocert.com

The **Humane Cosmetics Standard (HCS)** is the world's only international criteria for cosmetics or toiletry products that are "Not Tested on Animals." HCS was launched in 1998 by an international coalition of animal-protection groups from across the EU and North America, including the European Coalition to End Animal Experiments. HCS companies must not conduct or commission animal testing and must introduce fixed cutoff dates for ingredient purchasing. www.gocrueltyfree.org

The **Italian Organic Farming Association (AIAB)** and the **Institute for Ethical and Environmental Certification (ICEA),** together with a group of manufacturers, have developed standards for natural and organic cosmetics. www.aiab.it

The **National Association for Sustainable Agriculture Australia (NASAA)** is one of the leading organic certifiers in Australia. In recognition of the growing range of cosmetics seeking organic certification in the marketplace, NASAA developed a draft series of Health and Beauty Standards in August 2005. The standards vary depending on whether the company is the primary producer, manufacturer and distributor, or retailer. www.nasaa.com.au

The **Natural Products Seal** is a worldwide certification seal that was started by the Natural Products Association to help consumers determine what personal care products are truly made out of naturally derived ingredients. Under the new program, products must follow guidelines including:

- Be made up of at least 95 percent truly natural ingredients.

- Contain no ingredients with any suspected potential human health risks.

- Utilize no processes that significantly or adversely alter the purity/effect of the natural ingredients.

- Only contain ingredients that come from a purposeful, renewable, plentiful source found in nature (flora, fauna, mineral).

- Utilize processes that are minimal and don't use synthetic/harsh chemicals or otherwise dilute purity.

- Use non-natural ingredients only when viable natural alternative ingredients are unavailable and only when there are absolutely no suspected potential human health risks.

www.naturalproductsassoc.org/certifiednatural

People for the Ethical Treatment of Animals (PETA) has developed a "Cruelty Free" logo, which means no animal testing was done on the products bearing the bunny ears. www.peta.org

Soil Association Certification Limited (SA Certification) is the UK's largest organic-certification body. It launched its standards for health and beauty products in 2002 and now certifies a wide range of companies and products to these standards. A product that carries the Soil Association symbol and that is labeled "Organic" must contain a minimum of 95 percent organic ingredients. A product that carries the Soil Association symbol and is labeled "Made with XX percent organic ingredients" must contain a minimum of 70 percent organic ingredients, the exact percentage being specified on the label.

The remaining ingredients in the products must be proven to be non-GM and can only be used:

- If the organic version of that ingredient is not yet available, or

- The ingredients are from a restricted list of synthetic chemicals that have been assessed to determine that they have no detrimental impact on human health and minimal environmental impact.

The standards ban products or ingredients produced using nanotechnology. www.soilassociation.org

Though the **USDA Organic** label is most often found on food products, more and more cosmetics companies are meeting USDA Organic standards and certifying their products as such. This is largely due to the fact that there is no U.S. certifying body for organics strictly for cosmetics. Three separate types of labels may be used:

- "100 percent organic," where the product is composed exclusively of organic ingredients.

- "Organic," which means the product contains at least 95 percent organic ingredients.

- "Made with organic ingredients," indicating the product contains organic ingredients, but less than 95 percent. In this case, it is not possible to use the USDA Organic label.

www.usda.gov

The nonprofit organization Vegan Action administers the Certified Vegan logo, which is applied to foods, clothing, cosmetics, and other items that contain no animal products and are not tested on animals. www.vegan.org

Vegan Cosmetics is a newly formed certifying body and the only certifying agent exclusively serving the personal-care industry. Verified animal-free cosmetic, skin, bath, body, hair-care, and makeup products may use this logo. www.vegancosmetics.org

Further Reading

CLOSET CRAFTERS

Alabama Stitch Book: Projects and Stories Celebrating Hand-Sewing, Quilting, and Embroidery for Contemporary Sustainable Style. Natalie Chain and Stacie Stukin; photographs by Robert Rausch. Stewart, Tabori & Chang, 2008. 176 pgs.

Customizing Cool Clothes: From Dull to Divine in 30 Projects. Kate Haxell. Interweave Press, 2006. 128 pgs.

Fashion DIY: 30 Ways to Craft Your Own Style. Carrie Bladyes and Nicole Smith. Sixth and Spring Books, 2007. 136 pgs.

Generation T: 108 Ways to Transform a T-Shirt. Megan Nicolay. Workman Publishing Co., 2006. 272 pgs.

Rip It! How to Deconstruct and Reconstruct the Clothes of Your Dreams. Elissa Meyrich. Fireside Publishing, 2006. 208 pgs.

Sew What! Skirts: 16 Simple Styles You Can Make with Fabulous Fabrics. Francesca DenHartog. Storey Publishing, 2006. 128 pgs.

Threadbanger.com: A Web site devoted to the hippest DIY gear for the alternative crafter. This site offers up a refreshing approach to crafting what you wear.

BEAUTY BOOKS AND REPORTS

Business As Unusual: The Triumph of Anita Roddick. Anita Roddick. Thorsons Publishing, 2001. 304 pgs.

A Consumer's Dictionary of Cosmetic Ingredients: Complete Information about the Harmful and Desirable Ingredients Found in Cosmetics and Cosmeceuticals. Ruth Winter. Three Rivers Press, 2005. 576 pgs.

Not Just a Pretty Face: The Ugly Side of the Beauty Industry. Stacy Malkan. New Society Publishers, 2007. 177 pgs.

Not Too Pretty: Phthalates, Beauty Products, and the FDA. Jane Houlihan, Charlotte Brody, Bryony Schwan. Environmental Working Group, 2002. 19 pgs.

The Truth about Beauty: Transform Your Looks and Your Life from the Inside Out. Kat James. Atria Books/Beyond Words, 2007. 432 pgs.

SUSTAINABLE-STYLE BOOKS

Cradle to Cradle: Remaking the Way We Make Things. William McDonough and Michael Braungart. North Point Press, 2002. 208 pgs.

Environmental Impact of Textiles: Production, Processes, and Protection. K. Slater. CRC Publishing, 2003. 240 pgs.

Let My People Go Surfing: The Education of a Reluctant Businessman. Yvon Chouinard. Penguin Press HC, 2005. 272 pgs.

Threads of Labour: Garment Industry Supply Chains from the Workers' Perspective. Angela Hale and Jane Willis. Wiley-Blackwell, 2005. 288 pgs.

The Travels of a T-Shirt in the Global Economy: An Economist Examines the Markets, Power, and Politics of World Trade. Pietra Rivoli. Wiley Publishing, 2006. 288 pgs.

MAGAZINES AND WEB SITES

Anti-Apathy
This organization, based out of the UK, takes a creative approach to action. www.antiapathy.org

Clean Clothes Campaign
A Web site dedicated to improving working conditions in the garment industry. www.cleanclothes.org

The Daily Green
Hearst's consumer guide to Green stuff. www.thedailygreen.com

Eco-Chick
A girl's guide to Green: "Because Mother Earth is a woman," after all. www.eco-chick.com

Ecofashion World
A site that has all of the latest trends and designers. www.ecofashionworld.com

Ecorazzi
Catch celebrities Green-handed on this celebrity gossip blog. www.ecorazzi.com

Ecotextile News
The trade publication on environmentally correct textiles. www.ecotextilenews.com

Fashioning an Ethical Industry
A great Web site sharing information about sustainable-fashion publications and universities with an ethical-fashion focus. www.fashioninganethicalindustry.org

Good
A fresh view on social consciousness, this progressive magazine has cutting-edge commentary and top-notch articles. www.goodmagazine.com

Grist
Get your daily dose of eco-commentary from this award-winning online magazine and blog. www.grist.org

Haute
This Web and soon-to-launch hardcopy magazine highlights everything great about Green living, with a definite fashion edge. www.hauteidea.com

Ideal Bite
The *Daily Candy* of the Green world. www.idealbite.com

Inhabitat
An online blog covering the best in eco-design, from architecture to fashion. www.inhabitat.com

Labour Behind the Label
This is a campaign to help improve working conditions worldwide, including in the textiles industry. www.labourbehindthelabel.org

Lucire
This publication from New Zealand was the first fashion partner to the United Nation's Environmental Programme; *Lucire* was also the first international fashion publication to have a monthly editorial (Behind the Label) completely devoted to sustainable style. www.lucire.com

New Consumer
The UK's leading ethical-lifestyle magazine. www.newconsumer.com

Organic Exchange
Find the latest information on organic cotton and who is buying it. www.organicexchange.org

Pesticide Action Network
Find out more about the true costs of cotton. www.pan.uk.org

Planet Green
The Discovery network Web site that launched with their new Planet Green cable channel; check out the fashion and beauty section for some very helpful tips. http://planetgreen.discovery.com

S4
The sustainability trends in fashion newsletter; comes out twice a year. www.S4trends.com

Sprig
A smart and sassy eco–Web site, covering fashion, food, health, and home. www.sprig.com

Style, Naturally
The Web site devoted to all things having to do with this book, plus a host of information on great sustainable designers and beauty treats. www.stylenaturally.com

Style Will Save Us
Maybe style won't save us, but this online magazine might with its fun reviews and hot-to-trot style updates. www.stylewillsaveus.com

Sublime
A very style-forward magazine, covering all aspects of ethical lifestyle, with a special emphasis on in-depth reporting and fabulous fashion spreads. www.sublimemagazine.com

Sustain Lane
A great go-to site for Green product reviews. www.sustainlane.com

Sustainable Style Foundation
SSF has a great blog and magazine with a ton of the latest environmentally cool style resources. www.sustainablestyle.org

Treehugger
Quite possibly the best all-things-Green site on the Internet and definitely the most trafficked. www.treehugger.com

Retail Destinations

UNITED STATES

──── **ALABAMA, FLORENCE**

Alabama Chanin
www.alabamachanin.com
6534 County Road 200
Florence, AL
Tel: 256-760-1090

These are beautiful hand-quilted designs.

Billy Reid
www.billyreid.com
Pickett Place
438 N. Seminary Street
Florence, AL
Tel: 256-767-4692

Walk into this historic store and you will feel right at home. This is Southern hospitality at its finest. Seek out the design collaborations with Alabama Chanin.

──── **ARIZONA, PHOENIX**

Buffalo Exchange
www.buffaloexchange.com
730 E. Missouri Avenue
Phoenix, AZ
Tel: 602-532-0144

227 W. University Drive
Tempe, AZ
Tel: 480-968-2557

You'll find designer pieces and thrift finds in this second-hand and consignment shop.

TUCSON

Buffalo Exchange
www.buffaloexchange.com
2001 E. Speedway Boulevard
Tucson, AZ
Tel: 520-795-0508

6170 E. Speedway Boulevard
Tucson, AZ
Tel: 520-885-8392

See description under Phoenix, AZ.

Tucson Thrift Shop

319 N. 4th Avenue
Tucson, AZ
Tel: 520-623-8736

This store has some great vintage finds, ranging from clothes to accessories.

——CALIFORNIA, LOS ANGELES

Avita Co-Op

www.avitastyle.com
8213 W. 3rd Street
Los Angeles, CA
Tel: 323-852-3200

A small store with a nice selection of delicate, bamboo-based knits by Amanda Shi, shoes by Mink, and some other great eco-fashion finds.

Buffalo Exchange

www.buffaloexchange.com
131 N. La Brea Avenue
Los Angeles, CA
Tel: 323-938-8604

10914 Kinross Avenue
Westwood Village
Los Angeles, CA
Tel: 310-208-7403

14621 Ventura Boulevard
Sherman Oaks, CA
Tel: 818-783-3420

See description under Phoenix, AZ.

Catwalk

459 N. Fairfax Avenue
Los Angeles, CA
Tel: 323-951-9255

This is a vintage fashionista's heaven. From the moment you enter, you'll smell the sweet scent of some of the greatest vintage collections, including Gucci, Chanel, Pucci, Yves St. Laurent, Halston, Hermés, and other notables.

Deborah Lindquist

www.deborahlindquist.com
10500 Magnolia Boulevard
Tolouco Woods, CA
Tel: 818-762-7199

This is a lovely boutique with lots of light and floor space carrying Deborah's iconic bustiers, recycled cashmere sweaters, and bridal designs.

Decades

www.decadesinc.com
8214 Melrose Avenue
Los Angeles, CA
Tel: 323-655-1960

An upscale boutique with an eye-catching leopard-print staircase that leads to a vast selection of high-end vintage design, from Pucci to Missoni to Versace.

Green Rohini

www.greenrohini.com
13327 Ventura Boulevard
Sherman Oaks, CA
Tel: 818-981-0023

This little store has a mix of offerings, from Deborah Lindquist to yoga wear.

H Lorenzo

474 N. Robertson Boulevard

West Hollywood, CA

Tel: 310-652-0064

An eco-friendly boutique built with solar panels and reclaimed wood, H Lorenzo has some eco-friendly offerings for men and women and fine Japanese and indie designers.

Hidden Treasures

154 S. Topanga Canyon Boulevard

Topanga, CA

Tel: 310-455-2998

This whimsical little shop sells an eclectic mix of vintage clothes, accessories, quilts, and other stuff.

Natural High Lifestyle

www.naturalhighlifestyle.com

2400 Main Street

Santa Monica, CA

Tel: 310-450-5837

This is a nice little find, tucked away off Main Street in Santa Monica. It's a great shop for good-fitting yoga attire, casual athletic wear, and personal-care products.

Shop Regeneration

www.shopregeneration.com

1649 Colorado Boulevard

Los Angeles, CA

Tel: 323-344-0430

This cute shop has a lot of different knick-knacks and is a good place to find off-the-beaten-path jewelry, accessories, and girlie-girl footwear.

Slow Clothing

7474 Melrose Avenue

Los Angeles, CA

Tel: 323-655-3725

This vintage shop stands firmly on a popular Melrose Avenue corner with a host of funky finds from past eras.

Undesigned

www.undesigned.com

1953½ Hillhurst Avenue

Los Angeles, CA

Tel: 323-663-0088

A well-edited store in Los Angeles, with not only a beautiful store-brand collection but also great products and accessories from United Nude, Cruselita, OmbreClaire, Josh Jakus, Entermodal, Baggu Bags, and Ashley Watson.

Wasteland

www.thewasteland.com

7428 Melrose Avenue

Los Angeles, CA

Tel: 323-653-3028

1338 4th Street

Santa Monica, CA

Tel: 310-395-2620

Wasteland is one of the hottest places to browse a great selection of vintage. It was popularized when Angelina Jolie came down the red carpet in a $26 find from the store.

Visionary

8568½ Melrose Avenue
West Hollywood, CA
Tel: 310-659-1177

Visionary is a beautiful, inviting, rustic boutique with no shortage of eco jewelry, clothes, and personal care products.

SACRAMENTO

Sac's of Fruitridge

4220 Fruitridge Road
Sacramento, CA
Tel: 916-391-2402

This is a popular vintage destination, especially for those of us who love real vintage from past eras.

SAN DIEGO

Buffalo Exchange

www.buffaloexchange.com
Pacific Beach
1007 Garnet Avenue
San Diego, CA
Tel: 858-273-6227

Hillcrest
3862 Fifth Avenue
San Diego, CA
Tel: 619-298-4411

See description under Phoenix, AZ.

Frock You Vintage

www.frockyouvintage.com
4121 Park Boulevard
San Diego, CA
Tel: 619-220-0630

You can find this store on eBay, but if you happen to be in the San Diego area, check out their store. They have fun, funky, glam-rock, and glamour finds.

SAN FRANCISCO BAY AREA

AB Fits

www.abfits.com
1519 Grant Avenue
San Francisco, CA
Tel: 415-982-0406

40 Grant Avenue
San Francisco, CA
Tel: 415-982-0406

These stores have the best when it comes to up-and-coming, hot-off-the-street designers. They also carry eco-design cult favorites like Loomstate, Rogan, Edun, Del Forte, Eco*gan*ik, and Turk and Taylor.

American Rag

www.amrag.com
1305 Van Ness Avenue
San Francisco, CA
Tel: 415-441-0537

This store is crowded with fashions and antifashions. Chock-full of a wicked selection of vintage pieces, hand-picked by keen eyes, as well as some of the hottest new designers.

Atomic Garden

www.atomicgardenoakland.com
5453 College Avenue
Oakland, CA
Tel: 510-923-0543

This is a chic, minimalist boutique with a definite vintage feel. There is a vintage cash register and reclaimed shelving made from water towers. The racks are filled with the latest knits and denims from eco-friendly designers.

Azalea Boutique

www.azaleasf.com
411 Hayes Street
San Francisco, CA
Tel: 415-861-9888

The "Eco Azalea" section of this store provides a nice, edited selection of designers, ranging from denim masters like Loomstate, Del Forte, and Bread Denim to easy-to-wear pieces from Stewart and Brown, the Battalion, Panda Snack, and Edun.

Backspace

www.backspacesf.com
351 Divisadero Street
San Francisco, CA
Tel: 415-355-1051

This is a girlie-girl shop with a nice selection of designers, including some eco-designers.

Buffalo Exchange

www.buffaloexchange.com
2585 Telegraph Avenue
Berkeley, CA
Tel: 510-644-9202

1555 Haight Street
San Francisco, CA
Tel: 415-431-7733

1210 Valencia Street
San Francisco, CA
Tel: 415-647-8332

See description under Phoenix, AZ.

Collage

380 San Anselmo Avenue
San Anselmo, CA
Tel: 415-256-2562

A hip, edgy European-influenced boutique that carries some of the trendiest lines as well as a few good eco-brands.

Doe

www.doe-sf.com
629a Haight Street
San Francisco, CA
Tel: 415-558-8588

This is a local indie boutique meets art gallery. The cute little store stocks an eclectic mix of designers, with a particular emphasis on West Coast designers. Some favorites include She-Bible, Stewart and Brown, Prairie Underground, and Talla.

Dollhouse Bettie

www.dollhousebettie.com
1641 Haight Street
San Francisco, CA
Tel: 415-252-7399

This super-cute little shop is the place to go if you want to get your Ooh-la-la on. It has an outstanding selection of vintage lingerie, girdles, pinup-style ensembles, boudoir-style baby dolls, and exquisite hosiery and corsetry.

Eco Citizen

www.ecocitizenonline.com
1488 Vallejo Street
San Francisco, CA
Tel: 415-614-0100

This is a spacious store with a clean, minimalist appearance; it stocks eco-friendly, fair-trade clothes that share a similar, clean design.

EcoLogiQue

141 Gough Street
San Francisco, CA
Tel: 415-621-2431

This is a cute little shop with the freshest looks in eco-fashion and eco-beauty.

Embodies

www.embodies.com
1127 Magnolia Avenue
Larkspur, CA
Tel: 415-561-6462

This sweet boutique stocks a wide selection of eco-fashion clothing and accessories.

Mary's Exchange

1302 Castro Street
San Francisco, CA
Tel: 415-282-6955

This neat consignment shop has a great selection of brand-name clothes at reasonable prices. Clothes are arranged by style and color.

Mascara Vintage

www.mascaravintage.com
1747 Polk Street
San Francisco, CA
Tel: 415-378-0065

This is a tiny treasure trove of the cutest vintage finds.

My Trick Pony

www.mytrickpony.com
742 14th Street
San Francisco, CA
Tel: 415-861-0595

This is an awesome place to bring in a blank eco-shirt or bag and get your own custom print. Saying this shop is "cool" would be a vast understatement.

Porcelynne

www.porcelynne.com
487 14th Street
San Francisco, CA
Tel: 415-861-2647

A cute little co-op shop with unique, handmade designs, including Porcelynne lingerie and Oda shirts and dresses.

Red Dot

www.reddotshops.com
30 Miller Avenue
Mill Valley, CA
Tel: 415-383-6900

2176 Chestnut Street
San Francisco, CA
Tel: 415-346-0606

10 Main Street
Tiburon, CA
Tel: 415-435-2253

These stores, with hardwood floors and cute dollhouse-like decor, have a wide selection of some of the best vintage finds and local and eco-fashion designers.

Red Dragon Yoga

www.reddragonyoga.com
438 Miller Avenue
Mill Valley, CA
Tel: 415-381-3724

After you sweat off a few pounds doing Bikram yoga, cool down in the lounge area, and then cruise the retail shop for some easy-to-wear yoga pieces and other items from the likes of Panda Snack.

Self Clothing Company

1051 Bush Street
San Francisco, CA
Tel: 415-409-1821

This is a great store in San Francisco, especially if you are looking for custom one-off designs, usually made from vintage fabrics.

Self Edge

www.selfedge.com
714 Valencia Street
San Francisco, CA
Tel: 415-558-0658

Denim nerds and selvedge connoisseurs need look no further. Take a tour of this store to find the latest in eco-, vintage, and selvedge denim. Before you leave, you'll be talking denim jargon—from rivets to stitching to fabric weights.

Tela D Organics

www.teladorganics.com
51 Bolinas Road
Fairfax, CA
Tel: 415-455-9410

This is a cute little boutique with a wide selection of some of the latest eco-conscious finds. It's always updated and never overstated.

Ver Unica

www.ver-unica.com
2378 Hayes Street
San Francisco, CA
Tel: 415-431-0688

This is a fabulous store for the vintage elite. Since opening its doors in 1997, it has kept a number of repeat customers because of the unique, handpicked selection.

Wasteland

www.thewasteland.com
1660 Haight Street
San Francisco, CA
Tel: 415-863-3150

See description under Los Angeles, CA.

Wildlife Works

www.wildlifeworks.com
1849 Union Street
San Francisco, CA
Tel: 415-738-8544

This fun safari-decor store has a wide selection of African animal–inspired shirts, one-of-a-kind designer pieces, and work from local eco-friendly designers.

SANTA CRUZ

Once Around Lightly

871 41st Avenue
Santa Cruz, CA
Tel: 831-465-8393

This store on the beach has a nice little selection of period outfits and vintage finds.

Scout

1517 Pacific Avenue
Santa Cruz, CA
Tel: 831-427-3425

This is a nice little boutique filled with earth-friendly labels, with a particular emphasis on easy-to-wear clothes and activewear. It houses labels like Loomstate and PrAna.

OTHER CITIES IN CALIFORNIA

Arboretum Apparel

www.arboretumapparel.com
332 Healdsburg Avenue
Healdsburg, CA
Tel: 707-433-7033

This is an earth-friendly store with a boutique-meets–American Eagle feel. Shop for well-made accessory designs from Entermodal, Kim White, and Matt and Nat. They also have a nice selection of high-end eco-fashions, like Linda Loudermilk, Rag and Bone, Edun, Covet, and Loomstate.

Migrate Home

www.migrate-home.com
937 South Coast Hwy 101, Suite C103
Encinitas, CA
Tel: 760-632-8284

This is a sophisticated Green boutique, offering sustainable fashions, accessories, body products, and home decor. Catch brands like Twice Shy, TOMS shoes, Bambu, and Simple, as well as personal-care products from Pangea Organics and Nature Girl.

COLORADO, DENVER

Ace Dry Goods

46 Broadway
Denver, CO
Tel: 303-733-2237

This retro store has a lot of eclectic secondhand finds.

Buffalo Exchange

www.buffaloexchange.com

230 E. 13th Avenue

Denver, CO

Tel: 303-866-0165

See description under Phoenix, AZ.

DISTRICT OF COLUMBIA

Setchi Eco Boutique

www.shopsetchi.com

1614 Wisconsin Avenue, NW

Washington, DC

Tel: 202-333-5565

This sweet little eco-chic boutique has a nice selection of the cutest styles from Enamore, Stewart and Brown, and Ciel.

FLORIDA, BOCA RATON

Vintage 'N Vogue

1870 NW Boca Raton Boulevard

Boca Raton, FL

Tel: 561-750-5535

This vintage clothing store includes a wide selection of great finds from handbags, hats, and gloves to dresses, slacks, and shirts.

MIAMI

Barneys Co-Op

www.barneys.com

832 Collins Avenue

Miami Beach, FL

Tel: 646-335-0918

This is a worthwhile stop in order to check out their selection of great Green designers.

Beatnix Vintage Clothing

1149 Washington Avenue

Miami Beach, FL

Tel: 305-532-8733

A great store to find old rock tees and memorabilia as well as the latest in vintage finds.

Crimson Carbon

524 Washington Avenue, Ste. 101

Miami Beach, FL

Tel: 305-538-8262

Once a store by another name, Crimson Carbon has evolved into a nice eco-conscious boutique.

Steam on Sunset

www.steamstyle.com

5830 Sunset Drive

Miami, FL

Tel: 305-669-9991

This hip boutique is owned by celebrities and therefore often populated by celebrities. It carries all the latest fashions from top-echelon designers, including Alabama Chanin.

ORLANDO

Déjà Vu Vintage Clothing
1825 N. Orange Avenue
Orlando, FL
Tel: 407-898-3609

This store has fabulous vintage finds, from dresses to hats to jewelry, piled high in every corner.

Orlando Vintage Clothing Company
2117 W. Fairbanks Avenue
Winter Park, FL
Tel: 407-599-7225

Since 1995, this store has been stocking a wide variety of vintage, from period pieces up to glam rock.

Evolve Boutique
www.evolve-boutique.com
1581 N. Decatur Road
Atlanta, GA
Tel: 404-441-2351

This hip little boutique, right outside Emory University, carries a wide selection of indie-liscious earth-conscious finds, including Covet, Burning Torch, Zachary's Smile, and more.

Havens
www.havensonline.com
3209 Paces Ferry Place, NW
Atlanta, GA
Tel: 404-239-0411

This is a very well run store that stocks the latest designers and some eco-chic labels.

Ananas' East
109 N. Oak Park Avenue
Oak Park, IL
Tel: 708-524-8585

This high-end boutique carries a lot of the latest brands as well as some hot-off-the-street eco-brands like Lara Miller.

Buffalo Exchange
www.buffaloexchange.com
2875 N. Broadway
Lakeview/Lincoln Park
Chicago, IL
Tel: 773-549-1999

1478 N. Milwaukee Avenue
Wicker Park
Chicago, IL
Tel: 773-227-9558

See description under Phoenix, AZ.

The Daisy Shop
67 East Oak Street, 6th Fl.
Chicago, IL
Tel: 312-943-8880

This store is a vintage-Brandanista's dream. Get vintage Gucci, Hermés, and Yves St. Laurent.

Disgraceland

3338 N. Clark Street
Chicago, IL
Tel: 773-281-5875

Some resale shops sell high-end brand names. This one sells designers-within-reach and more common brand names like Gap and Banana Republic. Go here to get a whole outfit for under $30.

Flashy Trash

3524 N. Halsted Street
Chicago, IL
Tel: 773-327-6900

This is the place to go for the best of vintage. They specialize in everything from turn-of-the-twentieth-century through the 1960s.

Pivot Boutique

www.pivotboutique.com
1101 W. Fulton Market
Chicago, IL
Tel: 312-243-4754

Chicago's first eco-boutique houses an intense array of designers, from Beck(y) Bags—made out of recycled skateboards—to designers like Lara Miller, Ciel, Ryann, SANS, and Passenger Pigeon.

Robin Richman

2108 N. Damen Avenue
Chicago, IL
Tel: 773-278-6150

This is a popular place in Chicago to get Robin Richman designs, local design, vintage pieces, and European finds.

ShareWear Consignment Store

4703 North Damen Avenue
Chicago, IL
Tel: 773-596-5537

This is a great place to get designer clothes when you are on a budget.

Silver Moon

1755 W. North Avenue
Chicago, IL
Tel: 773-235-5797

Catch some nice vintage at this secondhand shop. Owners can also help you deconstruct vintage finds and modernize garments.

—— KENTUCKY, LEXINGTON

Argo

www.argostyle.com
214 W. Maxwell Street
Lexington, KY
Tel: 859-685-7752

Argo is one of the only boutiques in Kentucky that carries a wide selection of eco-based designers.

—— LOUISIANA, NEW ORLEANS

Buffalo Exchange

www.buffaloexchange.com
3312 Magazine Street
New Orleans, LA
Tel: 504-891-7443

See description under Phoenix, AZ.

Envi

www.shopenvi.com
164 Newbury Street
Boston, MA
Tel: 617-267-ENVI

Envi is a must-stop destination in the Boston area for eco-conscious styles.

Nomad

www.nomadcambridge.com
1741 Massachusetts Avenue
Cambridge, MA
Tel: 617-497-6677

This little shop sells great yoga wear and fair-trade garments.

Portobello Road

291 Buckminster Road
Brookline, MA
Tel: 617-922-4555

In case you can't get to London's version, hit up Portobello Road in Massachusetts to find some great one-of-a-kind garments.

——— MICHIGAN, DETROIT AREA

Ella's Vintage Clothing and Collectibles

157 E. Front Street
Traverse City, MI
Tel: 231-947-9401

Spend a whole day flipping through a wide selection of vintage.

Vintagey

141 E. Front Street
Traverse City, MI
Tel: 231-933-4207

This is another great vintage shop that pays homage to the '60s and '70s. Viva la revolution!

——— MINNESOTA, MINNEAPOLIS

Birch Clothing

www.birchclothing.com
2309 W. 50th Street
Minneapolis, MN
Tel: 512-436-0776

This shop has one of the widest selections of eco-designers, including Doie, EcoGanik, Edun, Loomstate, Vulcana, and Loyale, just to name a few.

Buffalo Exchange

www.buffaloexchange.com
2727 Lyndale Avenue S.
Minneapolis, MN
Tel: 612-871-9115

See description under Phoenix, AZ.

——— NEVADA, LAS VEGAS

Buffalo Exchange

www.buffaloexchange.com
4110 S. Maryland Parkway
Las Vegas, NV
Tel: 702-791-3960

See description under Phoenix, AZ.

Whole Body at Whole Foods

www.wholefoods.com

235 Prospect Avenue

West Orange, NJ

Tel: 973-669-3196

You can find a small collection of earth-friendly clothes at this boutique inside Whole Foods.

Buffalo Exchange

www.buffaloexchange.com

3005 Central Avenue NE

Albuquerque, NM

Tel: 505-262-0098

See description under Phoenix, AZ.

Amarcord

www.amarcordvintagefashion.com

223 Bedford Avenue

Brooklyn, NY

Tel: 718-963-4001

Though this shop doesn't have as robust a selection as its New York City counterparts, Amarcord in Brooklyn always has a fresh selection of vintage—from hats to shoes to jackets to party dresses.

Beacon's Closet

www.beaconscloset.com

88 N. 11th Street

Brooklyn, NY

Tel: 718-486-0816

This is the indie-hipster destination in Williamsburg. Get great music along with some great rock-inspired clothes. If you have something to sell, Beacon's Closet will buy your old clothes—offering 30 percent of the resale value in cash or 55 percent in store credit.

Blue Bass Vintage Clothing

431 DeKalb Avenue

Brooklyn, NY

Tel: 347-750-8935

This store sells handpicked vintage clothing and accessories as well as a nice selection from local designers.

Buffalo Exchange

www.buffaloexchange.com

504 Driggs Avenue

Brooklyn, NY

Tel: 718-384-6901

See description under Phoenix, AZ.

Catbird

www.catbirdnyc.com
390 Metropolitan Avenue
Brooklyn, NY
Tel: 718-388-7688

219 Bedford Avenue
Brooklyn, NY
Tel: 718-599-3457

Catbird owns two friendly boutiques in the heart of Williamsburg, each carrying completely different products. You'll find a nice selection of local designers and vintage pieces in both.

Diana Kane

www.dianakane.com
229B 5th Avenue
Brooklyn, NY
Tel: 718-638-6520

Head over to this cute little boutique for some signature handmade jewelry and sustainable collections from Loomstate, John Patrick Organic, Stewart and Brown, and Edun.

Fluke Vintage Clothing

86 N. 6th Street
Brooklyn, NY
Tel: 718-486-3166

Walk up the ramp to this store to find a fabulous window display and a small sales rack. The owner keeps the looks fresh and has an eye for pretty, vintage things.

Go Fish! Brooklyn

187 Sackett Street
Brooklyn, NY
Tel: 347-721-3401

This store has an eclectic selection of vintage items, including shoes and clothes.

Maiden Hong Kong

502 Lorimer Street
Brooklyn, NY
Tel: 718-388-8885

This wonderful gem stocks a wide selection of vintage clothes with an Asian twist for men and women.

Om Sweet Home

www.omsweethomenyc.com
59 Kent Avenue
Brooklyn, NY
Tel: 718-963-6986

This cozy little shop, overlooking the East River, carries a very well-edited selection of eco-fashion designs, from labels like Stewart and Brown, Kelly B, and Bahar Shahpar. It also has a small, regularly updated rack of vintage.

Sodafine

www.sodafine.com
119 Grand Street
Brooklyn, NY
Tel: 718-230-3060

This boutique carries a lovely handpicked selection of work from local and eco-fashion designers, like Passenger Pigeon, Panda Snack, Loomstate, Bahar Shahpar, and others.

Treehouse

www.treehousebrooklyn.com

430 Graham Avenue

Brooklyn, NY

Tel: 718-482-8733

This home-sweet-home boutique has racks of indie-fashion designers, vintage finds, and tons of one-of-a-kind jewelry pieces.

NEW YORK CITY

ABC Carpet and Home

www.abchome.com

888 Broadway

New York, NY

Tel: 212-473-3000

Walking into this store is like walking into the attic of a maharaja. It stocks a great collection of furniture, jewelry, and beauty products that are both exotic and sustainable.

Amarcord

www.amarcordvintagefashion.com

252 Lafayette Street

New York, NY

Tel: 212-431-4161

84 E. 7th Street

New York, NY

Tel: 212-614-7133

See description under Brooklyn, NY.

Blue Bag

266 Elizabeth Street

New York, NY

Tel: 212-966-8566

For those of us who love our handbags, this is the place to get one-of-a-kind vintage finds.

Ekovaruhuset

www.ekovaruhuset.se

123 Ludlow Street

New York, NY

Tel: 212-673-1753

Ekovaruhuset started in Stockholm, Sweden, but New York City was lucky enough to get one, too. This cute boutique sells some very nice handmade, organic finds. You will usually come across clothes in neutral colors with fine embroidery and attention to detail. Also get a pair of Kuyichi jeans, which are normally hard to come by in the States.

Eye Candy

www.eyecandystore.com

329 Lafayette Street

New York, NY

Tel: 212-343-4275

This shop has all of the latest bling, baubles, and other eye-catching vintage fashion accessories like hats, wallets, glasses, and bags.

Fisch for the Hip

153 W. 18th Street

New York, NY

Tel: 212-633-9053

Fisch for the Hip is a high-end consignment store with the best in current designer clothing, shoes, and accessories.

Gomi
443 E. 6th Street
New York, NY
Tel: 212-979-0388

This stylish boutique carries a great selection of eco-based designers and a beautiful line of handmade jewelry and bags, made by the owners themselves!

INA
www.inanyc.com
21 Prince Street
New York, NY
Tel: 212-334-9048

101 Thompson Street
New York, NY
Tel: 212-941-4757

208 E. 73rd Street
New York, NY
Tel: 212-249-0014

262 Mott Street (men's only)
New York, NY
Tel: 212-334-2210

15 Bleecker Street
New York, NY
Tel: 212-228-8511

INA has five locations and is the place in New York for the highest-quality brand-name vintage finds. It's possible to do all of your vintage shopping by just popping into each INA store.

Kaight
www.kaightnyc.com
83 Orchard Street
New York, NY
Tel: 212-680-5630

This is by far one of the best-edited eco-chic boutiques in Manhattan. Visit this shop to find designers like Linda Loudermilk, John Patrick Organic, Noir, Loomstate, Beyond Skin, and Charmoné.

Leontine
226 Front Street
New York, NY
Tel: 212-766-1066

Enter this spacious, open boutique to find the makings for a whole vintage lifestyle, with a dash of local designers.

Lindhardt Design
156 1st Avenue
New York, NY
Tel: 917-748-9000

This fresh, new jewelry boutique sells environmentally conscious fine designs, with a special emphasis on design that gives back to areas in need.

Lolli by Reincarnation
www.lolli-reincarnation.com
85 Stanton Street
New York, NY
Tel: 212-529-2030

This sweet little shop carries the latest in re-created vintage pieces—from scarves to hats to clothes.

M.A.D.

167 E. 87th Street
New York, NY
Tel: 212-427-4333

This is a hot spot for vintage couture pieces. If you're going to a fine event or just want to feel like you're on the red carpet, this is the place for you.

Michael's: The Consignment Shop for Women

www.michaelsconsignment.com
1041 Madison Avenue
New York, NY
Tel: 212-737-7273

For a few decades now, this upscale consignment shop has stood strong with a very well put together selection of threads.

NY Vintage Club Incorporated

www.nyvintageclub.com
346 E. 59th Street
New York, NY
Tel: 212-207-9007

All vintage fiends should head to the Vintage Club Incorporated to get unique finds.

Organic Avenue

www.organicavenue.com
101 Stanton Street
New York, NY
Tel: 212-334-4593

This small boutique is jam-packed with the latest organic threads and has a small organic beauty bar.

Poppet

www.poppetnyc.com
350 E. 9th Street
New York, NY
Tel: 212-924-3190

This shop has one of the freshest looks in vintage clothing (isn't that an oxymoron?) that New York has to offer. The founders' combined backgrounds in fashion and entertainment give this store a new swing.

Rags-A-GoGo

218 W. 14th Street
New York, NY
Tel: 646-486-4011

This store may get a C for decor, but it gets an A for thrift duds, especially in the men's category.

Rue Saint Denis Clothier Limited

170 Avenue B
New York, NY
Tel: 212-260-3388

Come here for great vintage finds that may never have been worn. The shop has a wide selection that you are bound to love.

SAKS

www.saksfifthavenue.com/main/green.jsp
611 5th Avenue
New York, NY
Tel: 212-644-1704

SAKS has recently opened up a SAKS "Green" section on their Web site and in the retail store. Find designers like Beau Soleil, Edun, John Patrick Organic, and Song.

Screaming Mimi's
382 Lafayette Street
New York, NY
Tel: 212-677-6464

This vintage store has the loudest and most colorful collection of vintage.

Sophie Roan
www.sophieroan.com
117 E. 7th Street
New York, NY
Tel: 212-529-0085

Here you can find limited-edition tops, vintage clothes, and great handmade jewelry, all in one place.

Tahir Boutique
www.tahirboutique.com
75 Orchard Street
New York, NY
Tel: 212-253-2121

This soft pastel-colored boutique's eclectic atmosphere matches its eclectic selection of hot vintage.

Takashimaya
www.ny-takashimaya.com
693 5th Avenue
New York, NY
Tel: 212-350-0100

This Japanese-style-infused shop is packed with products from all around the world. Plan to explore for a whole day, because you might find it hard to leave this art-gallery-meets-boutique.

Terra Plana
www.terraplana.com
260 Elizabeth Street
New York, NY
Tel: 212-274-9000

Come here to get the latest selection of Worn Agains, VivoBarefoots, and vegetable-tanned leather shoes by Terra Plana.

Yu
151 Ludlow Street
New York, NY
Tel: 212-979-9370

Designer vintage-ware for a fraction of the price draws a crowd to this boutique.

Zachary's Smile
www.zacharyssmile.com
9 Greenwich Avenue
New York, NY
Tel: 212-924-0604

317 Lafayette Street
New York, NY
Tel: 212-965-8248

These two welcoming stores have a wide range of re-created vintage clothes and a nice selection of vintage finds.

UPSTATE NEW YORK

Tuff Soul
www.tuffsoul.com
516 W. State Street
Ithaca, NY
Tel: 607-319-0083

This two-story store is a gem in downtown Ithaca and includes a wonderful selection of organic items and vintage finds.

NORTH CAROLINA

A Greener Shade of You
1130 Unit B Corolla Village Road
Historic Corolla Village
Corolla, NC
Tel: 252-453-6644

This store specializes in designer fashions made of organic cotton and bamboo. They also have a collection of accessories and handmade jewelry.

Sambuca
200 N. Front Street
Wilmington, NC
Tel: 910-343-0201

Take a jaunt to this store to find a small collection of eco-designers and beauty companies.

OHIO

Ecokiss
www.ecokissstyle.com
Mustard Seed Market
46 Shopping Plaza, #173
Solon, OH
Tel: 216-375-6700

Be sure to check out this little shop located in the Mustard Seed Market for some great eco-design finds for you and your home.

Revive
www.revivestore.com
2248 Lee Road
Cleveland Heights, OH
Tel: 216-371-2778

Right in the center of everything, this boutique carries a wide selection of fair-trade garments that are chic and ethical in equal measure.

Substance
www.fcpcares.com
783 N. High Street
Columbus, OH
Tel: 614-299-2910

Shop a wide range of selections of crafty-meets-fashion designs.

Buffalo Exchange
www.buffaloexchange.com
131 E. 5th Avenue
Eugene, OR
Tel: 541-687-2805

See description under Phoenix, AZ.

HOOD RIVER

Ruddy Duck Store
www.ruddyduckstore.com
504 Oak Street
Hood River, OR
Tel: 541-386-7411

For all the important guys in your life, this family-owned and -operated department store provides a nice selection of organic menswear.

PORTLAND

Avant Garden
2853 SE Stark Street, Ste. 7
Portland, OR
Tel: 503-283-4184

This store has great retro and punk finds, which is fitting considering their slogan is "Bitchin' Kitsch and Counter Couture."

Bombshell Vintage
811 E. Burnside Street
Portland, OR
Tel: 503-239-1073

Of course, with a name like Bombshell, you have to have some pretty sexy vintage finds.

Buffalo Exchange
www.buffaloexchange.com
1036 W. Burnside Street
Portland, OR
Tel: 503-222-3418

1420 SE 37th Avenue
Portland, OR
Tel: 503-234-1302

See description under Phoenix, AZ.

Decades Vintage Co.
www.decadesvintage.com
328 SW Stark Street
Portland, OR
Tel: 503-223-1177

Though not related to the Decades in Los Angeles, this shop totally holds its own when it comes to carrying a great selection of vintage.

Frock Incorporated
1439 NE Alberta Street
Portland, OR
Tel: 503-595-0379

For some good secondhand chic, pay a visit to this store.

The Greenloop

www.thegreenloop.com
8005 SE 13th Avenue
Portland, OR
Tel: 503-236-3999

This store was one of the first to open up as an eco-chic boutique and houses some of the greatest designers and beauty labels from Anna Cohen to Emily Katz.

Hattie's Vintage

729 E. Burnside Street, Ste. 101
Portland, OR
Tel: 503-238-1938

This is a super-cool and funky boutique that has a wide array of vintage and a very helpful staff.

Lady Luck Vintage

2742 E. Burnside Street
Portland, OR
Tel: 503-233-4041

This shop has an eclectic selection of vintage for those who want something unique.

Magpie

520 SW 9th Avenue
Portland, OR
Tel: 503-220-0920

This well-known store carries a nice selection of vintage that is conveniently organized by era and color.

Ray's Ragtime

1001 SW Morrison Street
Portland, OR
Tel: 503-226-2616

Visit this shop if you are looking for theatrical or period pieces. Some of this vintage actually dates back to the late 1800s.

Red Light

3590 SE Hawthorne Boulevard
Portland, OR
Tel: 503-963-8888

This large store carries a wide selection of vintage, neatly arranged for your convenience.

Xtabay Vintage Clothing Boutique

2515 SE Clinton Street
Portland, OR
Tel: 503-230-2899

This store has an unbelievable selection of one-of-a-kind jewelry and vintage clothes.

————— **PENNSYLVANIA, BETHLEHEM**

Clothesline Organics

www.clotheslineorganics.com
101 E. 3rd Street
Bethlehem, PA
Tel: 610-691-0111

This store carries some easy-to-wear pieces that also happen to be eco-conscious.

Antiquarian's Delight

615 S. 6th Street
Philadelphia, PA
Tel: 215-592-0256

This store has an upstairs and a downstairs, both filled with different vendors and incredible retro finds.

Arcadia Boutique

www.arcadiaboutique.com
819 North Second Street
Northern Liberties
Philadelphia, PA
Tel: 215-667-8099

Arcadia is a premier destination for fashion, including eco-designers such as Anna Cohen, Eco Ga'Nik, iWood, New Growth, and Rebe.

Buffalo Exchange

www.buffaloexchange.com
1713 Chestnut Street
Philadelphia, PA
Tel: 215-557-9850

See description under Phoenix, AZ.

Greene Street Consignment

700 South Street
Philadelphia, PA
Tel: 215-733-9261

This consignment shop promises great designer gems if you sift through the racks long enough.

Joan Shepp

www.joanshepp.com
1616 Walnut Street
Philadelphia, PA
Tel: 215-735-2666

Fashionistas will love this classy high-end store with a coveted selection of designers, including eco-based lines like Stewart and Brown, Linda Loudermilk, and Subversive Jewelry.

Maria Fe's Upscale Consignment

117 E. King Street
Malvern, PA
Tel: 610-407-4570

The store's name doesn't josh: This is a high-end consignment shop that only accepts and sells the highest quality secondhand clothes.

Retrospect

534 South Street
Philadelphia, PA
Tel: 267-671-0116

If you are looking for a good selection of vintage finds, try Retrospect on for size.

Studio 54½

54½ N. 3rd Street
Philadelphia, PA
Tel: 215-928-9250

This little store has great one-of-a-kind jewelry pieces and a nicely arranged selection of vintage clothes.

Vagabond

37 N. 3rd Street
Philadelphia, PA
Tel: 267-671-0737

This is touted as a hip vintage shop with handmade accessories and a well-edited selection of vintage.

PITTSBURGH

Crimes of Fashion

4628 Forbes Avenue
Pittsburgh, PA
Tel: 412-682-7010

Here you will find a nice selection of vintage, separated into two rooms.

Eons

5850 Ellsworth Avenue
Pittsburg, PA
Tel: 412-361-3368

You may have to squeeze your way through the narrow aisles, but Eons provides a heavy-hitting selection of vintage for the secondhand connoisseur.

Hey Betty!

5892 Ellsworth Avenue
Pittsburg, PA
Tel: 412-363-0999

With a few floors of vintage, you could peruse here all day long.

RHODE ISLAND

Orange Lola

www.orangelola.com
330 Main Street
Wakefield, RI
Tel: 401-284-4333

This shop carries a wealth of earth-toned fashions.

SOUTH CAROLINA

Izzi-B

www.izzi-b.com
315 Main Street, Ste. 1
Conway, SC
Tel: 843-488-3971

This smart little shop carries easy-to-wear eco-brands like Loomstate and Stewart and Brown.

Worthwhile

www.shopworthwhile.com
268 King Street
Charleston, SC
Tel: 843-723-4418

This cozy store has organic pieces tucked away among contemporary designs from around the world.

Clothing X Change
1817 21st Avenue S.
Nashville, TN
Tel: 615-463-0209

Here you can expect to find top brand-name and vintage clothing, as well as accessories, all at discounted prices. This store sells and trades items, so you can keep up with the latest trends.

Hip Zipper Vintage Clothing
1008 Forrest Avenue
Nashville, TN
Tel: 615-228-1942

This store may look unassuming from the outside, but it carries zany, retro clothes.

Tennessee Antique Mall
654 Wedgewood Avenue
Nashville, TN
Tel: 615-259-4077

This store is known for looking like a bazaar in India—bustling with people and completely disorganized, but everyone who comes here knows you can find great deals and wonderful vintage finds.

Venus and Mars
2830 Bransford Avenue
Nashville, TN
Tel: 615-269-8357

This converted bungalow carries a wide selection of crowd-pleasing vintage.

Vintage
411 Bridge Street
Franklin, TN
Tel: 615-397-0555

Vintage carries exactly that—vintage! And it happens to have pretty good secondhand finds, too.

Zelda
4100 Hillsboro Circle
Nashville, TN
Tel: 615-292-8045

Zelda is a well-designed boutique with a highly edited vintage selection, drawing a posh crowd.

Amelia's Retro-Vogue and Relics
www.ameliasretrovogue.com
2024 S. Lamar Boulevard
Austin, TX
Tel: 512-442-4446

This store features clothing reminiscent of a more glamorous time—with flapper gear and beautiful vintage hats.

Big Bertha's Bargain Basement
www.bigberthasbargainbasement.com/
frames.html
1050 S. Lamar Boulevard
Austin, TX
Tel: 512-444-5908

This store has a connection to Paramount Studios, so you'll find a lot of theatrical surprises here.

Bitch'in Threads/Kimono

1030 S. Lamar Boulevard, Ste. D
Austin, TX
Tel: 512-441-9955

This boutique has stood on Lamar Boulevard forever and carries bold vintage finds in one section and out-of-this-world antique kimonos in the other.

Blue Elephant

www.shopblueelephant.com
7801 N. Lamar Boulevard, Ste. E-194
Austin, TX
Tel: 512-371-3259

This shop carries a range of new, hip designers, including Stewart and Brown, and also some great beauty brands like Jurlique, Dr. Hauschka, and the Art of Shaving.

Buffalo Exchange

www.buffaloexchange.com
2904 Guadalupe Street
Austin, TX
Tel: 512-480-9922

See description under Phoenix, AZ.

Cream Vintage

www.creamvintage.com
2532 Guadalupe Street
Austin, TX
Tel: 512-474-8787

This is a hugely popular vintage store, with built-in alteration services to make certain your vintage finds fit to a T.

Flashback

1805 S. 1st Street
Austin, TX
Tel: 512-445-6906

This cute shop carries a nice selection of vintage dresses, lingerie, and evening wear.

Restyle Store

www.restylestores.com
7301 Burnet Road, Ste. 108
Austin, TX
Tel: 512-407-8861

This fun consignment shop has a warm and relaxed atmosphere. Here you can find well-organized second-hand clothes at reasonable prices.

Therapy

http://shop.therapyclothing.com
1113 S. Congress Avenue
Austin, TX
Tel: 512-326-2331

This little boutique includes a small eco-conscious collection.

Wildflower Organics Davenport Village

3801 Capitol of Texas Highway, D-180
Austin, TX
Tel: 512-732-2145

The store's signature style has evolved and expanded over the years to include healthy, quality, natural products for every room in the house.

Wildflower Organics Downtown

www.wildflowerorganics.com
908 N. Lamar Boulevard
Austin, TX
Tel: 512-320-0449

See description on facing page.

DALLAS

Buffalo Exchange

www.buffaloexchange.com
3424 Greenville Avenue
Dallas, TX
Tel: 214-826-7544

See description under Phoenix, AZ.

Counter Culture True Vintage

2707 Main Street
Dallas, TX
Tel: 214-698-0117

This is a store of rock-star-style vintage finds.

Gratitude Vintage Clothing

3714 Fairmount Street
Dallas, TX
Tel: 214-522-2921

This great little boutique houses secondhand chic and a friendly staff.

Zola's Everyday Vintage

www.zolasvintage.com
414 N. Bishop Avenue
Dallas, TX
Tel: 214-943-6643

You are guaranteed to find at least one and maybe two or three good finds in this store on any occasion, because each piece is handpicked by the owners.

HOUSTON

Buffalo Exchange

www.buffaloexchange.com
1618 Westheimer Road
Houston, TX
Tel: 713-523-8701

249 W. 19th Street
Houston Heights
Houston, TX
Tel: 713-868-240

See description under Phoenix, AZ.

Trudy's Boutique Resale

1927 Fairview Street
Houston, TX
Tel: 713-524-7888

This is an upscale boutique with almost-new pieces. Come here for a tasty wardrobe at half the price.

The Way We Wore

www.thewaywewore.net

2602 Waugh Drive

Houston, TX

Tel: 713-526-8910

If you're looking for a wild selection of retro and punk vintage, check out this funky store.

OTHER CITIES IN TEXAS

Restyle Store

5730 W. Broadway Street, Ste. 112

Pearland, TX

Tel: 281-997-9222

8700 Main Street, Ste. 160

Frisco, TX

Tel: 972-712-2267

See description under Austin, TX.

——— VIRGINIA, CHARLOTTESVILLE

Elsie Garden

www.elsiegarden.com

219 W. Main Street

Charlottesville, VA

Tel: 434-979-2888

This shop carries a nice selection of eco-designers, including Moral Fervor, Linda Loudermilk, Loomstate, and Panda Snack.

——— WASHINGTON, BELLINGHAM

Buffalo Exchange

www.buffaloexchange.com

1209 N. State Street

Bellingham, WA

Tel: 360-676-1375

See description under Phoenix, AZ.

SEATTLE

Buffalo Exchange

www.buffaloexchange.com

4530 University Way NE

Seattle, WA

Tel: 206-545-0175

See description under Phoenix, AZ.

Juniper

www.juniperinmadrona.com

3314 E. Spring Street

Seattle, WA

Tel: 206-838-7496

A neat little store that not only stocks a wide selection of designers—from Loyale to Souchi—but also a great selection of bags and homewares. Stop by if you are a cat lover. Juniper fosters cats that are up for adoption through the local Animal Shelter.

Les Amis

3420 Evanston Avenue N.

Seattle, WA

Tel: 206-545-9121

Find up-and-coming designers here, including eco-based brands like Souchi and Stewart and Brown.

CANADA

ALBERTA

Divine
720 17th Avenue SW
Calgary, AB
Tel: 403-228-2540

Try on chic secondhand garb in the seventies-inspired changing rooms at this shop.

Trend Fashions
120 10th Street NW
Calgary, AB
Tel: 403-283-1167

737 Main Street
Canmore, AB
Tel: 403-609-0021

This shop has a large selection of vintage clothing, ranging from Gap to high-end designers.

Vespucci Consignment Inc.
121 58th Avenue SW
Calgary, AB
Tel: 403-252-9558

Come here if you are looking for upscale designer wear, including evening gowns or business attire.

What's in Store
1600 Edmonton Trail NE
Calgary, AB
Tel: 403-276-3066

This little shop has a soft spot for disco-chic.

BRITISH COLUMBIA

Agnes Jean Boutique
www.agnesjean.com
38018 Cleveland Avenue
Squamish, BC
Tel: 604-892-9181

Check out this eco-conscious boutique with clothes, furnishings, and personal-care products.

Arezzo Consignment
127 1208 Homer Street
Vancouver, BC
Tel: 604-689-2830

Head over to this consignment shop for great accessories and high-quality thrift-store finds.

Burcu's Angels Funky Clothing Etc.
2535 Main Street
Vancouver, BC
Tel: 604-874-9773

Let the friendly staff at this shop take you through a vast selection of vintage clothes.

Changes Consignment Clothing Company
4330 W. 10th Avenue
Vancouver, BC
Tel: 604-222-1505

Here you will not only discover good consignment finds, but also a range of new designers from across Canada.

Deluxe Junk Company
310 W. Cordova Street
Vancouver, BC
Tel: 604-685-4871

This is one of the oldest vintage-clothing stores in Vancouver, housing a wonderful selection of castoffs from the past.

Discollection
324 W. Hastings Street
Vancouver, BC
Tel: 604-331-1244

Check out this shop to find a fine selection of vintage clothes.

Dream Designs
www.dreamdesigns.ca
956 Commercial Drive
Vancouver, BC
Tel: 604-254-5012

This retail shop carries a large selection of spa and eco-conscious clothing lines.

Legends
4366 Main Street
Vancouver, BC
Tel: 604-875-0621

Make a trip to this store if you are looking for a select collection of retro digs and accessories.

Mintage
www.mintagevintage.com
1714 Commercial Drive
Vancouver, BC
Tel: 604-871-0022

320 Cordova Street
Vancouver, BC
Tel: 604-646-8243

Mintage's two locations are chock-full of fresh new styles, as well as high-quality vintage pieces.

Not Just Pretty Modern Clothing
www.notjustpretty.com
1036 Fort Street
Victoria, BC
Tel: 250-414-0414

This boutique has one of the widest selections of eco-conscious wear in the area.

Sally's Trading Post, Antique, and Collectible Mall
3108 Jacklin Road
Victoria, BC
Tel: 250-474-6030

This is one of the largest antiques malls in Victoria. Explore both levels to find some great specialty items and accessories from the past.

True Value Vintage Clothing

710 Robson Street
Vancouver, BC
Tel: 604-685-5403

If you're looking for some classic Levi's or hard-to-get vintage, head downstairs and rummage through the racks at True Value.

Twigg and Hottie

www.twiggandhottie.com
3671 Main Street
Vancouver, BC
Tel: 604-879-8595

This shop sells both eco-conscious lines and up-and-comers, including Twigg and Hottie's signature line. They also sell a solid selection of others, including Grace and Cello, Mycoanna, Torn, and Twice Shy.

Used

831 Granville Street
Vancouver, BC
Tel: 604-694-032

Stop by Used to try on some of the coolest retro styles.

Woo Vintage Clothing

www.woovintage.com
321 Cambie Street
Vancouver, BC
Tel: 604-505-3567

This store has a fine selection of handpicked garments that will definitely Woo you.

--------ONTARIO

889 Yonge

www.889yonge.com
889 Yonge Street
Toronto, ON
Tel: 416-925-7206

If you're looking for an experience when shopping, drop by this shop, which has a boutique, spa, and live-DJ yoga classes. Find Ren and Astara beauty products, as well as organic and fair-trade clothes.

Asylum

42 Kensington Avenue
Toronto, ON
Tel: 416-595-7199

Housed in the Kensington Market, this shop has racks and racks of great vintage finds.

Brava

553 Queen Street W.
Toronto, ON
Tel: 416-504-8742

This store carries a nice selection of secondhand chic.

Bungalow

273 Augusta Avenue
Toronto, ON
Tel: 416-598-0204

Take a stroll through this store not only to find some of the latest retro fashions but also home decor.

The Cat's Meow

180 Avenue Road
Toronto, ON
Tel: 647-435-5875

Open the doors to this shop to find brand names like Furstenberg and Westwood.

Courage My Love

14 Kensington Avenue
Toronto, ON
Tel: 416-979-1992

Another great stop in the Kensington Market, this is a photogenic little shop with the finest collection of re-created vintage and high-quality gowns.

Divine Decadence Originals

www.divinedecadence.sites.toronto.com
136 Cumberland Street
Toronto, ON
Tel: 416-324-9759

Stop here for breathtaking vintage pieces from all over the world, including fine jewelry from throughout Europe. This is a favorite celebrity stop.

Gadabout

www.gadaboutvintage.com
1300 Queen Street E.
Toronto, ON
Tel: 416-463-1254

This shop carries all types of vintage, but look elsewhere if what you want is tees or denim. This shop carries only the finer things in past life.

Lileo

www.lileo.ca
55 Mill Street
Toronto, ON
Tel: 416-413-1410

This store is part gallery and part shop, housing a juice/snack bar and a very yoga-centric eco-conscious boutique.

Preloved

www.preloved.ca
613 Queen Street W.
Toronto, ON
Tel: 416-504-8704

Stop off at this shop for hip and sexy re-created vintage pieces.

—— QUEBEC

Boutique Seraphin

738 rue St-Jean
Quebec City, QC
Tel: 418-522-2533

Check out this store for its infamous selection of Levi's.

Ejust

www.ejust.ca
87 Wellington North
Sherbrooke, QC
Tel: 819-829-9928

This retail shop carries brands like Wildlife Works, Yellowport, Veja, Ecoganik, and Earth Speaks.

Preloved

www.preloved.ca
4832 boulevard St-Laurent
Montréal, QC
Tel: 514-499-9898

See description under Ontario.

EUROPE

──── **DENMARK, COPENHAGEN**

Commonzenz

www.commonzenz.dk
Jaegersborggade 14, DK-2200
Copenhagen N.
Tel: +45 3696 6645

Stop by this chic store to find the absolute sexiest ethical brands, including Aymara, Elsom, Katharine E. Hamnett, Noir BLAACK, Kuyichi, Veja, and others. This is also a good shop for eco-conscious beauty products.

Palace

www.palace-design.dk
Jægergårdsgade 7
8000 Århus C
Tel: +45 6126 2171

This little boutique carries items from their self-titled label, plus a number of other hip brands like Camilla Norrback and Edun.

──── **FRANCE, PARIS**

Colette

www.colette.fr
213, rue Saint-Honore
75001 Paris
Tel: +33 1 5535 3390

Colette is the chicest of boutique stores and is now housing some very sexy eco-fashion lines.

Galeries Lafayette

www.galerieslafayette.com
40, boulevard Haussmann
75009 Paris
Tel: +33 1 4282 3456

This is the major department store in France. In 2008, it launched an eco-fashion section, which makes it even more of a "must-stop" destination.

Sakina M'sa

www.sakinamsa.com
6, rue des Gardes
75018 Paris
Tel: +33 1 5655 5090

For a luxe selection of chic and sophisticated garments, stop at Sakina M'sa's little boutique and take a look at her splendid line.

IRELAND, DUBLIN

Mira Mira
www.miramira.ie
3 Sandymout Green
Dublin 4
Tel: +353 1 219 6668

This is a sweet little fair-trade boutique, where you can get wonderful accessories and clothes.

SWEDEN

Beyond Retro
www.beyondretro.com
Söder, Åsögatan 144
Tel: +46 (0) 8 641 3642

Souk, Drottninggatan 53
Tel: +46 (0) 8 641 3642

Souk, Mäster Samuelsgatan 56
Tel: +46 (0) 8 5591 3642

See description under United Kingdom.

Drömma
www.dromma.se
Östra Skansgatan 3C
413 02 Göteborg
Tel: +46 (0) 3 1711 3340

This well-designed store houses handpicked high-quality vintage and eco-conscious designs.

Ekovaruhuset
www.ekovaruhuset.se
Österlånggatan 28
111 31 Stockholm
Tel: +46 (0) 8 2298 45

See description under New York, NY.

Ingrid af Maglehem
www.ingridafmaglehem.se
Fersens väg 14
211 42 Malmö
Tel: +46 (0) 4 0611 4445

Drop by this store to find some of the latest eco-conscious brands like Spirit of Maya, Consequent, Denimwear, Machja, People Tree, and American Apparel.

Kunigunda
www.kunigunda.se
Skånegatan 76
116 37 Stockholm
Tel: +46 (0) 8743 0070

Come here to visit a very chic boutique with a hand-picked selection of vintage clothes, darling accessories, and great eco-conscious designers.

Mint and Vintage

www.mintandvintage.com
S:t Eriksgatan 48
112 34 Stockholm
Tel: +46 (0) 7 3533 5304

Karlssgatan 1B
252 24 Helsingborg
Tel: +46 (0) 4213 4610

This is the ultimate little shop; both locations sell the finest vintage clothes and a select number of eco-conscious designers like Katharine E. Hamnett and Camilla Norrback.

Selected Style

www.selectedstyle.com
Borganäsvägen 26
784 33 Borlänge
Tel: +46 (0) 2431 2320

For a handpicked selection of vintage and eco-labels, head over to Selected Style.

—— UNITED KINGDOM

162 Holloway Road

162 Holloway Road
Islington
London, N7 8DD
Tel: 020 7700 2354

Head over to this store to find a broad range of vintage and retro styles.

Absolute Vintage

15 Hanbury Street
London, E1 6QR
Tel: 020 7247 3883

This shop has the biggest secondhand shoe collection in Britain, so be sure to shop here if you're into shoes. There's also a nice collection of vintage clothes.

Admiral Vernon Antiques Market

141-149 Portobello Road
London, W11 2DY
Tel: 020 7727 5242

There are close to 200 stalls at this market, peddling a range of antiques and organic cotton frocks.

Annie's Vintage Clothes

12 Camden Passage
Islington
London, N1 8ED
Tel: 020 7359 0796

Visit Annie's if you're looking for cute frocks and evening wear.

Appleby

www.applebyvintage.com
95 Westbourne Park Villas
Notting Hill
London, W2 5ED
Tel: 020 7229 7772

Visit this shop for some very nice handpicked pieces; Appleby is largely known for quality suits and dresses.

Arkadash

www.arkadash.co.uk
103 Manchester Road
Chorlton, M21 9GA
Tel: 016 1881 9500

33 North Lane
Headingley, LS6 3HW
Tel: 011 3275 9674

Try out these two locations for some good fair-trade clothes and shoes.

Bertie Golightly

www.bertiego.co.uk
4 Kingsbury Street
Marlborough
Wiltshire, SN8 1HU
Tel: 020 7584 7270

This is a high-end dress agency that has all the top designers, from Hermés to Escada.

Bertie Wooster

284 Fulham Road
Chelsea
London, SW10 9EW
Tel: 020 7352 5662

This shop carries a line of bespoke tailor-made vintage clothes.

Beyond Retro

www.beyondretro.com
112 Cheshire Street
London, E2 6EJ
Tel: 020 7613 3636

58-59 Great Marlborough
London, W1 F7JY
Tel: 020 7434 1406

This is an enormous warehouse of vintage and retro fashions, covering a wide range of eras.

Biba Lives

www.bibalives.com
Wellers Auctions
70 Guildford Street
Chertsy, Surrey, KT16 9BB
Tel: 012 3256 8678

Once a storefront, Biba now sells a very pristine collection of vintage clothes and dead-stock items via auction houses.

Bolshie

www.bolshieclothing.com
57 Bank Street
Glasgow, G12 8NF
Tel: 014 1357 1777

This quaint little shop offers a number of organic and fair-trade choices.

Covet

www.covetbrighton.com
16 Gloucester Road
Brighton, BN1 4AD
Tel: 012 7360 9515

This store features women's wear from a number of chic designers, including fair-trade label People Tree.

The Dress Box

8-10 Cheval Place
Knightsbridge
London, SW7 1ES
Tel: 020 7589 2240

This dress agency sells some nice designer wear.

The Dresser

10 Porchester Place
Westminster
London, W2 2BS
Tel: 020 7724 7212

This little dress agency has a nice selection of designer castoffs.

Episode

26 Chalk Farm Road
Camden
London, NW1
Tel: 020 7485 9927

This shop has one of the best selections of retro wear and accessories, particularly from the '50s through the '80s.

Equa

www.equaclothing.com
28 Camden Passage
London, N1 8ED
Tel: 020 7359 0955

This is a great store if you're looking for a nice selection of ethical designers, including People Tree, Edun, Enamore, and Ciel.

Ethika

www.ethika.co.uk
25 Timber Hill
Norwich, NR1 3JZ
Tel: 016 0362 4891

This is a beautiful store, packed full of fair-trade clothes from Pakistan and marked by fine tailoring and sumptuous looks.

Exclusive Roots

www.exclusiveroots.com
Unit 6: Hatton Country World
Dark Lane, Hatton
Warwick, CV35 8XA
Tel: 019 2684 3897

Visit this store for a wide selection of fashion-forward fair-trade items for the body and the home.

Fabrications

www.fabrications1.co.uk
7 Broadway Market
Hackney
London, E8 4PH
Tel: 020 7275 8043

This independent gallery and shop has a particular emphasis on recycling clothes.

Gadjo Dilo

2 Church Street
Westminster
London, NW8 8ED
Tel: 020 7585 1770

This shop has a very nice selection of vintage from the most exotic parts of the world; you may also find them at the Portobello Market.

Greenway Stores

www.greenwaystores.co.uk
7 North Street
Leighton Buzzard
Bedfordshire, LU7 1EF
Tel: 015 2585 1744

Head over to this department store for all things organic, fair-trade items, and local products, including clothes, home-wares, linens, toiletries, and crafts.

Greenwich Market

www.greenwichmarket.net
11a Greenwich Market
Greenwich
London, SE10 9HZ
Tel: 020 8293 3110

This village market has a wide selection of secondhand clothes and a number of other exotic finds.

Handbag Café

8 Crescent Road
Wood Green
London, N22 7RS
Tel: 020 8881 8888

This tiny shop has an eclectic collection of handbags from the '50s through the '80s.

Howies

42 Carnaby Street
London, W1F 7DY
Tel: 020 7287 2345

If you are into outdoor sports, or if you're just looking for some fashion-forward athletic gear, check out Howies.

Junky Styling

www.junkystyling.co.uk
12 Dray Walk
London, E1 6RF
Tel: 020 7247 1883

Trawl the racks for great refurbished vintage finds. These one-of-a-kind pieces will please the most fashion-forward crafty types.

Lulie B

39B Sydney Street
Brighton, BN1 4EP
Tel: 012 7368 1721

This girlie-chic store provides a good overview of the ethical designers on the UK scene.

Marks and Spencer (M&S)

www.marksandspencer.com
Various locations
Tel: 084 5302 1234

M&S has well over 500 stores throughout the UK. Their largest store is at Marble Arch in London. The company has an additional 150 stores worldwide, including more than 130 franchise businesses, operating in 30 countries. M&S has become a big player on the fair-trade front, so visit one of their stores to check out their organic, fair-trade lines.

Mary Moore

5 Clarendon Cross
Kensington and Chelsea
London, W11 4AP
Tel: 020 7229 5678

Mary has been collecting vintage clothes for over forty years, so you can bet your bottom dollar that you'll find some exceptional pieces here.

Modern Age Vintage Clothing

www.modern-age.co.uk
65 Chalk Farm Road
London, NW1 8AN
Tel: 020 7482 3787

This clutter-free shop stocks lots of fabulous finds, ranging from ball gowns to suits.

One Ethical Boutique

www.responsiblygorgeous.co.uk
33 St. Paul's Square
York, Yo24 4BD
Tel: 019 0468 9627

This boutique stocks some of the UK's hottest Green labels, including Enamore and Emmeline 4 Re. Check out their shoe collection, too.

One of a Kind

253 Portobello Road
Notting Hill
London, W11 1LR
Tel: 020 7792 5853

A nice selection of vintage can be found here.

Oxfam

www.oxfam.org.uk
Unit 8 Smithfield
Manchester, M1 1JQ
Tel: 016 1839 3160

35/37 Bold Street
Liverpool, L1 4DN
Tel: 015 1709 6739

15/17 Duncan Street
Leeds, LS1 6DQ
Tel: 011 3246 8486

52 Bridlesmithgate
Nottingham, NG1 2GP
Tel: 011 5958 1057

127 Friargate
Preston, PR1 2EE
Tel: 017 7225 4870

7 Goodramgate
York, Yo1 7LJ
Tel: 019 0465 9001

70a High Street
Rochester, ME1 1JY
Tel: 016 3481 2576

These shops are great little places to find vintage and other one-of-a-kind pieces.

Pandora

16-22 Cheval Place

Knightsbridge

London, SW7 1ES

Tel: 020 7589 2240

This is a wonderful little corner shop with designer-label secondhand clothes.

Portobello Road Market

www.portobelloroad.co.uk

Portobello Road

London, W11 1LU

Tel: 020 7229 8354

Portobello Road Market is an adventure and a great place to find good vintage and unusual pieces from all over the world.

Rellik

www.relliklondon.co.uk

8 Golborne Road

London, W10 5NW

Tel: 020 8962 0089

This is a popular vintage hot spot with an eclectic mix of vintage chic.

Rokit

www.rokit.co.uk

101-107 Brick Lane

London, E1 6SE

Tel: 020 7375 3864

225 Camden High Street

London, NW1 7BU

Tel: 020 7267 3046

42 Shelton Street

Covent Garden

London, WC2 9HZ

Tel: 020 7836 6547

Rokit has a very fine collection of retro and vintage wear from all different eras; each store has a hip, street-funk vibe.

Sam Greenberg

www.samgreenbergrnwl.co.uk

Unit 1.7, Kingly Court

Carnaby Street

London, W1B 5PW

Tel: 020 7287 8474

This is a posh shop, filled with carefully selected vintage clothing.

Sheila Cook Textiles

www.sheilacook.co.uk

105-107 Portobello Road

London, W11 2QB

Tel: 020 7792 8001

This exceptional little vintage shop has a number of rare and exotic antique pieces.

Steinberg and Tolkein

193 King's Road
Chelsea
London, SW3 5ED
Tel: 020 7376 3660

This is one of the more well-known vintage shops in London. Explore its two floors of elegant vintage pieces from all eras.

Terra Plana

www.terraplana.com
124 Bermondsey Street
London, SE1 3TX
Tel: 020 7407 3758

See description under New York City

Thea

24 Chalk Farm Road
Camden
London, NW1
Tel: 020 7482 5002

This funky little shop carries loads of secondhand finds.

Tiger Lily

www.tigerlilyludlow.co.uk
22 The Bull Ring
Ludlow
Shropshire, SY8 1AA
Tel: 015 8487 9799

This cute little storefront houses the best in fair-trade accessories.

Topshop

www.topshop.com
Oxford Circus
216 Oxford Street
London, W1D 1LA
Tel: 020 7636 7700

Known for selling lots of trendy product, Topshop has begun embracing fair-trade and organic fashions.

Triad

www.traid.org.uk
39 Duke Street
Brighton
East Sussex, BN1 1AG
Tel: 012 7374 6346

2 Acre Lane
London, SW2 5SG
Tel: 020 7326 4330

199 King Street
London, W6 9JG
Tel: 020 8748 5946

324D Station Road
London, HA1 2DX
Tel: 020 8424 8198

375 Holloway Road
London, N7 0RN
Tel: 020 7700 0087

69-71 Kilburn High Road
London, NW6 6HY
Tel: 020 7328 1453

154 Uxbridge Road
London, W12 8AA
Tel: 020 8811 2400

61 Westbourne Grove
London, W2 4UA
Tel: 020 7221 2421

51-53 High Road
Wood Green
London, N22 6BH
Tel: 020 8888 0077

These stores cater to the young, fashionable crowd with vintage and TRAIDremade clothes.

Other Countries

AUSTRALIA

a-2-b
12-14 Oxford Street
Paddington
New South Wales 2021
Tel: 02 9360 0187

352 Darling Street
Balmain
Tel: 02 9810 9010

This store is for the gal who hikes and bikes. Stop here to find eco-conscious gear—from durable dungarees to Haul Bags.

Bird Textile
www.birdtextile.com
13 Banksia Drive
Byron Bay, NSW 2841
Tel: +61 2 6680 8633

380 Cleveland Street
Surry Hills, Sydney
Tel: +61 2 9699 8457

Take a jaunt over to these carbon-neutral stores, with whimsical collections of sustainable designs and unique prints.

Ethical Threads
www.stylewithsoul.com.au
267 Hay Street
Subiaco, Perth 6008
Tel: +61 2 9381 4641

This shop houses easy-to-wear, sweatshop-free, eco-conscious clothes, ranging from sweat suits to easy breezy summer dresses.

Grass Roots Eco Store
www.grassrootsecostore.com.au
160 Rusden St
Armidale 2350
Seymour
Tel: +61 02 6771 4406

This is a neat store with a vast selection of eco-conscious products from Down Under. Come here to find Bird Textile, Haul Bags, and Etiko.

Grok

www.grok.com.au
97 Military Road
Neutral Bay NSW 2089
Tel: +61 2 9908 5411

Stop at this store and café for a cup of fair-trade coffee or sustainable duds that help disadvantaged communities.

ICELAND

Borgarpakk

www.myspace.com/borgarpakk
Frakkastigur 7
101 Reykjavik

This is one of the first sustainable-style boutiques to open in Reykjavik. Head here to find anything from great street wear to high street styles.

JAPAN

Beams

www.beams.co.jp
3-25-15 Jingumae Shibuya-Ku
150-0001 Tokyo
Tel: +81 3 3470 2904

This trend-driven department store is constantly finding new high-quality designers. Stop by if you are in Tokyo.

NEW ZEALAND

Starfish

www.starfish.co.nz
128 Willis Street
Wellington
Tel: +64 4 385 3722

Stop by this store for carefree stylish gear, featuring a self-titled label and a few other good designers, including Howies, Veja, and Nice and Clean.

Untouched World

www.untouchedworld.com
20 High Street
Auckland
Tel: +64 9 303 1382

10 Brandon Street
Wellington
Tel: +64 4 473 2596

155 Roydvale Avenue
Christchurch
Tel: +64 4 357 9399

301 Montreal Street
Christchurch
Tel: +64 4 962 6551

1 The Mall
Queenstown
Tel: +64 3 442 4992

Untouched World is a Kiwi brand that has embraced organic fibers from the idea's inception. Visit their concept stores and be taken in by the surroundings.

Index

PHOTOGRAPHY CREDITS:

The images in this book are reproduced courtesy of the following. Used by permission.

Pages 2, 3 Photographer: Sarah Lockhart, Hair: Chrissy Tsang, Makeup: Elizabeth Gerbino, Models: Summer Rayne Oakes and Patrick Garms

4, 5 Photographer: Esther Havens

6, 7 Carolina K. Designs

8, 9 Photographer: Robert August, Hair: Crews, Makeup: Elizabeth Gerbino, Styling: Aleksandra Flora

11 Photographer: Emile Ashley for Ashley Studio

12, 13, 26, 27, 29, 140, 141, 174, 175, 190, 191, 272, 273, 280, 281, 282, 283 Photographer:Ann-Katrin Blomqvist, Model Camilla Norrback

17, 18 Katharine Hamnett Archives

19, 35, 143 Marks & Spencer

22, 23, 124, 166, 168 Photographer: Jon Moe, Hair/Makeup: Erica Gray

28 Nahui Ollin

34 Levis Strauss & Co.

39, 51, 55, 93, 129, 150, 152 Photographer: Jon Moe

41 Photographer: Jason Wallis, Design: Bay Bertea

42 Annie Mohaupt, Mohop, Inc. (yellow bar); Photographer: Jason Wallis, Design: Bay Bertea (maroon and pink bars)

43 Photographer: Jason Wallis; Design: Bay Bertea (salmon bar)

49 Nike, Inc.

52 Photographer: Paige Mycoskie

61 Belinda David-Tooze (light pink and dark pink bars); Photographer: Daniel Balmat (green bar); b. happybags, llc (salmon bar)

62 Photographer: Daniel Lorenze, World of Good, Inc. (yellow, light blue, and lime green bars)

63 Photographer: Josh Jakus (dark pink bar); Photographer: John Aitchison, Design: Helen E. Reigle (salmon bar); Photographer: John King (green bar)

66 Photographer: Ryan Sope, Design: Eli Reich (yellow bar)

67 Photographer: Daniel Lorenze, World of Good, Inc. (tan bar); Photographer: Doy Bags, Tasaram LTD (salmon bar); Photographer: Daniel Balmat (dark pink bar)

68 Doy Bags, Tasaram LTD (light blue bar); Photographer: Daniel Balmat (yellow bar); Photographer: Daniel Balmat (lime green bar)

69 Harveys Industries (dark green bar)

70 Harveys Industries (purple bar); Rachel Karaca (lime green bar)

71 Rachel Karaca (dark pink bar); Photographer: Peter Riddihough, Designer: Katja Aga Sachse Thom (dark green bar); Photographer: Tim Benko (light blue bar); Photographer: Lee Staples (tan bar); Lucuma Designs (salmon bar)

72 Maura Gramzinsu (light pink bar); Lucuma Designs (light blue bar); Katherine Rasmussen (lime green bar)

73 Martin Kluesener (salmon and dark green bars)

74 Photographer: Benjamin Montague, Designer: Jennifer Farrington (lime green bar)

76 Enamore (lime green bar)

77 Amy Kathryn Handbags (dark green bar)

83 John King (light blue and dark pink bars)

83 Greenwithglamour.com (lime green bar); Photographer: Melissa Kolbusz, Designer: [WIRED]/Melissa Kolbusz (lavender bar); Photographer: Mary Ann Alexander, Designer: [WIRED]/Melissa Kolbusz (dark green bar)

84 Photographer: Michael Brandt

85 Photographer: Hap Sakwa

86 (opening shot), 116, 117 Photographer: Robert Rausch www.gasphoto.net

88 Photographer: Terry Greene Photography, Designer: Kathleen Plate

89 Photographer: Christo Harvey

90, 91 Photographer: Esther Havens

97 Photographer: Jon Moe, Hair: Dennis Clendennen for Aveda, Makeup: Lotstar.com

99 Enamore (light blue and dark green bars)

100 Enamore (dark purple, yellow, and maroon bars)

101 Enamore (dark pink and dark green bars)

107 Photographer: Lois Bielefed, Hair/Makeup: Chris Newburg (lavender and tan bars); Photographer: Lois Bielefed, Hair/Makeup: Christle Chumney (dark green bar); Stella McCartney (dark pink and salmon bars)

108 Photographer: Ann-Katrin Blomqvist (dark blue bar); Photographer: Helen Berkun, missred.net (dark green and salmon bars)

115 Photographer: David Black

121 Photographer: Richard Burns

126, 127 Ethika Boutique, Rubana Ahmad

131 Photographer: Noel Spirandelli

133 Photographer: Zabou Carrière

134, 135 Photographer: Emile Ashley for Ashley Studio

137 Photographer: Henrik Adamsen

138, 139 Noir

145 Merkury Innovations, Art Director: Johanna Kuctek (red bar)

145 Stephen McMenamin (blue bar)

160, 163 Photographer: Akira Yamada

172, 173 Photographer: Ann-Katrin Blomqvist with overlay images courtesy of Lara Miller, Model Camila Norrback

179, 181, 189 Photographer: Sarah McColgan

195, Photographer: Robert August, Hair: Crews, Makeup: Elizabeth Gerbino

196 Styla, Inc. (pink, blight blue, and lime green bars)

199 Jamal Hammadi (dark pink bar); Photographer: Pat Dishinger; Graphic Designer: Anna Blazevich (dark green bar); Max Green Alchemy, Ltd. (salmon bar)

201 Intelligent Nutrients

202, 203 Photographer: Pat Dishinger, Graphic Designer: Anna Blazevich

204 Weleda North America (purple bar); Max Green Alchemy, Ltd. (pink bar); Styla, Inc. (light blue and lime green bars)

205 Max Green Alchemy, Ltd. (lavender and dark green bars); Styla, Inc. (salmon bar)

207 Weleda North America (dark pink bar)

209 Essential Care Organics Ltd. (dark pink bar); Lucky Duck Body Care LLC (green bar)

210 Ken Goudy (yellow bar); Myra Michelle Eby, Founder of Mychelle Dermaceuticals (maroon bar)

213 Osea Skin

216 Bob MacLeod, Owner of Kiss My Face (lime green bar)

217 Bob MacLeod, Owner of Kiss My Face (dark green bar); Essential Care Organics Ltd. (salmon bar)

218 Styla, Inc. (light pink bar)

219 Béla Temesváry (dark blue bar); Keys, Inc. (dark pink bar); Ian Dadash, Managing Director (dark green bar); Myra Michelle Eby, Founder of Mychelle Dermaceuticals (salmon bar)

220 Myra Michelle Eby, Founder of Mychelle Dermaceuticals (purple bar); Frank Ishman (yellow and pink bars)

221 Lora Leavenworth, Steve Tague, Rebecca Picard, Carlos de la Rosa (blue bar); Frank Ishman (salmon bar); Weleda North America (lavender bar)

223 Jerry Tan, Scott Ashton (salmon bar); Bob MacLeod, Owner of Kiss My Face (dark green bar)

225 Photographer: Esther Havens

227 Lora Leavenworth, Steve Tague, Rebecca Picard, Carlos de la Rosa (sky blue bar); Jeremy Clow (lavender bar)

229 Nvey Eco Organic Makeup (green bar); Jason Wynn (salmon bar)

230 Scott Sgide (lime green bar)

231 Jason Wynn (lavender bar); Lora Leavenworth, Steve Tague, Rebecca Picard, Carlos de la Rosa (dark pink bar); Nvey Eco Organic Makeup (green bar)

232 Jason Wynn (yellow bar); Nvey Eco Organic Makeup (blue bar)

233 Nvey Eco Organic Makeup (dark pink bar)

234 Lora Leavenworth, Steve Tague, Rebecca Picard, Carlos de la Rosa (purple bar)

235 Jeremy Clow (dark pink bar); Jason Wynn (salmon bar); Scott Sgide (lavender bar)

237 Nvey Eco Organic Makeup (dark green bar)

238 Bob Bretell (lime green bar)

239 Bob Bretell (salmon bar)

241 Auromere Ayurvedic Imports (dark green bar); Weleda North America (salmon bar)

242 Charlotte Vøhtz, Green People (purple bar)

243 Bob Bretell (dark green bar)

244 Bob Bretell (light pink bar); Photographer: Brigitte MacDonald; Hugo Saavedra; (yellow bar); Bob Bretell (lime green bar)

246 Kelly Evick, Biggs & Featherbelle (yellow bar); Bob MacLeod, Owner of Kiss My Face (lime green bar)

247 Photographer: Pat Dishinger; Graphic Designer: Anna Blazevich

249 Essential Care Organics Ltd. (dark green bar)

250 Photographer: Brigitte MacDonald; Hugo Saavedra (purple bar); Kelly Evick, Biggs & Featherbelle (lime green bar)

251 Bob Bretell (yellow bar)

252 Photographer: Pat Dishinger; : Graphic Designer: Anna Blazevich (purple bar); Photographer: James Hahn (yellow bar); Vince O'Connell (lime green bar)

253 Catherine Gaffney (green bar)

256 W.S. Badger Balm Company (pink bar); Keys, Inc. (blue bar)

258 Ken Goudy (maroon bar); Myra Michelle Eby, Founder of Mychelle Dermaceuticals (lime green bar)

249 Photographer: Thomas O'Hara; Dr. Tony Kovacs (dark green bar); Max Green Alchemy Ltd. (salmon bar)

261 Bob Bretell (sky blue bar); Lora Leavenworth, Steve Tague, Rebecca Picard, Carlos de la Rosa (dark green bar)

262 French Transit, Ltd. (pink bar); Bob MacLeod, Owner of Kiss My Face (sky blue bar)

263 Charlotte Vøhtz, Green People (dark pink bar); Weleda North America (lavender bar); James Hahn (dark green bar)

264 Iouley & Tsi-La (maroon bar); Mandy Aftel (light blue bar)

265 Valerie Bennis for Essence of Vali (sky blue and lavender bars); Lucky Duck Body Care LLC (dark green bar)

267 Photographer: Eric Striffler

268 Bob MacLeod, Owner of Kiss My Face (light blue and lime green bars)

269 Aromafloria, Inc. (lavender, dark green, and salmon bars)

270 Ying Chun Liu (purple and lime green bars); Anise Cosmetics, LLC (yellow bar); W.S. Badger Balm Company (dark green bar)

271 Aromafloria, Inc. (sky blue bar); PeaceKeeper Cause-Metics (lavender bar); W.S. Badger Balm Company (dark green bar); Vince O'Connell (salmon bar)